Palgrave Studies in the History of Finance

The study of the history of financial institutions, markets, instruments and concepts is vital if we are to understand the role played by finance today. At the same time, the methodologies developed by finance academics can provide a new perspective for historical studies. Palgrave Studies in the History of Finance is a multi-disciplinary effort to emphasise the role played by finance in the past, and what lessons historical experiences have for us. It presents original research, in both authored monographs and edited collections, from historians, finance academics and economists, as well as financial practitioners.

Larry Neal

The Forgotten Financiers of the Louisiana Purchase

European Bankers, the US, and the Rise of International Finance

palgrave
macmillan

Larry Neal
Emeritus Professor of Economics
University of Illinois
Columbus, OH, USA

ISSN 2662-5164 ISSN 2662-5172 (electronic)
Palgrave Studies in the History of Finance
ISBN 978-3-031-56276-1 ISBN 978-3-031-56277-8 (eBook)
https://doi.org/10.1007/978-3-031-56277-8

Cover illustration: P C Labouchere by an unknown artist, undated, oil on board. Reproduced courtesy of the Baring Archive Limited

This Palgrave Macmillan imprint is published by the registered company Springer Nature Switzerland AG
The registered company address is: Gewerbestrasse 11, 6330 Cham, Switzerland

Paper in this product is recyclable.

'To the archivists—past, present, and future—of the Baring Archive'

Preface: Behind the Scenes of the Finance of the Louisiana Purchase

This book is the happy result of a visit I first made to the Baring Archive in London in 1996 near the end of my sabbatical leave at the London School of Economics & Political Science. My first book, *The Rise of Financial Capitalism: International Capital Markets in the Age of Reason*, (Cambridge University Press, 1990) argued that the London Stock Exchange, formally organized in 1800 to market more effectively the huge increase in sovereign debt issued by the British government to finance their role in the French Revolutionary and Napoleonic Wars, was also the preferred "safe haven" for flight capital fleeing the French armies on the European continent. Relying on the records kept by the Bank of England, which was in charge of sequestering foreigners' holdings of British national debt when they were in territories controlled by French forces, my estimates of such "flight capital" were said by one critic to be "pitiably small." Knowing that the firm of John & Francis Baring had been a major dealer-jobber in 3 Per Cent Consols at the time and had extensive relations with Hope & Co., the largest merchant banking firm in the Netherlands, I booked a visit to the Baring Archive to see what transactions Barings had handled for European clients during that period.

The archivist on duty, Jane Waller, presented me a full day's worth of materials dealing with the financial transactions of the firm of John & Francis Baring during the period 1789–1812. What I found, instead of my hoped-for large-scale private (and confidential) transfers of European funds to London, were large flows from the newly formed United States to London, and then to Paris and Amsterdam—quite different than what I had hoped to find. As archivist Waller escorted me out, however, she noted that as an American I might be interested to know that the Baring Archive had a lot of material dealing with the financing of the Louisiana Purchase. She remarked, "Someone should take a look at it sometime!"[1]

Nearly thirty years later, after checking the literature that celebrated the 200th anniversary of the Louisiana Purchase, which was much less weighty than the efforts that went into celebrating the 200th anniversary of the Lewis and Clark expedition that followed up the Louisiana Purchase at much less expense and much greater consequence, I decided to check up on the Baring Archive's material dealing with the Louisiana Purchase. The current archivist, Clara Harrow, pulled out a large folder that the second Lord Northbrook, Francis George Baring, had arranged and listed at the time of the centenary of the Louisiana Purchase in 1903.

The Northbrook Business Papers cover the globally ranging activities of Sir Francis Baring, the founding partner of the house of Barings, from his initial efforts to his death in 1810. One folder, in particular, focuses on his letters and memoranda that dealt with the Louisiana Purchase. It begins with an extended letter by Pierre Cesar Labouchere (one of Sir Francis' sons-in-law) to Alexander Baring (the second son of Sir Francis) in mid-January 1803. The letter makes clear that these two young men put a great deal of planning into initiating and then carrying out the specific details of the financing of what became the Louisiana Purchase in May 1803. They developed their plan in consultation with Sir Francis and his friend and colleague, Henry Hope, together the two richest merchant bankers in Europe in 1803. All this was done well before the political decision-makers who are typically associated with the Louisiana Purchase, Thomas Jefferson and Napoleon Bonaparte, could get their agents into formal negotiations in Paris in mid-April 1803. Especially striking was Pierre Cesar's initial proposal to "grease the wheels" of the deal by bribing the main political ministers who would be making and signing the formal agreements, one of whom remained anonymous.

[1] Indeed, an illustrated pamphlet, "The Financing of the Louisiana Purchase: A Landmark Real Estate Transaction Funded by the Amsterdam and London Capital Markets 200 Years Ago," was produced by Tim Schantz of the History Factory in Washington, D.C., and published in 2003 by ING and FORTIS, the Dutch companies that acquired Barings in 1995. The current website of the Baring Archive has an online exhibit as well: https://baringarchive.org.uk/exhibition/the-louisiana-purchase/.

Since that visit pre-pandemic, I have re-visited the Baring Archive several times in person and many times digitally to take advantage of the ongoing digitization project, which continues while being overseen by archivist Harrow. To overcome the restrictions of the COVID pandemic, I enlisted the services of Danielle Wilson, graduate student in History at American University to undertake digitization of the relevant Baring manuscripts at the Library of Congress, which helped me follow-up initial work done many years ago by Ralph Hidy (1949).

Piecing together the adventures of the two most active agents involved in the financing of the Louisiana Purchase, as revealed in the Northbrook folder, has led to a number of seminars at the London School of Economics & Political Science, Louisiana State University, the University of Michigan, University of Pennsylvania, Vanderbilt University, Wittenberg University, and University College of London. Especially valuable have been comments on successive drafts by Olivier Accominotti, Jeremy Atack, Joan DeJean, Rui Esteves, Marc Flandreau, Virginia France, Michael Haupert, Eric Hilt, Joan Labouchere, Joseph Mason, William Oelman, Albrecht Ritschl, Mark Stumpf, John Wallis, and Eugene White. Their general consensus was that my successive drafts had to become a book, not an article. My patient wife, Margaret (Peg) Doherty Neal, has diligently insisted all along that I complete it!

The podcasts organized by Carmen Hoffman, European Association for Banking and Financial History, https://podcasters.spotify.com/pod/show/carmen-hofmann/episodes/The-Louisiana-Purchase-e1j8jnl/a-a816v4m, and Mitu Gulati, University of Virginia Law School, https://soundcloud.com/clauses-controversies/ep-80-ft-larry-neal, also helped me focus more on the main theme: the importance of individual efforts and ingenuity of two young men, Alexander Baring in London and Pierre Cesar Labouchere in Amsterdam. They conceived the financial details of the deal in the first place, persuaded their seniors to back them, then persuaded the French Treasury minister, François Barbé-Marbois, to accept their deal, and finally convinced the American Secretary of the Treasury, Albert Gallatin, to accept the specific number and form of the bonds they would market in Amsterdam and London. The decisions and actions by these four individuals were responsible for completing the finance of the Louisiana Purchase, very much as originally designed in Paris during the temporary Truce of Amiens (October 31, 1801–May 17, 1803) despite the disruptions of renewed war between Britain and France, and then between American and Britain. The consequences of the territorial acquisition initiated by the Louisiana Purchase were of historic importance for the United States, but so also were the consequences of the success of its financing by Baring and Hope.

The two young men accomplished all this in the midst of the ongoing Napoleonic Wars in Europe, which led to reciprocal blockades of trade and finance between Britain and France as well as the War of 1812 between the United States and Britain. After Waterloo, the two men in their maturity then played key roles in sustaining the postwar transitions in the finance of sovereign debt for both France and the United States. Along the way, they also encountered some of the more interesting players in the financial turmoil of that era, men whose personal ambitions to seize the potential profits arising from the economic disruptions of the time have largely been overlooked, or dismissed as inconsequential in the subsequent historiography, even by financial historians such as myself. While arranging the financing of the Louisiana Purchase, Alexander Baring and Pierre Cesar Labouchere took the success of the Dutch and British examples of marketing sovereign debt to customers beyond the Netherlands or the United Kingdom and applied it on behalf of Spain, Portugal, and the United States. Marketing the sovereign debt of the United States, seen at the time as a "Hercules in the cradle," (Edling, 2014) proved to be one of several successes for the two men. Their role in creating the conditions for credible international markets in national sovereign debts, while also serving in effect as nursemaids to the infant Hercules, deserves a modern hearing as well and I hope readers of the following pages will agree.

Columbus, USA Larry Neal

Contents

1 **Behind the Scenes of the Louisiana Purchase** 1
The Houses of Baring and Hope 11
References 15

2 **Setting Up the Finance for the Louisiana Purchase** 17
Financing the Louisiana Purchase Seen as an American Triumph 22
References 30

3 **"The Present Order of Things" in January 1803** 31
References 50

4 **Baring & Hope Anticipate Financing the Louisiana Purchase** 53
How Alexander Baring Set the Ball Rolling 56
Pierre Cesar Labouchere's Initial Plan 58
Calculating the "Financials" Ahead of Time 65
The "Final Plan" Agreed by Sir Francis Baring and Henry Hope 74
What Happened in the Meantime? 77
References 82

5 **All the Players Were Important** 83
References 113

6 **Daniel Parker, Expatriate Extraordinaire** 115

References 133

7 The Deal Is Done, But Problems Arise Everywhere: America, London, Paris, and Amsterdam 135
Problems in America 135
Problems in London 141
Problems in Paris 144
Problems in Amsterdam 145
Complications in London 146
Problems Between the Houses of Hope and Baring 151

8 Meanwhile, More Trouble Back in Paris 159
Reference 174

9 The Financial & Personal Crises of 1810–1811 175
Alexander Baring 176
Pierre Cesar Labouchere 181
References 187

10 The War of 1812 and the Financiers of the Louisiana Purchase 189
Vincent Nolte 190
David Parish 195
Alexander Baring 197
References 202

11 Lessons Learned, Applied, and Ignored 203
References 211

12 Curtain Call: All the Players Should Take a Bow 213

Appendix A. The U.S. Certificates for the Louisiana Purchase 219

Appendix B. Initial Transfers of Louisiana 6% Stock by Baring Bros. (from Library of Congress, Baring mss. MMC 2475) 223

Appendix C. Examples of Stock Certificates 225

Appendix D. Addington's Order for Barings to Stop Payments 227

Appendix E. The Dutch Plan for Selling and Managing the U.S. Bonds 229

Appendix F. Sir Francis Baring's "Estimate" of Profits 233

References 235

Index 247

Time Line for the Finance of the Louisiana Purchase (Events Important for the Finance Players Are Highlighted)

1783 September 3	Peace of Paris, three treaties signed that end Britain's wars with America, France, and Spain
1784 mid-August	**Daniel Parker, major U.S. army contractor, leaves United States for the Netherlands**
1788 June 21	U.S. Constitution formally adopted
1789 July 14	Fall of the Bastille, French Revolution becomes violent
1790 January 9	Alexander Hamilton's *First Report on the Public Credit*
1790 March 23	**Daniel Parker and Sir Francis Baring sign Deed of Trust to establish tontine in England for U.S. "liquidated debts"**
1790 September	**Pierre Cesar Labouchere joins Hope & Co. in Amsterdam**
1790 December 14	Alexander Hamilton's *Second Report on the Public Credit*
1791 August	Slave revolt begins in St. Domingue, in response to French Revolution proclaiming rights of man
1794	**Alexander Baring arrives in Amsterdam to learn Hope & Co. business**
1795 January 16	Alexander Hamilton's *Report on a Plan for the Further Support of Public Credit*
1795 January 18	**Pierre Cesar and Alexander flee Amsterdam for London**
1795 November	**Alexander Baring arrives in the United States to deal with William Bingham and U.S. debt**
1797 September 4	Coup of 18 Fructidor, Year V, that exiles **Barbé-Marbois**, Pichegru, Du Pont, and many others who will return to power under Napoleon

1800 September 30	*Treaty of Mortefontaine*, United States and France ends Quasi-War, French liabilities for United States losses to French privateers deferred
1800 October 1	*Treaty of San Ildefonso*, Spain "conditionally" cedes Louisiana to France
1801 mid-January	Toussaint L'Ouverture invades Santo Domingo, controls all Hispaniola
1801 February 9	*Peace of Lunéville*, ends war b/n France and Holy Roman Empire
1801 February 16	Pitt resigns as Prime Minister in GB, replaced by Henry Addington
1801 March 4	Thomas Jefferson takes office as U.S. President
1801 March 21	*Treaty of Aranjuez* confirms Spanish cession of Louisiana to France
1801 May 1	Rufus King's letter to Jefferson confirms the cession
1801 June 6	*Treaty of Badajoz*, bn Spain and Portugal, ends "War of the Oranges" Portugal gives Fr. part of Brazil in S. America
1801 (mid-July)	Toussaint L'Ouverture's constitution for Hispaniola outrages Napoleon
1801 September 29	*Peace of Madrid* forces Portugal to pay 20 million FF to France
1801 October 1	Truce of Amiens agreed between Britain and France
1801 October 31	LeClerc's formal instructions from Napoleon to seize St. Domingue assume British acquiescence and American cooperation
1801 November 10	**Robert R. Livingston** lands in France (with entire family and servants and provisions)
1802 March 25	Truce of Amiens formally announced bn France and Britain
1802 April	**Alexander Baring** purchases remaining Bank of U.S. stock held by Fed'l gov't & pays off remaining Dutch loan to United States
1802 April	Napoleon arranges possession of Louisiana by appointing head of army, navy, and government.
1802 April 18	Jefferson's open letter to **Livingston**, carried by **Du Pont de Nemours**, emphasizes strategic importance of New Orleans to the United States
1802 May 1	Toussaint and his generals meet LeClerc, who arrests Toussaint 1 month later and sends him as prisoner to France
1802 May 20	Napoleon re-establishes slavery in French colonies, black revolt intensifies

1802 August 2	confirmed as First Consul for life, with power to appoint successor
1802 August 20	Napoleon confirms Pierre-Clement Laussat as colonial prefect of Louisiana and Claude Perrin Victor as captain general
1802 October 15	Carlos IV finally signs off on the cession of Louisiana to France, after receiving French ambassador's promise in July that Napoleon would never alienate Louisiana!
1802 October 16	Morales, Spanish Intendant of New Orleans, withdraws U.S. right of deposit.
1802 November 2	Gen'l Charles Leclerc dies in Haiti of yellow fever, replaced by Rochambeau
1803 January 11	Jefferson calls for Congress to appoint **James Monroe** to join Robert R. *Livingston* in an effort to purchase New Orleans from France. Congress appropriates $2 million to support their efforts.
1803 January 19	**Alexander Baring proposes financing the U.S. purchase of New Orleans**
1803 January 30	**Pierre Cesar Labouchere sets "nut shell" for financing by Baring & Hope**
1803 February 15	**Sir Francis Baring & Henry Hope approve Labouchere plan from London, leave final details to be arranged by Alexander in Paris**
1803 March 1	Ohio was admitted as the first state from the Northwest Territory.
1803 March 11	Monroe finally departs NY for France with his family and Madison's instructions.
1803 March 26	Pierre Laussat arrives in New Orleans to take possession for France
1803 March 30	Napoleon learns of death of Leclerc from his sister, Leclerc's widow, when she returns to Paris with Leclerc's body from Haiti
1803 April 7	Toussaint L'Ouverture found dead in French prison
1803 April 11	Monroe and family arrive in Paris to begin negotiations, **Parker tells Monroe about loan commitment by Baring & Hope**; Talleyrand raises the possibility of selling Louisiana to Livingston
1803 April 30	***Barbé-Marbois*, *Livingston*, and *Monroe* sign the 3 conventions for the Louisiana Purchase**.
1803 May 11	Whitworth, British Ambassador leaves Paris, signals war will resume
1803 May 18	Great Britain declares war on France

1803 May 23	Talleyrand sends letter to Pichon in the United States, telling him of sale of La. to the United States
1803 June 20	Jefferson's letter to Meriwether Lewis describes his mission for the Corps of Discovery to the Pacific Ocean
1803 June (??)	**Alexander Baring and James Monroe** each leave Paris for London
1803 June 22	Napoleon leaves St. Cloud, to prepare for invasion of England.
1803 (mid-summer)	**Daniel Parker** purchases his country estate, Draveil, on the outskirts of Paris
1803 July 4	Jefferson and Madison in DC inform Lewis and Clark of Louisiana Purchase
1803 August 17	Pierre Laussat writes Pichon to tell him a letter from Decrès and informs him that La. has been ceded to the United States
1803 October19	Treat of Subsidies signed in Paris, Spain to pay 6 million pesos monthly to France while maintaining neutral status
1803 October 20	U.S. Senate ratifies the Louisiana Purchase, House then authorizes issuance of U.S. bonds to cover purchase price, $11.25 million.
1803 November 18	Rochambeau's final defeat in Haiti, Battle of Vertières
1803 November 30	In New Orleans, Spain formally cedes control of Louisiana to France
1803 December 20	In New Orleans, France formally cedes control of Louisiana to the United States
1804 January 1	Dessalines, new ruler of Haiti, proclaims its independence
1804 January 10	**Alexander Baring receives 1/3 of the 6% Louisiana bonds in DC**
1804 January 16	Jefferson's address to Congress describes his plans for Louisiana
1804 February 7	**William Bingham dies in Bath, England**
1804 February 13	**USN Midshipman John Nicholson receives 2/3 of the 6% La. Bonds in NY**
1804 February 19	Pichegru arrested in Paris, part of a plot against Napoleon
1804 February	Edward Livingston, younger brother of Robert R. Livingston, fleeing NY for embezzling funds arrives in New Orleans
1804 March 9	Cadoudal, sent to kill Napoleon, arrested, with General Moreau

1804 March 10	St. Louis formally transferred from Spain to France to United States, Lewis and Clark are present at the start of their Corps of Discovery.
1804 April 21	**Barbé-Marbois** signs two agreements with **Labouchere** in case bonds don't arrive; then purchases Chateau de Noyers in Normandy (273,000 francs)
1804 April 25	**Robert R. Livingston receives 2/3 of the 6% La. bonds from U.S. Lt. Leonard**
1804 May 4	Napoleon is acclaimed as Emperor of the French by the French Senate
1804 May 10	William Pitt the Younger resumes office as Prime Minister, replaces Addington
1804 May 18	Napoleon proclaimed Emperor of France
1804 July 25	**Alexander Baring** informs **Gallatin** of financial procedures for paying interest on the Louisiana 6% bonds.
1804 September	Gabriel-Julien Ouvrard arrives in Spain to arrange tribute payments
1804 October 5	British frigates capture Spanish treasure fleet, seizing £900,000 worth
1804 November 3	First Treaty of St. Louis between the United States and various Native American tribes
1804 November 18	Jefferson re-elected for second term; **Robert R. Livingston** replaced as minister to France; returns to his estate in Clermont, NY
1804 November 26	Charles IV grants Ouvrard sole rights over trade bn Spain and colonies, including monopoly over treasure shipments
1804 December 2	Napoleon formally crowned as Emperor of France
1804 December 12	Spain was forced to declare war on Britain, then ceased subsidy to arm its own forces
1804 December 18	Ouvrard receives 20 million piastres in notes drawn on colonies to pay his advances to Spain. **Barbé-Marbois** demands half for the French treasury
1804 December 26	Charles IV signs order to collect funds in colonies for service of Dutch loans, repayment of Ouvrard's advances, and to cover military expenses
1805 April 11	Gt. Britain and Russia sign treaty, Br. to pay £1,250,000 for every 100,000 troops
1805 May 6	Ouvrard signs contract with Hope & Co. to ship Mexican silver to Europe
1805 August	Vincent Nolte, Armand Lestapis, and David Parish arrive in the United States, NY, and Philadelphia

1805 October 21	Battle of Trafalgar, Nelson destroys combined Spanish and French fleets
1806 January 27	Napoleon convenes his Conseil, replaces **Barbé-Marbois** as Treasurer with Mollien
1806 April 6	Nolte arrives in New Orleans to receive shipments of Mexican silver
1806 April 18	Jefferson's Non-Importation Act, against Britain
1807 August	Nolte leaves New Orleans, works with Parish in Philadelphia, witnesses Fulton's steam boat, the *Clermont*, succeed on Hudson River
1807 September 28	Napoleon recalls **Barbé-Marbois** to be head of new *Cour des Comptes*
1807 October 27	Treaty of Fontainebleau, b/n Napoleon & Charles IV to invade Portugal
1807 December 22	Jefferson's Embargo Act, against all nations
1808 August	Both Charles IV and Ferdinand VII deposed as Spanish monarchs, replaced by Joseph Bonaparte
1809 April	Nolte returns to England from the United States to settle accts with Baring & Hope
1810 September 11	**Death of Sir Francis Baring**
1811 February 25	**Death of Henry Hope**
1812 April 30	Louisiana becomes the 18th state in the United States
1812 June 18	United States declares war against Britain (War of 1812)
1812 June 24	Napoleon declares war on Russia
1812 July 18	Treaty between Russia and England
1815 January 8	Andrew Jackson defeats British in Battle of New Orleans
1815 February 17	Treaty of Ghent ends War of 1812
1817 July 24	Baring Bros. & Hope & Co. agree to underwrite French occupation loan
1820 October 21	**Final certificates of Louisiana stock paid off in the United States**
1821 January 10	Credit remains to the United States for £703.3.11 Louisiana Dividends in Baring Bros.

List of Figures

Fig. 1.1	The expansion of the United States after independence in 1783 (*Source* https://www.ilibrarian.net/history/louisiana_purchase_map_lg.jpg)	2
Fig. 1.2	Historical panel in the Louisiana State Archives Building (The original map of that territory is shown on the scales, balanced by a small amount of species. The three figures prominent in the negotiations to obtain this large land mass in 1803: Robert Livingston, Thomas Jefferson, and Napoleon. Also depicted are William C. C. Claiborne, the first colonial governor of Louisiana, and Andrew Jackson, the hero of the Battle of New Orleans in 1815. *Source* https://www.sos.la.gov/HistoricalResources/PublishedDocuments/HistoricalPanels.pdf)	8
Fig. 3.1	French 5% rentes (monthly average on Paris Bourse) and British 3% Consols on London Stock Exchange. Prices as percentage of par	32
Fig. 3.2	Yields of French rentes compared to British Consols, 1798–1823	32
Fig. 3.3	Exchange rates of pound sterling, 1789–1805 (Amsterdam: schellingen banco. Hamburg: schillingen banco. Paris: pence sterling per livres [1789–1798]; franc, centimes per pound [1801–1805])	33
Fig. 5.1	François Barbé-Marbois (*Source* https://en.wikipedia.org/wiki/François_Barbé-Marbois#In_the_Revolution)	84

Fig. 5.2 Albert Gallatin (Portrait by Gilbert Stuart, 1803. https://upload.wikimedia.org/wikipedia/commons/b/b6/Albert_Gallatin_%28by_Gilbert_Stuart%29.jpg) 89
Fig. 5.3 *Alexander Baring* (*Source* https://baringarchive.org.uk/exhibition/baring-portraits/) 95
Fig. 5.4 Pierre Cesar Labouchere (*Source* https://www.wikitree.com/photo/jpg/Labouchere-1) 99
Fig. 6.1 Chateau de Draveil (*Source* Chateau de Draveil, front view, http://www.chateau-fort-manoir-chateau.eu/chateaux-essonne-chateau-a-draveil-chateau-de-paris.html) 131
Fig. 7.1 Sample certificate for Louisiana Purchase bonds (*Source* https://lewis-clark.org/media/loupur_stock-certif.jpg, accessed March 6, 2023. This rare specimen appears to be a certificate transferred to a group of Amsterdam investors in place of one (or more) of the original certificates issued in Amsterdam. After Napoleon's Continental Blockade made it difficult to collect interest payments in Amsterdam, the Dutch proprietors could shift payments to London. While interest was payable in London, the bond "is transferable only by appearance in person, or by attorney, at the proper office, according to the rules and forms indicated for that purpose." The exchange rate of the dollar to the pound is still fixed at the original rate agreed in 1803. One of the owners, Willem Borski, died in February 1814, which may be why this replacement certificate still exists in the U.S. archives.) 136
Fig. 7.2 Amsterdam Advertisements for various American securities, December 25, 1804 (Source *Amsterdamsche Courant*, December 25, 1804) 146
Fig. 7.3 The baring prospectus for the Louisiana bonds in London (*Source* Baring Archive, NP1.4.45, "1804, Apr: Prospectus for Louisiana 6% Loan.") 148
Fig. 10.1 Vincent Nolte confronts General Andrew Jackson, 1815 (*Source* Historical New Orleans Collection, http://hnoc.minisisinc.com/THNOC/SCRIPTS/MWIMAIN.DLL/128817035/5/1/217840?RECORD&UNION=Y, accessed July 8, 2022) 192
Fig. 10.2 American funds on the London Stock Exchange, 1811-mid-1817 (*Source* Edward Wetenhall, *The Course of the Exchange*. 1811–1817) 199

Fig. 11.1 Yields of French 5% and British 3% bonds, 1810–1821 (*Source* Wetenhall, *The Course of the Exchange,* 3% Consol, & Courtois (1877), average of French *rente* high/low prices monthly, Paris bourse) 204

List of Tables

Table 1.1	The full cast of players	14
Table 4.1	Alexander Baring's Plan, January 19, 1803	57
Table 4.2	Plan by Pierre Cesar Labouchere, January 30, 1803	59
Table 4.3	Counterfactual estimate of profit from actual arrangement, with initial assumptions of Baring & Hope	77
Table 7.1	General estimate	154
Table 9.1	American flour exports to Spain and Portugal, 1808–1815	181

CHAPTER 1

Behind the Scenes of the Louisiana Purchase

Signed off in Paris on April 30, 1803, the Louisiana "Purchase" may have been the greatest land deal in history, at least for the United States. In fact, the United States did not *purchase* the "land" of the Louisiana Territory. Instead, it paid to assume the authority to negotiate the acquisition of the land from its current occupants. The United States simply replaced the British, French, or Spanish authorities who had claimed that authority previously. The so-called process of "preemption" from Native Americans would take another $2.6 billion and two centuries to accomplish.[1] Rather than referring to the Louisiana Purchase, it might be more accurate to say that for $15 million, the United States immediately acquired the "Louisiana Preemption." Whatever, the deal for 530 million acres of land (2.83 cents per acre) doubled the territory for potential settlement of the United States and laid the basis for further expansion (Fig. 1.1).

Textbook accounts of the Louisiana Purchase summarize the financial details, if they even bother, by stating simply that the United States issued $11.25 million of 15-year bonds bearing 6% interest annually and committed another $3.75 million to pay the accumulated claims of American merchants against France. While the United States was committed to pay interest semi-annually for the life of each bond, it also committed

[1] Lee (2017).

L. Neal, *The Forgotten Financiers of the Louisiana Purchase*, Palgrave Studies in the History of Finance,
https://doi.org/10.1007/978-3-031-56277-8_1

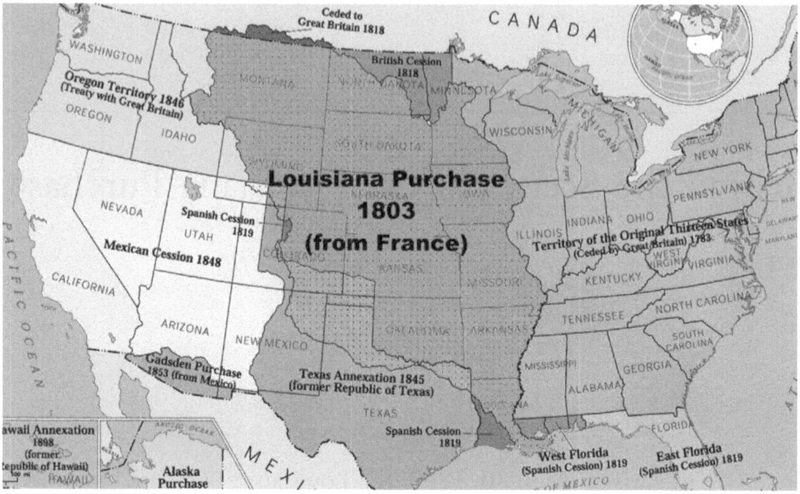

Fig. 1.1 The expansion of the United States after independence in 1783 (*Source* https://www.ilibrarian.net/history/louisiana_purchase_map_lg.jpg)

not to redeem the bonds for 15 years, and then only one-fourth of the outstanding bonds annually over the following four years. Given that the Federal government of the United States would be collecting a growing amount of tariff revenues from its increased trade through New Orleans in the meantime, however, this was a very good financial transaction for the United States at the time. Even Albert Gallatin, Jefferson's Secretary of the Treasury, committed to retiring within ten years all the debt that Alexander Hamilton had assumed for the Federal government, acknowledged that he could still meet that goal and then pay off the Louisiana debt in the following years.[2] Barely mentioned are the terms arranged for the remaining \$3.75 million that the U.S. government agreed to pay to its own citizens in lieu of requiring the French government to make restitution for the losses American merchants had suffered during the Quasi-War of 1796–1800 between the United States and France. The

[2] Albert Gallatin, *Report on the Finances, October 1803*, "The new debt will neither impede nor retard the payment of the principal of the old debt; and the fund will be sufficient, besides paying the interest on both, to discharge the principal of the old debt before the year 1818, and that of the new one within one year and a half after that year."

Treaty of Mortefontaine, September 30, 1800, which ended the Quasi-War, had agreed that France would make compensation, but had left the amount and terms unspecified, to be determined later.

France, eager to replenish Napoleon's war chest so he could continue his pursuit of military glory, could cash in the American bonds, but only if a ready market could be found for them. Only if he could offload the bonds in a secondary market, would the finance of the Louisiana Purchase be a good deal as well for France. Only then, by implication and rarely mentioned, might this also be a good deal for the merchant bankers who just happened to be in Paris at the moment to seize the opportunity to manage this side of the finance of the Louisiana Purchase. Such is the standard treatment accorded to the role played by the two merchant banking firms that managed the financial details—John & Francis Baring & Co. of London and Hope & Co. of Amsterdam. As the historian of Barings put it pithily: "What in fact happened was that the two banks bought Louisiana from France and resold it to America."[3]

The statement is accurate, and Ziegler rightly moves on to more interesting parts of the history of Barings as the company became famous as "the sixth great power" of Europe after the defeat of Napoleon at Waterloo. The financial arrangements of the Louisiana Purchase proved satisfactory on all three sides—the United States, France, and the two firms of Barings and Hope. All three parties moved on to other, more interesting, issues for themselves. After taking possession of Louisiana, the United States had to deal with the challenge of absorbing the huge and as yet unexplored and unknown territory. Napoleon turned to the challenge of invading Britain, while consolidating his authority over continental Europe. Barings focused on dealing with the explosive rise in British national debt, becoming the lead underwriters in 12 successive issues, each one of which far exceeded the $15 million the United States paid for the Louisiana Territory. Hope & Co. had to cope with ever-changing governments in the Netherlands while continuing to provide the means for Napoleon's successive satellite kingdoms to pay their required tributes to the French empire. The possible question of just why and how these two firms happened to be in Paris at such an opportune time and prepared as well to assume the double role of buying Louisiana from France and

[3] Ziegler, p. 71.

then reselling it to America, when so much else was happening in Europe is never posed, much less answered.[4]

Material in the Baring Archive, in the process of being re-organized and digitized for greater use by the scholarly community, however, reveals that the presence of Barings and Hope was not just accidental at Easter-time in Paris in 1803 when the deal was struck. Moreover, Barings had been involved with investing in American securities as early as 1790, thanks to initiatives by the American expatriates Daniel Parker and Gouverneur Morris as well as efforts by William Bingham (Alexander Baring's father-in-law). Further, in the Spring of 1802, Alexander Baring had arranged a major purchase of Bank of the U.S. stock in the form of the remaining debt of the Federal government to the Bank. In the process, he also provided Albert Gallatin the funds needed to pay off the remaining debt the United States owed to Dutch financiers. Moreover, as early as January 1803, when Jefferson was inducing James Monroe to go to France with his family to undertake negotiations to purchase just the area of New Orleans, Alexander Baring and his brother-in-law in Amsterdam, Pierre Cesar Labouchere, were plotting how to arrange the financing between France and the United States. None of their hard work in planning and then carrying out the complicated finance that emerged by the end of 1803 (and was only completed in 1821) has been given the attention it deserves.

According to the retrospective account by François Barbé-Marbois (1830), the French minister entrusted by Napoleon with the negotiation of the Louisiana Cession, however, it took some time before the terms could be agreed between him and the two American envoys. After some bargaining, the Americans finally consented to the full price set at 80 million francs, but only if 20 million were paid in a timely fashion to the American merchants to settle their claims against France for losses they had suffered during the Quasi-War of 1796–1800. That would settle any remaining claims of American merchants against France, which Napoleon had already agreed to cover. The American envoys, however, had only been authorized to offer up to 50 million francs, albeit only for New Orleans and the Floridas, not the entire Louisiana Territory that extended

[4] Even studies of Barings earlier (Hidy 1949) and later (Orbell 1985; Austin 2007) give the episode short coverage. Ditto for the magisterial study of Hope & Co. (Buist 1974), which moves on quickly to other, larger, and more consequential projects undertaken by Pierre Cesar Labouchere.

to the headwaters of the Mississippi and Missouri Rivers. Their problem was how to assure France that the U.S. government would agree to that increased amount.

Barbé-Marbois states firmly that no French bank was willing to take on this commitment, not even the newly empowered Banque de France, "afraid of rendering it dependent on an authority that was too ready to interfere in matters of which a reciprocal confidence ought to constitute the basis." Further, "the American ministers were very desirous that the payments should be made through the intervention of the most stable house in Europe" the combination of Baring & Co. in London and Hope & Co. in Amsterdam.[5] In an appendix added by the translator, a letter from the retired ex-President James Monroe affirmed "It is just to state, that the frank, candid, and friendly conduct of the two great houses of Hope, of Amsterdam, and of Baring, of London, by offering to us loans to any amount we might require, at the usual interest, rendered to the U.S. essential service in the negotiation. We had reason to believe, that the knowledge of their offers, and the confidence with which it inspired the French government, that our stock might be converted through them into cash, at a fair price, aided us in prevailing on that government to accept the payment in stock, and to lessen the amount demanded for the territory ceded."[6] In Monroe's memoirs, moreover, he mentions that upon his arrival in Paris, an agent of Baring & Co. had visited him to assure him that the two banking houses were willing to back up to $10 million of U.S. debt toward the purchase of New Orleans. Monroe dismissed the offer at the time, saying he did not anticipate needing that assurance. In later correspondence between Monroe and Livingston, when Monroe was in London as the American minister, however, he mentions the agent, Daniel Parker, by name and recommends him to be one of the American commissioners appointed to distribute the 20 million francs among the American claimants. Daniel Parker will appear again (Chapter 6) as an important "influencer" and promoter of many possible opportunities for profit in the ongoing relations between France and the United States.

In summary, the first-person accounts of the negotiations by Livingston, Monroe, and Barbé-Marbois, the three signatories to the

[5] Barbé-Marbois (1830, pp. 309–310).

[6] Barbé-Marbois (1830, pp. 309–310, p. 425, p. 54 of Appendix).

conventions that comprised the Louisiana Purchase, simply take for granted the role played by the two banking houses. All three ministers were persuaded that the financial details of the transaction were in good hands and would be carried out faithfully and completely. Indeed, that was the case as well for Jefferson in the United States (advised by Gallatin) and Napoleon for France (advised by Talleyrand and Barbé-Marbois), the two authorities who had to approve the formal treaty to make it binding. The contented comments of both Monroe and Barbé-Marbois in his 1830 book put aside the role of finance to emphasize many other, much more important for later government officials, aspects of the Louisiana Purchase.

Implicit in all the discussions at the time was the assumption that France was well into the process of reclaiming sovereign title to all of the Louisiana Territory that it had claimed before 1763 by the internationally accepted (at least by European powers) "Doctrine of Discovery." Title under the doctrine of discovery, as understood at the time, however, "was not a complete fee title of ownership and possession *until* (emphasis added) the Euro-Americans extinguished the Indian title of occupancy and use and actually occupied the land."[7] Extinguishing the Native Americans' title of occupancy, however, required making some accommodation with the current occupants. This could range from periodic gift exchanges, through the purchase of defined parcels of territory, to a "just war" to subjugate or remove the Native Americans. Paying $11.25 million to France for the privilege of taking on the future burden and expense of extinguishing the title of occupancy of Native Americans had to be weighed against the alternative: removing the few and scattered Spanish forces holding minor posts between St. Louis and New Orleans by military force, using either the U.S. Army or Kentucky and Tennessee militias.

Such military action, strongly recommended by some in Congress and even by Alexander Hamilton in one of his published opinions, however, would have played into the Federalist goal of strengthening the central government. While it might have been less expensive in the long run, it would have been more costly in the short run than the 6% annual interest payments to foreign bondholders. Clearly, even before Livingston and Monroe seized the opportunity of the Louisiana Purchase in Paris,

[7] Miller (2008, p. 72).

Jefferson, Madison, and Gallatin had in mind to use the Doctrine of Discovery to expand the territorial limits of the new country. They had already set into motion the Corps for Discovery of a northern river debouching on the Pacific Coast. The Lewis and Clark expedition was already in preparation even as Livingston was asked by Jefferson and Madison to bargain with France for the sale of New Orleans.

Beyond that, little else is said about the role played behind the scenes, as it were, of the bankers providing the finance for the Louisiana Purchase. Standard histories of both Barings and Hope pass over the deal as a minor episode in the history of those two distinguished merchant banking houses, the leading financiers in London and Amsterdam at the time.[8] For each firm, the Louisiana Purchase was only one of several major funding operations carried out during the years preceding and following the French Revolutionary and Napoleonic Wars. Further, it was neither the most profitable nor the most troublesome operation for either house. Consequently, the Louisiana Purchase fades into the background of the histories of the companies involved. That it turned out to be successful on its own terms, for both the finance companies and the two countries involved, means that historians generally (*mea culpa!*) put it aside to deal with more interesting phenomena.

First and foremost in the minds of the political and financial players in the process was making the transfer of European-American title from Spain to France. This process that had already begun in New Orleans on March 26, 1803, with the arrival of Pierre Laussat, the civilian governor sent by Napoleon to take possession of New Orleans and the rest of the Louisiana Territory. Two weeks later, James Monroe arrived in Paris to begin the negotiations for transfer of title ("right of preemption") from France to the United States. Consequently, the existing historiography on the Louisiana Purchase focuses on the network of *political* players who responded in the United States and France to the political and military pressures that led them to make their final deal, the deal now known as "The Louisiana Purchase." Hence, the mural that celebrates the Louisiana Purchase in the state capitol of Louisiana in Baton Rouge

[8] Buist, pp. 57–60, covers the Dutch side of the Louisiana loan from the perspective of Hope & Company, with intriguing details on Labouchere's activities relegated to his footnotes. Ziegler, pp. 70–74, focuses on the concerns of Sir Francis Baring that his firm share equally in the profits with the Dutch partners.

Fig. 1.2 Historical panel in the Louisiana State Archives Building (The original map of that territory is shown on the scales, balanced by a small amount of species. The three figures prominent in the negotiations to obtain this large land mass in 1803: Robert Livingston, Thomas Jefferson, and Napoleon. Also depicted are William C. C. Claiborne, the first colonial governor of Louisiana, and Andrew Jackson, the hero of the Battle of New Orleans in 1815. *Source* https://www.sos.la.gov/HistoricalResources/PublishedDocuments/HistoricalPanels.pdf)

today features Napoleon Bonaparte, Thomas Jefferson, and Robert R. Livingston (Fig. 1.2).

Assuredly, these three men were the key political decision-makers who made Louisiana part of the United States. Napoleon, First Consul of France at the time, decided to cede all of the Louisiana Territory to the United States, two and one-half years after he had wrested it back, if only conditionally, from Spain (in the Third Treaty of San Ildefonso, October 1, 1800). Jefferson, President of the United States, finally decided to offer buying New Orleans from France, but only after he faced increased pressure from restless settlers in Kentucky and Tennessee when the port of New Orleans was closed temporarily to Americans in October 1802. The American minister in Paris, Robert R. Livingston, initially sent just to settle the claims of American shippers for their losses to French privateers as agreed under the Treaty of Mortefontaine (1800), gradually broadened his mission to attempt to purchase both New Orleans and the Floridas from France as well.

James Monroe is missing from the mural in Baton Rouge, but he was called into action by Jefferson to make the actual offer in 1803 for reasons that can only be inferred from the domestic political calculations that Jefferson made at the time. The commemorative stamp issued in 1953 by the U.S. Postal Service, however, featured Monroe, Livingston, and François Barbé-Marbois, the three men who actually signed the treaty in Paris. Bizarrely, Monroe and Livingston were the two "ministers plenipotentiary" to France from the United States, each with full powers to act on behalf of the United States, so each had to sign the treaty on behalf of the United States. (Monroe had the additional title of "envoy extraordinary.") The two ministers who became co-signatories on behalf of the United States to the definitive treaty that brought the Louisiana territory into the United States would then spend the rest of their lives each man trying to take credit for the deal from the other.

François Barbé-Marbois, also missing from the mural in Baton Rouge, was the sole French representative to sign the treaty on behalf of Napoleon. All historians find his presence unusual as previous treaties under Napoleon's rule as First Consul had been signed off either by brothers of Napoleon (Joseph for the Treaty of Mortefontaine and Louis for the Treaty of San Ildefonso), or Talleyrand (the Treaty of Amiens). As with Monroe for the United States, the best explanation for the presence of Barbé-Marbois is that domestic political considerations determined Napoleon to replace Talleyrand with Barbé-Marbois. The relationship of Barbé-Marbois with Livingston predated Talleyrand's by 15 years and had been more personal. In 1783, both men and their wives were in Philadelphia, Barbé-Marbois as consul-general and acting *chargé d'affaires* for France while Livingston was Secretary of Foreign Affairs for the U.S. Congress of the Confederation. Talleyrand did not arrive in the United States until 1794 after being expelled from England. In September 1796, he circuitously returned to France in time to become foreign minister under Napoleon in July 1797. Further, all three alternative representatives for Napoleon—Joseph, Louis, and Talleyrand—were opposed to ceding Louisiana at the time.[9] And, perhaps Napoleon thought Barbé-Marbois would siphon off less bribe money from the Americans than Talleyrand.[10]

[9] Roberts, pp. 324–326.

[10] So conjectures Deviosse, pp. 330–339.

In any event, François Barbé-Marbois has been celebrated in later years as *The Man Who Sold Louisiana* (E. Wilson Lyon, 1942) and *L'Homme qui vendit la Louisiane* (Jean Deviosse, 1989). As the recently appointed Minister of the Public Treasury in 1801, Barbé-Marbois was responsible for government expenditures and management of the public debt, at least until he was summarily dismissed by Napoleon in January 1806. In later years, Barbé-Marbois published "[t]he most authoritative French treatment of the cession in his *Histoire de la Louisiane*, published in 1829, with an English translation appearing in 1830."[11] The latter work included some additional material provided by James Monroe, apparently intended to downplay the role of Robert R. Livingston in accomplishing the purchase.[12]

In neither work, however, does Barbé-Marbois say anything about the efforts of Alexander Baring, the agent of the house of Barings who set the terms for the finance of the purchase in the negotiations that took place in Paris in April 1803. Nor does he mention the working relationship he had established earlier with Pierre Cesar Labouchere, the agent of the house of Hope, to speed up payments to the French Treasury, first in September 1803 and then, crucially, in March 1804. Without the ability of these two individual agents for the firms of Baring and Hope to adapt to the rapidly changing political circumstances created by Napoleon at the time by changing the timing and form of payments to France, it is conceivable that Napoleon might have reneged on the cession of Louisiana, as he threatened to do from time to time.

As one follows the forays of these two financial agents, Alexander Baring and Pierre Cesar Labouchere, into international finance as recorded by Sir Francis Baring,[13] one learns not only the risks that merchant-financiers faced at this defining moment in the history of sovereign finance, but also how the various political players and decision-makers could be persuaded (or purchased) to agree to the terms of finance. Further insight into the factors that facilitated widespread marketing of sovereign bonds in London and Amsterdam at the height of the Napoleonic Wars is also found in the Baring Archive. The merchant banker houses of Baring and Hope combined to market the Louisiana

[11] Chase (1929, foreword).

[12] Deviosse, p. 437.

[13] The Baring Archive, NP1.A, "The Northbrook Business Papers."

Purchase bonds in Amsterdam and London in 1804 and then maintained their marketability through the War of 1812 between Britain and the United States. This was the financial breakthrough that later enabled the success of the Rothschild brothers to market other sovereign bonds, such as the Prussian loan of 1818, which were issued while the Louisiana bonds were being successively paid off in Amsterdam and London.[14] Even the designated price-current issued by the London Stock Exchange at the time, Wetenhall's *Course of the Exchange*, listed the U.S. sovereign bonds starting in 1811, the first foreign government bonds to be listed. Further, dividends were payable in pound sterling in London, as well as Dutch guilders in Amsterdam. Some bondholders, however, preferred to let the house of Baring collect interest on their behalf in the United States until the wartime income tax in Britain was repealed in 1816.

The Houses of Baring and Hope

The key development on the financial side that led to the success of the Louisiana Purchase, all accounts agree, at least in passing, was the previous affiliation of the two most eminent merchant banking firms in Europe—Hope & Co. in Amsterdam and Baring & Co. in London. The heads of the two firms, Sir Francis Baring in London and Henry Hope, first in Amsterdam and then in London after 1795, had established cordial relations during the American Revolution, relations that were put on hold briefly during the Fourth Anglo-Dutch War (1780–1784). Afterward, their relations resumed, especially in commerce in the West Indies, at least until the 1790 Patriot revolution in Holland eventually forced Henry Hope to leave Amsterdam permanently in October 1794 to relocate in England.[15] Earlier, Henry Hope had moved his art collection from his country estate in Welgelegen, a villa built in 1784 now housing the government of North Holland, to his East Sheen estate in England.

Before Henry Hope's move to England, however, Sir Francis had tried to establish a stronger personal tie with Henry Hope by sending

[14] The *Gentleman's Magazine* in 1819 asserted this primacy for Nathan Rothschild, and is the basis for the assertion that this was the start of the international sovereign bond market in London by the Rothschild Archive web site: https://www.rothschildarchive.org/exhibitions/timeline/.

[15] A house in Harley Street, off Cavendish Square in London, and the East Sheen estate outside Richmond (Buist, 49–50).

his second son, Alexander, at age 20 to receive training in the affairs of Hope & Co. in Amsterdam in 1794. There, Alexander came under the tutelage of Hope & Co.'s chief clerk, Pierre Cesar Labouchere, age 22, which began a relationship that would endure to the end of their lives. It did not last long in Amsterdam, however, for the two junior clerks, left to manage affairs of Hope & Co. after Henry Hope had departed for London, were themselves forced to flee in turn in January 1795. That winter the French army was able to complete their invasion of Amsterdam across the frozen polders and rivers. The two young men were soon separated again, however, as each was sent by their respective firms to explore new possibilities for facilitating capital flight from Europe, increasingly convulsed by the turmoil created by the French Revolution's destruction of traditional property rights.

Sir Francis Baring and Henry Hope sent Alexander to the United States in 1795, equipped with a letter of credit for £100,000 and their joint power of attorney. His primary mission was to check out the prospects for purchasing extensive lands in the north woods of Maine, then a part of Massachusetts, that Senator William Bingham of Philadelphia had offered to sell, repeatedly without success to various French, British, and Dutch investors, including Sir Francis in 1794.[16] With Henry Hope's desire to place some of his wealth beyond the reach of European governments at war with each other, however, the possibility now seemed worth exploring by Sir Francis in partnership with Henry Hope. While that was Alexander's main mission, he was clearly meant to determine as well what prospects lay in the realm of American public finance and in financing the booming overseas trade that American ships were enjoying with their privileges of neutrality while France and Britain were at war. Alexander surely was also given the mission to determine the possible success of Alexander Hamilton's re-financing of American government debt in which Sir Francis had taken a substantial position earlier in partnership with Daniel Parker as described in Chapter 3. Daniel Parker's role in American-European financial relations, moreover, continued well afterward as will be described in Chapter 6.

Pierre Cesar would be sent by Henry Hope to represent Hope & Co. when and wherever a new problem or opportunity for the firm's affairs arose. His duties took him to Hamburg in 1798, to Surinam in 1799,

[16] The tortuous history of Bingham's Maine lands is covered in detail in Allis, 1954. "William Bingham's Maine Lands 1790–1820."

back to Amsterdam at the end of 1801, and then to Portugal in 1802 before returning to Amsterdam. The two men who worked together to make the financing of the Louisiana Purchase possible in 1803 and who would become the leading financiers of the early nineteenth century laid the basis for their future successes by exploring separately the possibilities for international finance at the end of the eighteenth century whether in North America (Alexander) or continental Europe and the West Indies (Pierre Cesar). They combined their separate networks of political and financial contacts in January 1803, when Alexander posed a possible financial deal to Pierre Cesar, a deal that would lead to the financing of the Louisiana Purchase by the two merchant banking houses of Sir Francis Baring & Company in London and Hope & Company in Amsterdam.

These two individuals should be added to the already well-known "cast of characters" who were critical players in the finance of the Louisiana Purchase, whether they played a role as political agents or principals, financial agents or principals, and whether they were American, British, Dutch, or French. In the story that follows, the starring roles are played by the "Finance Principals," Sir Francis Baring and Henry Hope, who made the strategic decisions for initiating the financial arrangements. But, the "Finance Agents," Alexander Baring and Pierre Cesar Labouchere, had to make strategic decisions as well over the course of carrying out their respective assignments. Alexander had to persuade the American Secretary of the Treasury, Albert Gallatin, that his personal contract with the three political agents who signed the formal agreements in Paris was binding on the American government as well. Meanwhile back in France, Pierre Cesar had to speed up the advance payments to France as insisted upon by Napoleon, to the satisfaction of François Barbé-Marbois, the French equivalent of Gallatin.

The other financial players in the background are mainly the Dutch merchant bankers, who continued to satisfy their customer base with the new Louisiana 6's that served to replace their earlier holdings of American sovereign debt. Servicing the interest payments to their customers, however, required them to devise surreptitious modes of access to the facilities offered by the Baring Bros. firm in London, thanks to the enforcement of the Continental Blockade by France and the enforcement of Orders in Council by the British government. One Daniel Parker, never mentioned in the historiography of the Louisiana Purchase, may also have played a critical role, at least according to evidence found in the Baring Archive. All the actors, political and financial, had to perform their roles during the turbulent times of the French Revolutionary and Napoleonic Wars (Table 1.1).

Table 1.1 The full cast of players

United States
Thomas Jefferson, President of the United States
James Madison, Secretary of State
[Political Principals]
Robert R. Livingston & James Monroe, both Ministers Plenipotentiary, but Monroe a further "Envoy Extraordinary"
[Political Agents]
William Bingham, Director, Bank of the United States
Thomas Willing, President, Bank of the United States
[Financial Principals]
Albert Gallatin, Secretary of the Treasury
[Financial Agent]
Daniel Parker, American expatriate
[Financial Promoter]
France
Napoleon Bonaparte, First Consul
[Political Principal]
Charles Maurice de Talleyrand-Périgord
[Political Agent]
François Barbé-Marbois
[Financial Agent]
Pierre Samuel du Pont de Nemours
[Financial Promoter]
Netherlands
[All Merchant Bankers]
Willink Bros. & Co.
De Smeth Bros. & Co.
Van Staphorst Bros. & Co.
Hope & Co.
Finance, principals
Sir Francis Baring (London)
Henry Hope (London)
Finance, agents
Alexander Baring (London)
Pierre Cesar Labouchere (Amsterdam)

References

Austin, Peter E. 2007. *Baring Brothers and the Birth of Modern Finance*. London: Pickering & Chatto.

Barbé-Marbois, François. 1830. *The History of Louisiana, particularly the cession of that colony to the United States of America with an introductory essay on the Constitution and government of the United States* (tr. William Beach Lawrence). Philadelphia.

Buist, Marten G. 1974. *At Spes Non Fracta: Hope & Co. 1779–1815*. Amsterdam: Bank Mees & Hope NV.

Chase, Eugene Parker. 1929. *Our Revolutionary Forefathers: The Letters of Francois, Marquis de Barbé-Marbois, during his Residence in the United States as Secretary of the French Legation, 1779–1785*. New York: Duffield & Co.

Hidy, Ralph W. 1949. *The House of Baring in American Trade and Finance: English Merchant Bankers at Work, 1763–1861*. Cambridge, MA: Harvard University Press.

Lee, Robert. 2017. "Accounting for Conquest: The Price of the Louisiana Purchase of Indian Country." *The Journal of American History* 103 (4): 921–942.

Miller, Robert J. 2008. *Native America, Discovered and Conquered: Thomas Jefferson, Lewis and Clark, and Manifest Destiny*. Lincoln and London: University of Nebraska Press.

Orbell, John. 1985. *A History of Baring Brothers to 1939*. London: Baring Brothers & Co., Limited.

CHAPTER 2

Setting Up the Finance for the Louisiana Purchase

Amsterdam, January 30, 1803

I reply, my dear Alexander, to your letter 19 inst. by Samuel[1] without having as yet maturely considered, how to forward to you my letter. I think I perfectly understand the subject you treat upon, it is of the utmost magnitude and importance, might stagger us in ordinary times, and in the present would hardly attract the serious attention of many. But much and long as I have been a skeptic respecting the permanency of the present order of things, I find strong inducement to vary the grounds of my opinions, and to reconsider with yourself what is than what may be. Thus the operation appears to me in a double point of view and which induces me to blend the whole in laying it before our London friends for their acceptance or refusal.

(*The Baring Archive, NP1.A4.3*)

Pierre Cesar Labouchere's response to Alexander Baring's letter of January 19, 1803, from Paris shows both his enthusiasm for the project and his affection for his brother-in-law. Further proof of his enthusiasm,

[1] Samuel was likely Samuel Pierre Labouchere, younger brother of Pierre Cesar Labouchere.

L. Neal, *The Forgotten Financiers of the Louisiana Purchase*, Palgrave Studies in the History of Finance,
https://doi.org/10.1007/978-3-031-56277-8_2

in addition to the hasty scrawl,[2] is the detail and precision of the instructions he gives to Alexander over the next five pages on just how to set up and then carry out an unprecedented financial deal. The deal, simply put, would be to transfer New Orleans from France to the United States on the one hand and to settle the accumulated claims of American merchants against French privateers on the other hand. In January 1803, however, neither country had a well-established government with a credible record of financial commitments, much less a record of making binding diplomatic relations with one another. Consequently, Labouchere argues, each government should be more willing to deal with a private third party, a credible intermediary capable of taking on the risk that either sovereign government might find it preferable to default rather than fulfill an agreement. Indeed, each government had a recent history of demanding the other country recall its ambassador or designated representative. In this case, Labouchere was anticipating the later comments of Barbé-Marbois and James Monroe.

Citizen Genêt, appointed as Minister to the United States by the Girondins in revolutionary France, arrived in South Carolina in April 1793. He immediately began outfitting privateers to attack British shipping with French letters of marque, very much against President Washington's policy of neutrality. When Washington formally asked the French government to recall Genêt, the new revolutionary powers declared him under arrest. Fearing for his life if he returned to France, Genêt pleaded for asylum in the United States, which Washington, on the advice of both Hamilton and Jefferson, granted him in 1794. Meanwhile, Gouverneur Morris, the U.S. Minister to France during the Terror, was declared persona non grata by the First French Republic in April 1794 due to his public sympathy for a constitutional monarchy. His eventual successor, James Monroe, was recalled as well by Washington as American minister to France in December 1796. Monroe's enthusiasm for the French Revolution ran counter to Washington and Hamilton's policy of strict neutrality with respect to wars in Europe. Further, John Jay's Treaty with Great Britain, signed in London late in 1794, outraged the French

[2] Unlike most of the correspondence in the Baring Archive, this letter was not transcribed in a fine hand by a trusted clerk. At the end, Labouchere apologizes for his "hasty scrawl" due to the press of time as a confidential agent is just then available to deliver the letter in person to Alexander. For reasons described below, the carrier was possibly Daniel Parker, an American expatriate from Boston.

government when its terms became known and their privateers increased their captures of American merchant vessels in the West Indies.[3]

Agreement between American and France would be even more difficult at the time because the French government was openly corrupt and the American government was politically (and financially) restrained from paying bribes. In 1798, the three commissioners sent by John Adams to negotiate the withdrawal of French privateers from attacking U.S. merchant ships, later termed the Quasi-War of 1798–1800, were denied access to Talleyrand, the French Minister of Foreign Affairs. Instead, they were approached by various private individuals, later identified as W, X, Y, and Z. The terms dictated by these individuals were for a side-payment to Talleyrand, a low-interest loan to France, and the United States to compensate itself the damages sustained by American merchants. Outraged, the Americans refused to deal with these intermediaries, although one American, Elbridge Gerry, stayed on later to arrange at least a cease-fire with Talleyrand. This deal probably came with the assistance of an American Quaker pacifist, George Logan, who had approached Talleyrand directly. The Logan Act of 1799, still in force, was then passed to criminalize any private citizen's diplomatic negotiations with a foreign power.

Consequently, Labouchere had to work up a detailed arrangement for financing a complex deal between France and the United States in which neither country would deal directly with the other. Instead, the two banking houses in Amsterdam and London would interpose their agents between the two countries. Three months later in Paris, Alexander Baring would modify Labouchere's plan sufficiently to accomplish the financing of the Louisiana Purchase.

Labouchere's letter, which continues for another four pages of detailed calculations and recommendations, however, highlights just how uncertain were the times, especially for international finance. Further, the responses to Labouchere's initial letter, contained in a special folder in the Baring Archive created by Lord Northbrook in 1903 to commemorate the centennial of the Louisiana Purchase,[4] highlight the difficulties that confronted the financiers. The folder dedicated to the Louisiana Purchase is filled with detailed instructions and advice that Pierre Cesar and Sir

[3] See Unger (2005, Ch. 10, "The War with France," for details).

[4] *Baring Archive*, Northbrook Business Papers, NP1.A4.7.

Francis Baring each gave to Alexander in Paris well before the arrival of James Monroe on April 11, 1803, the American "Envoy Extraordinary" sent by Jefferson specifically to purchase New Orleans for the United States.

There is a gap in the Baring file during the actual negotiations in Paris, however, probably due to the precautions taken on the advice of Sir Francis to destroy all the letters after reading them. Coverage resumes, however, when problems with completing the deal arise, first from Napoleon and then from the British prime minister in late 1803. As the implications of the deal for financing the upcoming war became clearer to both governments, each put pressure on the financiers—France to speed up the payments, Britain to cut them off. (While Addington, the British Prime Minister, preferred the United States to possess New Orleans, he balked at sending British funds to Napoleon after the war was declared.) The Baring Archive reveals how Sir Francis coped with pressures from all sides, largely with the aid of timely interventions by Pierre Cesar on the Continent.

Most of the remaining material in the Baring Archive, however, deals with Sir Francis' response to the claim by Hope & Co. in Amsterdam in late 1804 (after the bonds had arrived in Amsterdam and London and been sold off at premium prices and the payments to France had been completed) that they should take two-thirds of the profits, leaving Baring & Co. in London with only one-third. Sir Francis then recovered copies of the original correspondence to make his case that the profits of the deal should be split equally between the houses of Baring and Hope, a case that he was willing to take to an English court of law if the partners in Hope & Co. in Amsterdam refused to concede.

To make his case, Sir Francis revealed more insights into the various obstacles that had to be overcome by the financiers before the purchase could be completed. Ultimately, he demonstrated to his satisfaction, and perhaps that of Henry Hope as well, that the risks borne by the London side, especially by Alexander Baring, were at least equal to those overcome by Pierre Cesar Labouchere on the Amsterdam side. Exhausted by his efforts, which succeeded to keep the Baring share equal to the Hope share, Sir Francis then retired from the firm. It was left to Alexander and Pierre Cesar to carry on the affairs of both firms after Sir Francis died in September 1810 and Henry Hope died in February 1811. The two brothers-in-law would then share more financial adventures, first using their access to American shipping to drain the Mexican mint of silver to finance both Napoleon and Wellington, then arranging the finance of the French occupation loan in 1817. Their joint efforts would confirm London as the center of international finance for the next century, while establishing American government debt as a worthy complement to European sovereign debts.

Other materials in the Northbrook Business Papers in the Baring Archive, moreover, shed even more light on the contingencies that continually confronted both Alexander and Pierre Cesar in the period leading up to their success. In those perilous times of continued war and revolution, the emergence of internationally marketable sovereign debt proved to be a "safe haven" for investors faced with extortion, expropriation, and, possibly, execution. Providing access to these assets for private investors was a worthy challenge to a new class of international financial intermediaries, the merchant bankers of Europe. Providing worthy assets by the respective governments, on the other hand, proved to be much more difficult and required repeated experiments and failures by the respective governments. The Baring Archive reveals the difficulties of governments in the United States, Spain, France, Portugal, Austria, the Netherlands, and Prussia encountered while attempting to emulate Britain's financial success. The archive also reveals some of the marketing techniques used by Barings to provide access to the London market for the sovereign debt issued by the new Federal government of the United States.

To appreciate the measure of the success of Alexander and Pierre Cesar in confronting and overcoming the obstacles to creating marketable sovereign debt during the French Revolutionary and Napoleonic Wars, one has to contrast the apparently flawless execution of the financing of the Louisiana Purchase, as uncovered in American government sources, with the disruptions to international finance at the time. The political revolutions of the Atlantic world, starting in 1775 with the Boston Tea Party, convulsed the rest of the Atlantic world until at least 1825. International finance endured repeated shocks throughout this period with governments and investors making repeated experiments in reaction.

Over the course of the careers of Alexander Baring and Pierre Cesar Labouchere, the two men participated in the financial responses of the warring powers to unprecedented demands of war finance. They saw at first hand the remarkably sustainable public finance of Great Britain, the authoritarian attempts by Napoleon first to replicate and then to undercut Britain's financial system, the various attempts of other European states to replicate the British success, and, finally, the emergence of sundry experiments in the financial system of the United States—experiments that continue to the present day. With the benefit of over two hundred years of hindsight, perhaps we can discern better than was possible for people at the time just why some of the many financial experiments undertaken succeeded while others failed.

In particular, it will emerge that the success of the Louisiana Purchase was a last legacy of Alexander Hamilton. Hamilton's financial program, sustained by Albert Gallatin, restructured the public finance of the new, truly United States. It was not merely a lucky outcome of Thomas Jefferson's "noble gamble" due to fortuitous circumstances as argued in most recent accounts. Even the presence of the financial intermediaries from Amsterdam to London was not at all fortuitous. The apparent triumph of American finance of the Louisiana Purchase from the perspective of the Virginia dynasty of Presidents Jefferson, Madison, and Monroe is a marked contrast to the disruption of international finance during the Napoleonic Wars that followed and the agonizing decision-making by the Anglo-Dutch financiers who actually accomplished the deal. A lot of people were involved, and none worked more diligently toward the success of sovereign debt finance than Alexander Baring and Pierre Cesar Labouchere, as we shall see.

Financing the Louisiana Purchase Seen as an American Triumph

The fullest account of the American side of the financing of the Louisiana Purchase, based on materials that turned up accidentally a century ago, is still the *Louisiana Historical Quarterly* article by James E. Winston and Robert W. Columb, "How the Louisiana Purchase was Financed."[5] In their account, there were $11.25 millions in U.S. bonds elaborately printed up in Washington, D.C., as 5071 separate certificates in 13 different denominations of dollars and signed by Joseph Nourse, Registrar of the U.S. Treasury. They were never delivered to the French Treasury, however. Instead, one-third of the printed certificates were consigned directly to Alexander Baring in Washington, D.C., as the representative

[5] Winston, James E. and Robert W. Columb (1929). "How the Louisiana Purchase Was Financed." *Louisiana Historical Quarterly* 12: 189–237.

of the London house of Sir Francis Baring & Company. He may have distributed a few in Philadelphia and Baltimore to American investors,[6] but took the bulk with him to London for distribution by the house of Sir Francis Baring & Company. The other two-thirds of the bonds were sent by American warship to the U.S. envoy in Paris, Robert R. Livingston. Unmentioned in the Winston-Columb article is that Livingston then turned them over to Pierre Cesar Labouchere, representative of the Amsterdam house of Hope & Co. In Amsterdam, Labouchere distributed them to his partners, the firms of Willinks & Co. and De Smeths & Co. Robert R. Livingston, the American Minister to France, who remained in Paris after James Monroe left to take up duties as Minister to the Court of St. James in London, then released the 92 signed and legally binding bills of acceptance that committed the two firms, Sir Francis Baring & Co. in London and Hope & Co. in Amsterdam to the French Minister, François Barbé-Marbois. These formal, legally binding bills of exchange committed the two firms to pay 52 million French francs to the French Treasury over the next 3 1/3 years in bi-weekly installments.

Also not mentioned in the Winston-Columb paper is that while waiting for the arrival of the U.S. bond certificates in London and Paris, Labouchere had replaced the acceptances previously signed by Alexander Baring with a variety of payments that satisfied the French Minister in less than two years.[7] In sum, rather than the United States purchasing the Louisiana Territory from France, instead, the United States issued bonds to international investment bankers who sold them in turn to their clients in London and Amsterdam. Further, none of the bonds remained in France. The bankers took on the responsibility to distribute the semi-annual interest payments on the bonds to the ultimate holders in Amsterdam and London over the next 18 years while taking a sizable commission for themselves. (Gallatin, on the American side, would argue that the bankers' commission was excessive; Barbé-Marbois, on the French side, that it was reasonable given the times.) In

[6] Winter, p. 923, fn. 72, states that Alexander had already sold $200,000 in America to Willing and Francis and $100,000 to Daniel Ludlow & Co., and another $200,000 had been offered to the public, citing letter by Alexander to Hope & Co., March 9, 1804, Hope Papers. Nevertheless, Gallatin remitted the interest payment on all $11,250,000 bonds to Barings in March 1804.

[7] Indeed, Labouchere is not mentioned at all. Full details are in the Baring Archive, but the basic arrangements made by Labouchere are found in an article by one of his descendants (Labouchere, 1916) and discussed in Chapter 5.

preparation, however, the bankers had clearly anticipated the desires of their ultimate retail investors by specifying exactly how many certificates were to be printed up in each denomination for their respective clients in Amsterdam and London.

The French Treasury, moreover, received a handsome advance payment upon Napoleon's ratification of the treaty in Paris as discerned from the American side, but from the Baring and Hope financiers, not from the U.S. government, which had not yet ratified the treaty much less approved the bond issue necessary to fulfill it. Only after the U.S. Congress had ratified the treaty, the U.S. Treasury had printed up the bonds, and Jefferson had received official confirmation that the transfer of New Orleans from Spain to France and then from France to the United States had taken place without incident, were 1/3 of the bonds shipped by sea to London and 2/3 to Paris. They arrived in both cities in April of 1804. For nearly one year after the agreements between France and the United States for the Louisiana Purchase had been signed, therefore, the houses of Baring and Hope made advance payments to France before they had possession of the bonds that they could then market and start to receive interest payments from the United States. Once the bankers had the packets of bonds, they (not the American representatives) began payments to France of the remaining 34.5 million francs to complete the Louisiana Purchase. Ultimate payment by the United States was delayed for 15 years, but the bankers had immediately committed to pay France the equivalent over 3 and 1/3 years, a commitment they actually completed in 2 years.

There is no formal bill of sale for the Louisiana Territory from France to the United States in 1803, nor was there any payment of dollars by the United States to France. This did not set a precedent for subsequent purchases of territory by the United States from sovereign powers, however. The purchase of the Floridas in 1818 from Spain, the Gadsden Purchase in 1854 from Mexico, and Alaska from Russia in 1867 were all settled directly with payments in U.S. dollars.[8] The success of the U.S. government in servicing and then redeeming the

[8] While the history museum in Anchorage, Alaska displays a check for the $7.2 million paid by the United States to the Russian Tsar, it must be noted that formal authorization of the payment was not made by the House of Representatives, and no treaty was submitted to the U.S. Senate, quite the reverse of the sequence of events for the Louisiana Purchase. (Thanks to Mark Stumpf for calling this interesting factoid to my attention!)

Louisiana debt, therefore, established U.S. debt as an acceptable payment thereafter in international settlements, the enduring legacy of Alexander Hamilton's service as the first Secretary of the Treasury of the United States. According to the most definitive published account of the financial arrangements for the Louisiana Purchase, and the official records of the United States and France now available online, what happened in that case was more complex and deliberately obscure.[9]

Instead of a simple land sale, Robert R. Livingston and James Monroe for the United States and François Barbé-Marbois for France signed three separate documents in Paris on April 30, 1803. The first, the formal treaty, simply specified that France ceded the Louisiana Territory that it had received from Spain by an earlier treaty to the United States; the second, called the "First Convention," said the United States would issue bonds to the sum of $11,250,000 bearing interest at 6% annually payable in Paris, London, or Amsterdam; and the third, called the "Second Convention," said that the claims of U.S. merchants for their losses to French privateers in the preceding conflict from 1798 to 1800 (the Quasi-War between France and the United States) would be assumed by the U.S. Treasury to a limit of 20 million French francs.[10]

The first document, the actual treaty itself, has only ten articles and none, by design, deal with the terms of payment. The initial article makes formal cession of the Louisiana Territory, as previously ceded by Spain to France by the Treaty of San Ildefonso in 1800, from France to the United States. The remaining articles specify the reciprocal legal responsibilities of the United States and France regarding navigation rights of the

[9] James E. Winston and Robert W. Columb (1929), "How the Louisiana Purchase Was Financed." *Louisiana Historical Quarterly* 12: 189–237. The authors copied and translated papers out of a book entitled, "Papers Appertaining to the Purchase of the Louisiana Province," collected and edited by the U.S. Treasury Department in 1875 for use in the Centennial Exposition at Philadelphia. While the authors state that there were two editions of the book, one given to the Louisiana Historical Society, and the other to the Howard Memorial Library at Tulane University, I have not found either book in these libraries or elsewhere to date. Perhaps the papers are in the National Archives, https://catalog.archives.gov/id/593574.

[10] The three conventions, in English and French, are at: https://memory.loc.gov/cgi-bin/ampage?collId=llsl&fileName=008/llsl008.db&recNum=213:226; and: https://www.archives.gov/milestone-documents/louisiana-purchase-treaty%20-%20:~:text=In%20this%20transaction%20with%20France,Mississippi%20River%20for%20%2415%20million. The French versions are reprinted in Barbé-Marbois (1829, pp. 431–446) and the English versions in Rodriguez (2002, pp. 408–412).

Mississippi, the rights of the existing residents, and relations with Native Americans.

The second and shortest of the three documents, the First Convention, has only three articles: (1) that the United States will pay 60 million francs to France, (2) the United States will create a stock of $11,250,000 in 15-year bonds denominated in dollars, paying 6% interest annually in either Amsterdam, London, or Paris, and (3) that the dollar will be fixed at an exchange rate of 5 1/3 francs per dollar. The second article in this convention has an additional paragraph that states that France, in order to receive full payment in a shorter period of time, will act to keep the market value of the U.S. bonds as high as possible. Implementation of that commitment turns out to have been the complete responsibility of the Anglo-Dutch banking firms of Baring and Hope, which will be our focus below based on materials in the Baring Archive.

The third and longest by far of the three documents, the Second Convention, is the least important from the financial perspective of the Louisiana Purchase, although the political ramifications persisted for many years afterward. It merely mentions that up to a further 20 million francs will be set aside by the U.S. Treasury to make restitution to American merchants for losses they suffered during the years prior to 1800 from seizures by French privateers. Nevertheless, it takes 13 articles to specify how American losses would be determined and compensation made to U.S. claimants. This third document became the most contentious for the Americans for years to come, but nothing in it concerned either France or the role of the English and Dutch merchant banks in financing the Louisiana Purchase.

The source of the heated and prolonged conflict between Robert R. Livingston and James Monroe over the manner in which the American commissioners awarded claims to the aggrieved American merchants, however, which has fascinated American historians ever since, may also have been initiated inadvertently by the Barings. Circumstantial evidence in The Baring Archives suggests that when Sir Francis Baring began to make the initial payments to France before formal ratification of the three conventions had occurred in the United States, he explicitly gave priority to Monroe's preferences for committing Napoleon to honor the agreement over Livingston's preferences to begin immediate restitution of the losses of American merchants, as agreed in the Second Convention.[11]

Most interesting for financial historians, however, is the private contract between the three individuals who signed the three conventions with a fourth, private, individual—an English citizen married to an American heiress, with no diplomatic or political standing, but who happened to be in Paris at the time enjoying the Christmas and Easter holidays with his family: Alexander Baring.[12] The fourth document[13] was a contract between the French Republic and Francis Baring & Co. of London and Hope & Co. of Amsterdam "for underwriting the stock to be issued by the United States in settlement of the Louisiana Purchase." Article 1 confers all the rights of the French government for possessing the U.S. bonds amounting to $11,250,000, as specified in the First Convention, to the "bankers Hope and Baring, or such other person or persons as they may designate." Further, Article 2 specifies that one-third of the bonds shall be delivered directly to Alexander Baring (or his attorney) in the United States and the remaining two-thirds sent to the American representative in Paris. Article 3 states that "the total and complete payment of the stock of $11,250,000, shall be made to the public treasury of France by Hope & Co. and Baring & Co., who reserve to themselves the interest and benefits resulting therefrom in consideration of Fifty-Two Million Francs."[14]

The payments of the 52 million francs to the French government, not 60 million, were specified to begin with 6 million francs paid within 30 days after formal notification had been received in Paris that the bonds had been delivered to Baring or his attorney in the United States. After that initial payment, the remaining 46 million francs were to be paid 2

[11] *Baring Archive*, NP1.A4.35 ff. 4–6, Propositions made to the Minister of the [French] Public Treasure by P C Labouchere, agent of the house of Hope & Co of Amsterdam.

[12] Winston and Columb, pp. 215–218.

[13] Oddly, I did not find a copy of this contract in the Baring Archive but it is reproduced in the Winston and Columb article, and it is referred to by Gallatin in a letter to Jefferson while they awaited the arrival of Alexander Baring in America to complete the financing.

[14] Note that Alexander Baring had already negotiated a commission of 8 million francs to compensate the two firms for their risk of not being able to sell the bonds at par within the time needed to pay the 52 million francs to France.

million each month over the next 23 months. In short, the United States took a long-term loan of $11,250,000 from the Hope and Baring partnership that the United States promised to repay in annual installments of one-fourth each year after 15 years while paying 6% interest annually in the meantime. The loan would be completely redeemed after 19 years. Meanwhile, Hope and Baring committed their firms to pay France the equivalent in francs within two years, while deducting a commission of 13 1/3%. Those payments were to be made weekly in bills of exchange of one-half-million francs each.

Alexander Baring, using his power of attorney from Sir Francis Baring & Co. in London and Hope & Co. in Amsterdam, personally accepted each bill and legally committed the two firms for each of the future payments. He signed a total of 92 separate bills of exchange, making each one an undated acceptance. He then left them with Robert R. Livingston, the American envoy, to be handed over to François Barbé-Marbois, the French Treasurer, whenever Livingston received the bonds in Paris for 2/3 of the purchase price. At that time, specific dates would be written into each bill so they could be cashed seriatim by the French Treasury over the following weeks. Livingston, in turn, would deliver the bond certificates to Labouchere or his agent in Paris to take back to Amsterdam for sale to his partners and clients.

Later exhibits in the article by Winston and Columb show that the total number of individually printed certificates came to 5071. The bonds were further broken down into six separate bundles destined either to London or Amsterdam. None were meant for Paris and only a few remained in the United States, taken by close associates of the Barings (Appendix A). Each certificate specified the agent in either Amsterdam or London who was responsible for paying the semi-annual interest to the bearer of the bond. In sum, the financing of the Louisiana Purchase from the American perspective was straightforward. Marketing the numerous bonds in their various denominations was left up to the brokers employed by the various merchant banks in Amsterdam and London. True, the American government was bound to pay semi-annual interest in dollars that were fixed at a constant rate relative to the French franc, which, in turn, had recently been stabilized in terms of gold and silver. The American payments, however, would be to the Dutch and English financial houses, who would distribute them to the current holders of the various certificates. The total outlay for the U.S. Federal government over the following years came to $23,527,872.57, still only about 4 cents an acre.[15] It was up to the respective merchant banking firms of Baring and Hope to make the payments in French francs to the French treasury in bi-weekly bills over the next three plus years, not the U.S. government.

From the perspective of those two private firms, however, carrying out the details of the financing would turn out to be quite complicated and risky, especially given "the present order of things." Moreover, the deal struck by Alexander Baring in Paris was quite different than the one planned originally by Pierre Cesar Labouchere in his letter of January 30, 1803, or the modified plan that was eventually approved by the senior partners in London and Amsterdam in April 1803.

The contract brought by Alexander Baring from Paris to Washington, D.C., in 1803 and published by Winston and Columb in 1926 was altered in its implementation, moreover, for reasons that did not concern the U.S. Treasury over a half-century later when they compiled the papers for the Philadelphia Centennial celebration of 1876. That is why the Winston and Columb article omits the details of the financing of the Louisiana Purchase from the French side, or from the Dutch or English side for that matter. These were the devilish details, however, that occupied most of the efforts by Baring and Hope to initiate and then complete the financing of the Louisiana Purchase under duress. The lessons they learned along the way, moreover, laid the basis for the future success of sovereign bond financing for governments able to tap into the international capital market of the nineteenth century that followed. Especially noteworthy were the respective successes of the American and French governments in acquiring the organizational capacity and financial expertise necessary to make their sovereign debts marketable in the international financial markets that emerged after the French and British wars. Alexander Baring's role as an instructor to the American Secretaries of the Treasury, especially Albert Gallatin, explaining how they could maintain access to European capital markets was an important ingredient in the American success, which ensured that Hamilton's legacy would endure. Meanwhile, Pierre Cesar Labouchere, as a central financial intermediary on the European continent, was laying the basis for the later success of European sovereign debts.

[15] As calculated by Van Meter, p. 253.

References

Barbé-Marbois, François. 1829. *Histoire de la Louisiane et de la cession de cette colonie par la France aux États-Uniés de l'Amérique Septentrionale: précédé d'un discourse sur la constitution des aux États-Unis.* Paris: Firmin-Didot.

Labouchere, M. G. 1916. "L'Annexion de la Louisiane aux États-Unis et les Maisons Hope et Baring." *Revue d'Histoire Diplomatique* 29 (1): 423–455.

Rodriguez, Junius P., Editor, 2002. *The Louisiana Purchase: A Historical and Geographical Encyclopedia*. Santa Barbara, CA: ABC-CLIO.

Unger, Harlow Giles. 2005. *The French War Against America: How a Trusted Ally Betrayed Washington and the Founding Fathers.* New York: John Wiley & Sons.

CHAPTER 3

"The Present Order of Things" in January 1803

Labouchere's letter to Alexander went on to assess "the present order of things" as he saw them from his vantage point in Amsterdam, mid-January 1803. The political implications of the American and French Revolutions and the wars that ensued shook profoundly the European worlds of trade and finance over the half-century after 1776. The formal signing of the Treaty of Amiens (March 25, 1802), however, allowed all parties to catch their breath and reassess the possibilities for the future. The Truce of Amiens actually began at the end of October 1801 when word spread of the negotiations underway between Britain and France. Figures 3.1, 3.2, and 3.3 highlight the financial benefits of that short-lived period of peace. For example, the price of the benchmark security on the London Stock Exchange, the Three Per Cent Consol, immediately jumped several points at the news of the truce before falling again once the war was declared by Britain on May 17, 1803 (Fig. 3.2). At the same time, even the price of the newly stabilized French *rente* (arbitrarily set at one-third of its capital value by the French Directory in 1796) also rose to levels comparable to the British Consol. Investors, however, required higher yields for the newly stabilized French sovereign debt than for Britain's well-established sovereign debt throughout the course of the French Revolutionary and Napoleonic War, as shown in Fig. 3.3 (cf. Bordo and White 1991).

L. Neal, *The Forgotten Financiers of the Louisiana Purchase*, Palgrave Studies in the History of Finance,
https://doi.org/10.1007/978-3-031-56277-8_3

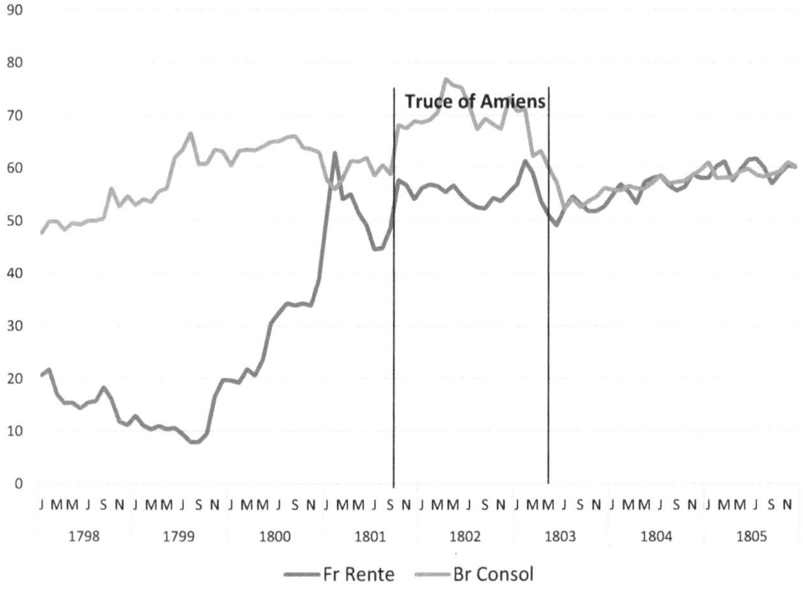

Fig. 3.1 French 5% rentes (monthly average on Paris Bourse) and British 3% Consols on London Stock Exchange. Prices as percentage of par

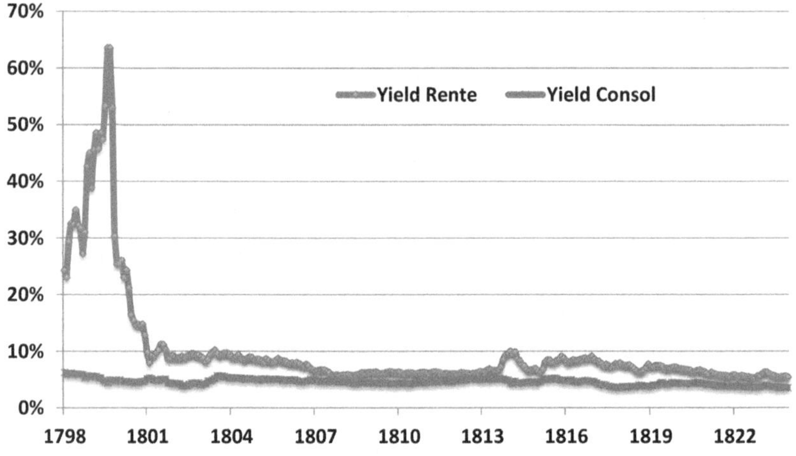

Fig. 3.2 Yields of French rentes compared to British Consols, 1798–1823

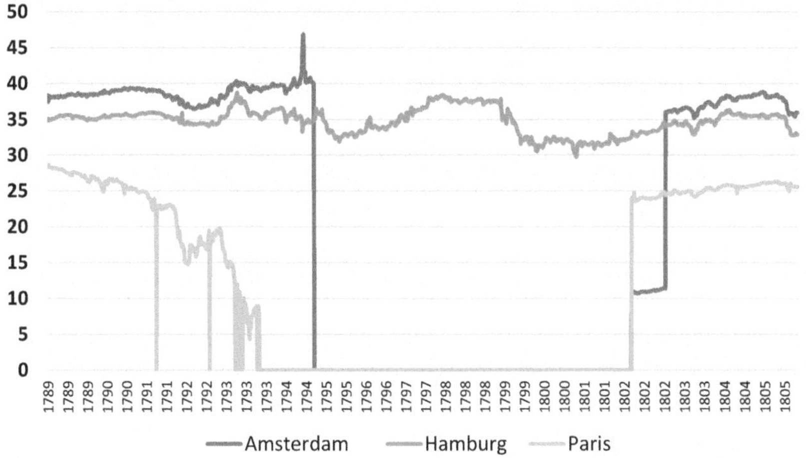

Fig. 3.3 Exchange rates of pound sterling, 1789–1805 (Amsterdam: schellingen banco. Hamburg: schillingen banco. Paris: pence sterling per livres [1789–1798]; franc, centimes per pound [1801–1805])

More important for the calculations of international financiers at the time was the disruption to exchange rates caused by the increasing demands of war finance and revolutionary governments. Figure 3.3 highlights the failure of the French experiment with *assignats* as the number of pence sterling needed to purchase one *écu* (=3 livres) plummeted until the market ceased altogether in the week of October 4, 1793 (as the British Navy laid siege to Toulon in the War of the First Coalition against France). Even the traditional ties with Amsterdam were broken in the week of January 20, 1795, when French troops occupied that city with the aid of the Dutch Patriot Party. Only with the actual signing of the Treaty of Amiens in March 1802 could the most important foreign exchange market in the world for the previous two centuries re-open.

Meanwhile, the port of Hamburg prospered as the remaining entry for licensed and illicit trade between Britain and Europe despite the later attempts by Napoleon to establish a Continental Blockade (which did weaken the pound, much as intended). Such were the times that Labouchere had experienced when he developed the plan of action for the respective houses of Hope and Baring to undertake the finance of the Louisiana Purchase.

The Truce of Amiens, therefore, was the brief interval of time within which the negotiations for the financing of the Louisiana Purchase took place in Paris and during which the correspondence took place between Sir Francis Baring and Henry Hope in London and Pierre Cesar Labouchere in Amsterdam with Alexander Baring in Paris. It was also, however, the period when Napoleon launched a massive invasion of St. Domingue in his ultimately futile effort to restore French central control of that colony. He intended to restore slave labor on the sugar plantations that had made Haiti such a wealthy possession for France before the slave revolt that began in 1791. By 1802, however, the military expertise demonstrated by the newly emancipated slaves led by Toussaint L'Ouverture enabled them to drive off the French forces,[1] who were weakened by tropical diseases, which probably killed more of them than the Haitian forces. After Toussaint himself had been tricked into being captured and sent to France, the other Haitian leaders expelled the remaining French forces. The ultimate success of the Haitian revolution, leading to the declaration of Haiti's independence on January 1, 1804, was not welcomed at the time, however, by Jefferson. (Although he and Monroe speculated that Haiti could become a preferred destination for emancipated American slaves, in preference to West African destinations such as Sierra Leone or Liberia.) The failure of Leclerc's expedition to restore slavery in Haiti helped decide Napoleon to sell off, not just New Orleans as the Americans had been asking, but the entire Louisiana Territory. Why, however, did he think that finance would not be a problem for the United States?

The much earlier political revolutions in the Netherlands and Great Britain in the mid-seventeenth century had, over time, established their legitimacy by creating new financial systems that benefited both their domestic economies and their military strength (Neal 1990, 2015). In 1802, however, the recent revolutions in the United States and France were still in the early stages of establishing the financial legitimacy of their respective governments. Each government explicitly looked to the essential features of the Dutch and British financial systems and then created in their own image the basic foundations they took to be the source of Dutch and British success (Neal 2015, Ch. 6). The salient features were: a public bank, a funded sovereign debt readily traded on stock exchanges,

[1] Many, perhaps 40,000, of the recently acquired slaves by French proprietors in Saint-Domingue had been warriors captured by coastal tribes in Africa.

and a stable unit of account for the domestic money supply. All three features of a successful *financial* revolution had to function within a stable legal and political system.

In France, it took Napoleon's accession to power as First Consul in 1800 that enabled him to establish in quick succession the Bank of France, re-vitalize a Sinking Fund (*Caisse d'Amortissement*) to maintain the market value of the re-financed national debt traded on the re-established Bourse de Paris, and establish a unit of account defined in internationally recognized values of gold and silver. He did all this in the first two years of his rule as First Consul between 1801 and 1803 (Neal 2015, Ch. 6). Mere imitation of the outward symbols of Britain's successful financial system, however, was not enough to accomplish parity with it. Rather than use the new financial resources to subsidize Continental allies as became the guiding principle for British war finance, Napoleon continued to extract tributes from his satellite kingdoms and potential conquests, such as Spain and Portugal, eventually culminating with his disastrous campaign against Russia in 1812.

As we shall see, Sir Francis and Pierre Cesar devoted some effort toward enabling all three countries—Spain, Portugal, and Russia—to finance either their initial tributes to France or their eventual resistance movements to Napoleon's forces. Indeed, the efforts of the houses of Baring and Hope on the European continent to enable continued tributes from the satellite kingdoms far overshadowed in quantity the flow of funds they channeled from the United States to France to finance the Louisiana Purchase. (This may well be another reason why the financing of the Louisiana Purchase has received so little attention in the subsequent historiography.)

In the United States, by contrast to France, Alexander Hamilton, under his imaginative interpretation of the new Constitution of the United States in 1789, managed to install the Bank of the United States and convert all outstanding state war debts (which had been issued in a wide variety of forms, currencies, and denominations) into Federal debts available in three basic forms—Three Per Cents, Six Per Cents, and Deferred (until 1802) Six Per Cents—all backed by revenue of the Federal government derived from customs duties, excises, and occasional land sales. Combined, these sources provided the Federal government the revenues it needed. All of these elements of Hamilton's system were denominated as well in a unit of account defined in terms of fixed amounts of silver or gold. Hamilton accomplished all this by the time he retired as Secretary of the Treasury in 1795, leaving it to his successors to carry on, which they did. That is, they did until Albert Gallatin was finally forced to resign as Secretary of the Treasury in 1813 to take up a lead role in negotiating terms for ending the War of 1812 with Great Britain.[2] Even then, however, Gallatin continued to play a major role in maintaining the public credit of the United States thanks to his relationship with Alexander Baring, as we shall see in the chapter dealing with the War of 1812.

Under the pressures of continued war finance in the 1790s, however, all four financial systems responded to the new challenges in different and largely unexpected ways. The long-established Dutch system proved unable to resist invasion by French troops in 1795. The Patriot Party tried to revamp existing financial structures in the Netherlands under the tutelage of revolutionary France, which only disrupted matters more (Schama 1992). Britain's symbiotic financial relation with the Netherlands, which had been severely shaken during the Fourth Anglo-Dutch War of 1780–1784, was severed as a result.[3] The Dutch East India Company and the Exchange Bank of Amsterdam both collapsed, leaving open the Asian trade to the English East India Company and European finance to the Bank of England.

Napoleon's eventual stabilization of the French monetary system created new drains on the British money supply, which forced the Bank of England to suspend convertibility of its bank notes into specie (silver or gold) in February 1797. Until the previous gold standard of the British pound sterling was restored in 1819–1821, the British financial system was anchored to the "paper pound" as managed by the Bank of England,

[2] The details of the "American financial revolution" initiated by Alexander Hamilton have been covered in admiring detail by recent scholars starting with Wright (2002a, b, 2008), Perkins (2004), and Sylla (2009, 2011, 2016). The brilliant musical "Hamilton" created by Lin-Manuel Miranda and based on the biography by Chernow (2005), assures Hamilton's role in history.

[3] The Baring Archive includes NP1.A6, "In 1795 Sir Francis Baring was appointed chairman of a committee formed to represent the interests of "Merchants and Others connected with Holland. These are Sir Francis' papers dealing with the working of the committee." The committee terminated remittances on accepted bills to Holland, "under the present situation of the two countries" (Feb. 5, 1795, circular to Dutch merchants in London). The work of Quinn and Roberds (2024) argues that 1784 was the critical break point for the Bank of Amsterdam.

which created new issues for the continued development of the British financial system.[4]

Hamilton's system in America proved to be the most resilient, however, thanks to a trade boom for American merchants as long as the United States remained neutral in the conflicts among the Europeans. Thomas Jefferson, who had opposed Hamilton's system vigorously even while serving in Washington's cabinet as Secretary of State, took steps to undermine it when he assumed office as the third President of the United States in March 1801. Most seriously, Jefferson eliminated the internal taxes that Hamilton had initiated and John Adams had continued. Thereafter, Jefferson's Secretary of the Treasury, Albert Gallatin, furthered Jefferson's goal by doing his best to pay off all of the Federal debts left by Hamilton. As Gallatin diligently pointed out repeatedly in his annual reports, however, the fiscal resources of the Federal government came almost entirely from the customs revenues collected at the ports of the eastern seaboard. Any interruption to the profitable foreign trade that had expanded rapidly when the European war broke out in 1793 would require the restoration of taxes while drawing down accumulated surpluses in the U.S. Treasury. Proven examples of the U.S. ability to redeem its initial debt, however, would enable the government to issue new debt in the event of renewed war, in Gallatin's opinion.

Gallatin, the elected Republican for the House of Representatives from western Pennsylvania, made his reputation among the Republican party leaders with his lengthy and repeated attacks on Hamilton's administration of the country's finances in the 1790s. Not receiving the annual reports from Hamilton as required for the House of Representatives to fulfill its constitutional duty to oversee Federal taxes and appropriations of revenues, Gallatin ferreted out his own data. These, he argued, showed that the Federal government had taken on much more debt than needed by assuming the war debts of each state under Hamilton's system. Whereas Hamilton had argued that having a large amount of outstanding, marketable sovereign debt was necessary for the new country to fulfill its enormous promise of economic development, Gallatin argued (along with

[4] See works by Antipa, Gent, Hotson, MacDonald, and O'Brien and Palma.

Jefferson and Madison) that such a large amount of funds at the government's disposal would simply encourage the rise of a military power, which in turn would benefit only the wealthy elite.[5]

Hamilton's plans for the new American system of public finance were tested repeatedly in the ten years between the signing of the Treaty of Paris in 1783, which ended the war between Britain and the American colonies, and 1793, which saw the next declaration of war between France and England. The classic work of E. James Ferguson (*Power of the Purse*, 1961) focuses on the speculative gains made by insiders who gambled during this period on the success of Hamilton's assumption of state debts. These were men like William Bingham, Senator from Philadelphia, who bought up the depreciated state debts wherever and however they could before Hamilton's scheme was formally enacted, and then held them to maturity when they were paid off at face value with the accumulated interest of 6% annually. Ferguson mentions incidentally an American expatriate, Daniel Parker, as well. Parker, moreover, may have been eventually the prime promoter of the financing arrangements for the Louisiana Purchase, as we shall see in Chapter 6.

Ferguson does give Parker credit for changing the general attitude European investors had toward U.S. government debt. He notes that Parker arrived in Europe in 1784 bringing with him "a bag of securities and an indubitable talent for negotiation. His primary mission was to acquire title to the assets of a bankrupt Dutch company, with whom he had been doing business, by offering public securities to the company's creditors as a guarantee of their claims."[6] Ferguson refers to Parker's later contract with Sir Francis Baring in March 1790, but without details of that contract (p. 288). If Ferguson could have had access to the Baring Archive, however, he would not have failed to note that the March 1790 contract established the investment vehicle in U.S. sovereign debt for

[5] Sylla (2011), pp. 74–80, summarizes the Hamilton–Gallatin debate as "The Financial Policy Debate of the 1790s." Managing the size of the Federal debt, as opposed to maintaining the marketability of that debt, was really the main difference in their philosophies. Like Hamilton, Gallatin supported the First Bank of the United States and was concerned with control of customs revenues as well as Federal land sales.

[6] Ferguson, p. 260. Ferguson's account of Parker and his subsequent dealing with the Dutch broker, Pieter Stadnitski was later incorporated bodily into the text of the article by James Jan Kaminski, "Pieter Stadnitski: America's Principal Broker and Land Developer," *Polish American Studies* Vol. 44, No. 1 (Spring 1987), pp. 56–66.

Baring and his partners as a tontine,[7] and was structured precisely as the one suggested by Alexander Hamilton in his January 1790 report on Public Credit. Ferguson leaves open the question of why Parker could be so persuasive with the merchant banker already acknowledged as the leading house in Britain, but Sir Francis' notes provide the answer, which is worth reproducing in full.

Exhibit 1: Sir Francis Baring's Notes on U.S. Debts, 1789

The liquidated debts of America, are those which result from an examination & an immense depreciation of debts contracted during the War, by the different states in their separate capacity, by Congress &c. and are at present consolidated into one fund, under the title of "The liquidated debts of the United States of America," at an interest of 6 pcent per annum. {*The formal title of the new Federal debt restructured by Hamilton to absorb the existing debts of the individual states.*}

These funds or stock have been sold at various prices, & loans negotiated in Holland during & since the war depending on the same security for the payment of interest that is the good faith & regularity of remittances from the States of America & bearing only 5 % per annum as appears from a certificate of Brokers of issuance in Amsterdam & are now worth in Holland 94 ½ pcent. {*Information conveyed by Parker, but also readily available to Sir Francis in the Dutch newspapers.*}

The interest has hitherto been paid in paper called indents & not in specie. These indents are allowed to be received in certain cases for the payment of duties & taxes at par; but when they cannot be so applied, those indents have been at a very heavy discount.

One of the first objects of the new government in America, appears to have been, to pass a revenue bill, for the purpose of imposing duties throughout the continent, to raise a sum of money sufficient to discharge the interest of their debts, & to defray the expense of their government.

The duties they propose to levy, appear to be so moderate, as to afford a reasonable expectation that the plan will be accomplished.

Under these circumstances, it is apprehended that in a reasonable time, provision will be made for the payments of interest in America in Specie, in lieu of indents and in the meanwhile Messrs. P & R [*Parker & Rogers*] who are the proprietors in this business will have secured in the 3 pct.

[7] A tontine is an annuity shared by subscribers to a loan or common fund, the shares increasing as subscribers dies until the last survivor enjoys the whole income. Jennings et al. (1988) argue that Hamilton's proposal shows he was in favor of retiring the entire Federal debt, although it is as likely that Hamilton favored retiring mainly the debt owed to foreigners.

consolidated annuities a sum sufficient (at the present value of that stock) to pay the interest to the subscribers to the Tontine for 5 years, {*Sir Francis lays off some of the recent issue of British 3% Consols to Parker and Rogers, who commit, under the supervision of Sir Francis and his two partners, to using the securities to start the regular payments of interest to the tontine investors until the U.S. securities are slated to be redeemed in specie*} which stock will be vested in the names of the Trustees, who are to be empowered to sell a sufficient sum half-yearly for the purpose of paying the interest to the subscribers to the Tontine as the sums may become due.

As the funds for the payment of interest are effectually secured for 5 years in England, (*with the interest payments on the British 3% Consols*) it is presumed that before the expiration of that period, the government of America will be so far established, as to be enabled to collect a sufficient sum in money by duties & taxes for the purpose of discharging the interest due to the creditors of the state (instead of paying them in indents); the more so as it appears to have been one of the first objects after they assembled under their new form of government. (*The speculation will be repeatedly confirmed by direct correspondence of Sir Francis and then Alexander with Albert Gallatin.*)

(*Baring Archive*, NP1.A7.1.13, "Note in hand of Sir Francis Baring concerning the liquidated debts of the US and the aims of the new government.")

These notes in Sir Francis' hand, moreover, read like an English translation of Pieter Stadnitski's "An Explanatory Report Regarding the Funds Called "Liquidated Debt,"" published for his Dutch clientele in 1787.[8] Further, Stadnitski's success in marketing his investment fund in the "liquidated debt of the United States" with his Amsterdam clients was noted by Sir Francis in the dossier. Sir Francis had taken the precaution of inquiring of a friend in Amsterdam, Charles Wilkieson, about the credibility of Parker and the certificates he claimed were available on the American debt. Wilkieson's reply (July 21, 1789) reassured Sir Francis that American stocks were held in high regard on the Amsterdam market and that the reputation of the owners of the certificates he had asked about was sound. Further, he added in a follow-up letter, Parker had made quite a nice sum from a previous deal with Dutch merchants, and

[8] Veru (2021a).

Peter Stadnitski had successfully marketed a large amount of the U.S. certificates to his clientele in Amsterdam, largely Anabaptists.[9]

The file in the Baring Archive, NP1.A.7.1 "1789–92: US Tontine Papers," goes on to include a formal indenture to set up the tontine to be invested in the "liquidated debts of the United States" purchased for the accounts of Samuel Rogers and Daniel Parker and then administered by the trustees: Edmund Boehm, Thomas Hinchman, and Sir Francis Baring.[10] The deed of trust explicitly states that Rogers and Parker will place the liquidated debts of the United States in the names of the three trustees: Baring, Boehm, and Hinchman. This provision avoided a continued issue of dispute between William Bingham and the Willink Bros. of Amsterdam. That dispute arose because while Willink had loaned Bingham the funds needed to purchase a substantial amount of the liquidated debts, Bingham kept them in his name. Later correspondence between Bingham and Sir Francis, intermediated eventually by Alexander Baring when he arrived in the United States, consisted of Bingham's pleas to Sir Francis to reassure the Willink Bros. that he would pay Willink Bros. in full when the debts were redeemed. (See letters by Bingham in Library of Congress, Baring Mss.)

The plan of the U.S. tontine created by Sir Francis follows very closely the tontine Alexander Hamilton proposed in his report to Congress on public credit in January 1790, which in turn was modeled on the British government tontine of 1789. The Parker–Baring tontine had two ten-year classes under 20 years of age while Hamilton's proposal had only one class for insurees under 20 years of age. Hamilton's tontine had 4.2% interest paid on the youngest class, rising incrementally for each subsequent cohort of 10 years to a maximum of 6.4%.

Exhibit 2: Parker's Proposed Tontine for U.S. Liquidated Debts, March 1790

The plan of a tontine to consist of 1000 shares at £100 each to be divided into 7 Classes as follows, the dividend of each Class to increase by survivorships

[9] TBA NP1.A17.1-3 Amsterdam Charles Wilkieson to Francis Baring, July 21, 1789.

[10] *Baring Archive*, NP1.A7.14, 1790 23 Mar: Deed of Trust between Baring, Boehm, Henchman, Samuel Rogers, and Daniel Parker.

1st Class on Lives under 10 years of Age..	170 Shares	@£6.2 for each £100	£1037
2nd do. above 10 & under 20 years of Age	170 Do	@ 6.4 Do	£1054
3rd do. above 20 & under 30 years of Age	170 Do	@ 6.6 Do	1071
4th do. above 30 & under 40 years of Age	140 Do	6.10	910
5th do. above 40 & under 50 years of Age	130 Do	7.0	910
6th do. above 50 & under 60 years of Age	120 Do	7.7	882
7th do. above 60 years of Age	100	8.3	815
			£6679.00

Every subscriber to mention the class in which he will subscribe & to pay £25 on every £100 subscribed into the hands of the Treasurers Messr. Lockhart Bankers in Pall Mall the remaining £75 per cent to be paid on the 1st of December next when the name age & description of every nominee shall be given in the Deed of Trust executed.

The annuities to be paid half yearly at the Treasurers to commence on the 1st of July 1789 and the first half yearly payment to be made on the first Wednesday in January 1790 and to be paid half yearly on the 1st Wednesday in July and January every year.

To secure the regular payment of the Annuities 600,000 Dollars in the Funds of the United States of America which at the par of Exchange are equal to £135,000 sterling bearing an interest of 6 percent per annum until the full reimbursement of the 600,000 Drs. will be vested in Francis Baring, Edmund Boehm, & Thomas Hinchman Esqs. of London in Trust to receive the Interest on the same & to pay to the Treasurers such part thereof as will discharge the annuities.

The funds to be legally vested in the said Trustees & by them declared so to be & the deed securing the payment of to the Treasurers of so much of the interest they may receive on the 600,000 Dollars as will discharge & pay the annuities to be enrolled in one of his Majesty's courts of record at Westminster.

By the desire of the Proprietors a Sale of the First 7 Years Interest has been made by the Trustees whereby the punctual payment of the first 14 half yearly payments are secured to the Treasurers Messrs. Lockhart in London whose positive engagements for the regular payment of the said 14 half yearly payments of £3339.10 are lodged with the Trustees as also

their engagements for the faithful application of all such further sums as may be paid them by the trustees for account of the subscribers.
(*Baring Archive*, NP1.A7.1)

Parker and Baring, however, taking as their model an earlier British tontine that was already offered to the investing public in Britain in 1789, offered over 6% for the youngest class, rising in decadal stages to just over 8%. The higher returns made their tontine more competitive relative to the British tontine, a copy of which is filed in the Baring Archive with the materials on American securities. (And a copy of which is compared to Hamilton's proposal in Jennings et al. 1988.)

Exhibit 3: Hamilton's Proposed Tontine

As an auxiliary expedient, and by way of experiment, the Secretary would propose a loan upon the principles of a tontine.‡

To consist of six classes, composed respectively of persons of the following ages:

First class, of those 20 years and under.
Second class, of those above 20, and not exceeding 30.
Third class, of those above 30, and not exceeding 40.
Fourth class, of those above 40 and not exceeding 50.
Fifth class, of those above 50, and not exceeding 60.
Sixth class, of those above 60.

Each share to be two hundred dollars. The number of shares in each class, to be indefinite. Persons to be at liberty to subscribe on their own lives, or on those of others, nominated by them.

The annuity	upon a share in the first class to be	8	40
	upon a share in the second	8	65
	upon a share in the third	9	0
	upon a share in the fourth	9	65
	upon a share in the fifth	10	70
	upon a share in the sixth	12	80

The annuities of those who die, to be equally divided among the survivors, until four-fifths shall be dead, when the principle of survivorship shall cease, and each annuitant thenceforth enjoy his dividend as a several annuity during the life, upon which it shall depend.

These annuities are calculated upon the best life in each class, and at a rate of interest of four per cent. with some deductions in favor of the public. To the advantages which these circumstances present, the cessation of the right of survivorship on the death of four-fifths of the annuitants, will be no inconsiderable addition.

The inducements to individuals are, a competent interest for their money from the outset, secured for life, and the prospect of continual encrease, and even of large profit to those, whose fortune it is, to survive their associates.

Source https://founders.archives.gov/documents/Hamilton/01-06-02-0076-0002-0001

Hamilton's suggested tontine was not taken up by Congress, so the historical literature ignores the possibility of such an investment. Hamilton, however, had suggested that the tontine would be designed for foreign investors, not domestic U.S. investors. Further, the purpose of the tontine would be to bring the mass of "Liquidated debts of the United States of America" up to comparable prices to existing sovereign debt issues available to investors in Europe, especially in the Netherlands. It was the success of Parker and Stadnitski's marketing efforts in Amsterdam that managed to accomplish this goal without the benefit of the proposed tontine in London (Veru 2021b).

Before "fleeing" to Europe in 1784, Daniel Parker had been an active business partner in military contracting with William Duer and John Holker in the closing years of the Revolutionary War. At one point, while serving as one of the three commissioners in New York to oversee the departure of the British forces in 1784, Parker paid Alexander Hamilton a sum of £6.8s. to represent a Captain Smith "before the Council."[11] At the time Parker made his proposal to Sir Francis Baring in 1790, Duer was serving as private secretary to Alexander Hamilton, who had just assumed his position as the first Secretary of the Treasury of the United States. It is not surprising, then, that Parker would have exactly such a scheme laid out for the benefit of British investors. Both Parker and Hamilton (as well as William Duer, Parker's former partner and Hamilton's current secretary) also had access to the details of the British government tontine of 1789.

Sir Francis' interest in the U.S. tontine was also apparently stimulated by the publicity that attended the 1789 British government tontine, one of the various schemes advanced by the British government to pay down

[11] Dated March 11, 1784. https://founders.archives.gov/documents/Hamilton/01-03-02-0007, accessed October 10, 2021.

the excessive debt accumulated over the course of the American Revolutionary War. After the British government's painful experience with their first tontine in 1693, they had never tried this financial technique again until launching the 1789 tontine. The earlier one had failed to attract much interest at the outset, and then it proved expensive for the government as there were unusually long lives for the nominees in that tontine. Most likely, this had been the result of substituting replacements with the same name for the recently deceased. Consequently, "in the (last) British tontine launched in 1789, the founding act stipulated a long and complicated process for proving that a nominee was still alive."[12] Presumably, the tontine for U.S. securities would have used those same procedures put in place for the British tontine. The procedures laid out for subscribers making their nominations for which life was to be insured were the same for both the British tontine of 1798 and the tontine on American securities chartered by Sir Francis and associates. It may be the case, however, that neither the British nor the American tontine was entirely successful.

The Baring Archive also has clippings about a similar private tontine that was promising much higher yields to subscribers, who then became increasingly upset that they were not getting the promised returns, or any at all.[13] At a meeting called by a group of subscribers held in the London Tavern in December 1806, the promoter, Mr. William Ludlam, apparently caused quite a commotion when the attending shareholders demanded their money back. After throwing the dishes and cutlery laid out for dinner at them, he jumped through an open window and fled down the street. Later, he was committed to a lunatic asylum, from which he escaped in 1808, shouting to passersby, "I am William Ludlam, they say I am insane, but I am perfectly well!" (*Coventry Herald*, 24 June 1808).

Moreover, there would be some difficulties to overcome that arose with the operation of the U.S. tontine. Samuel Rogers, Parker's original partner in the purchase of U.S. "liquidated securities," was sued for bankruptcy in London. While Parker's arrangement with the Dutch bankruptcy trustees continued to drag on, he remained on good terms with the Dutch bankers who had been the primary bankers for the United States during the revolution. The Staphorsts were seeing considerable

[12] Milevsky, p. 95, where he argues they should be made legal again.

[13] *Baring Archive*, NP1.A7.3. 1806 plan of Annuities by William Ludlam.

gains in their extensive holdings of U.S. Revolutionary War debt. Their success surely enabled Parker to parlay a similar arrangement with Sir Francis Baring and his associates for the U.S. tontine in March 1790. Another scheme that Parker had proposed to Baring and associates in collaboration with Gouverneur Morris, namely, to re-finance the U.S. debts owed to France, was, however, rejected by Sir Francis and the bankers in London.

Gouverneur Morris and Daniel Parker had proposed a plan for re-financing American debt to the French government (still the monarchy of Louis XVI) to Jacques Necker in early 1789. While Necker rejected it, Gouverneur nevertheless had expressed interest in joining with Parker on any other speculative venture that he might bring to light. In 1790, Gouverneur went to London himself, reportedly to straighten out a mess that Parker had gotten into London, presumably due to the unexpected bankruptcy of Samuel Rogers, Parker's partner in the tontine proposal. This accounts for the letter by Gouverneur Morris to Sir Francis dated March 6, 1792.[14] The letter begins by assuring Sir Francis and his partner Thomas Hinchman that he would return to them the accounts of Samuel Rogers (Parker's original partner, who had been declared bankrupt shortly after the tontine was indentured), while assuring them that the "six percent Stock standing in your names" was not liable at all to Mr. Parker's debts, which fear apparently had motivated Sir Francis and Hinchman to ask Gouverneur if he would arrange for their holdings to be transferred to Mr. Warder. Beyond that assurance, however, Gouverneur was upset that Baring and Hinchman had not used his friends in America, meaning Robert Morris, to purchase the liquidated securities for them. He had counted on Robert Morris to pay him his share of the appropriate commissions on the sale of the obligations to Baring and Hinchman, which was why he had forgone any claim of commission originally. Now, however, he felt that they should provide him some commission for the services he was providing their affair, and most of the letter is devoted to his argument.

The bankruptcy of Samuel Rogers in the meantime, however, had apparently forced Parker and Morris to reduce the size of the tontine to just over a quarter of the original size—from the original £500,000 to £135,000. Consequently, the scale of the emoluments to be allowed to

[14] *Baring Archive*, NP1.A7.1.8.

the trustees—Baring, Boehm, and Hinchman—had to be reduced proportionally.[15] Nevertheless, it appears that the remaining American securities were held and rose to par value over the following years even if the proposed tontine project failed.[16] In Gouverneur Morris's "Waste Book," where he kept meticulous accounts of his expenses and assets, he recorded large profits from the sales he had made in Europe. In Antwerp, where he had used the services of Charles John Michael de Wolf to acquire title to $59,246.60 of "liquidated securities," he had gained $16,499.45 by August 26, 1793, on his own account.

This gain, however, had to be shared with Robert Morris, who was credited with $11,875.00, leaving Gouverneur with only $4441.70 on this venture. In London, however, on February 1, 1791, he recorded two transactions with Samuel Rogers and Daniel Parker for $250,994.22 and $106,558.05, with a net profit of $15,555.20 and $6000.00 on them. On June 25, 1791, he recorded a large affair of $335,842.15 that he shared equally with Robert Morris and William Constable, and on which he pocketed a profit of $68,584.76. Further, despite his complaint to Sir Francis and Thomas Hinchman in his letter of March 1792 about losing their commission business, he recorded a deal with Baring, Boehm, and Hinchman of $33,333.33 (£7500) on October 7, 1794. His gain was $6622.48, which he shared again with his associates in America, Robert Morris and William Constable.[17]

Clearly, Gouverneur Morris profited consistently by putting European investors into possession of the "liquidated securities of the United States" when they were selling in the United States at a price well below par, so much so that when he finally was recalled as the American ambassador from France in 1794, he was able to rent an entire merchant ship, *Le Superbe*, for carrying the treasures he had purchased at bargain prices from the royal, ecclesiastical, and noble estates that had been seized by the Convention for auction back to Morrisania, his American estate (Fiechter, Ch. XIII, "Morrisania-sur-Seine"). *Le Superbe* had arrived in La Rochelle with a cargo of flour and tobacco sent by Robert Morris. The cargo was sold for their joint profit, another source of profiteering for Americans

[15] *Baring Archive*, NP1.A7.1.3.

[16] No public announcement appears in London papers, nor any notices in the London Gazette. The British government tontine, itself, was judged a failure by Charles Compton (1833), given the low actual returns to annuitants that remained by 1829.

[17] Fiechter, loc. 2180–81, in Ch. VI, "Les Speculations Internationales."

capable of commissioning the necessary shipping services, men like Daniel Parker, who remained in France to continue exploiting his mercantile shipping contacts (Chapter 6).

While the original deed of trust between Parker and Sir Francis Baring was funded for seven years, when the American securities would start to be redeemed, no further mention of the tontine can be found in the Baring Archive. Further, the British Parliament put an end to tontines with the British Life Annuity Act in 1808. That act also re-introduced government-issued life annuities to the public as an extra inducement to take up fresh issues of government debt to finance the resumption of war with Napoleon. Thereafter, the interest of the Baring firm was focused much more on the sovereign debt issued successively by the British government over the course of the Napoleonic Wars. Parker's interest in sovereign debt, in turn, seems to have turned from speculating on the rise of prices of American Revolutionary War debt with the help of the Dutch bankers toward, instead, helping the French Revolutionary government deal with its financial problems, while doing very well for himself. Sir Francis Baring's interests in the future of American sovereign debt continued, however, as did his business relations with Daniel Parker.

The pressures of war were relieved briefly when hostilities ceased with the signing of the Treaty of Amiens, March 25, 1802. While the most reliable indicators of financial pressures at the time, the London prices of British Three Per Cent Consols, and the London exchange rates with Europe (Figs. 3.2 and 3.3) responded positively to the Peace of Amiens, they also show that investors were well aware of the dangers that the peace would not persist. Indeed, they had anticipated the end of the Treaty well before May 18, 1803, when Britain declared war again on France. During this peaceful interval of uncertain duration, however, the financial terms of the Louisiana Purchase were worked out and agreed upon by the American and French negotiators in Paris on April 25, 1803. Ratification of their agreement by their political superiors (Napoleon in France and Jefferson and Congress in the United States) took several more months, and actual implementation of the terms of the contracts would take yet another several months. Nevertheless, the actual implementation of the initial contract occurred very much as it had been written out, in French and English, in Paris on April 25, 1803.

The ensuing stability of the financial arrangements over the following 18 years is remarkable given that:

1. war between Britain and France resumed within one month of the initial contract,
2. revenues for the U.S. government dropped sharply with Jefferson's Embargo Act at the end of 1807,
3. the lending powers of the Bank of the United States ended when it was closed in 1811,
4. the United States faced unexpected large expenses to fight the War of 1812 against Great Britain, which required even larger issues of new debt.

Also remarkable is that the durable financial arrangements of the Louisiana Purchase were agreed upon very quickly, within two weeks of the arrival of James Monroe at Le Havre, France on April 8, 1803. Monroe arrived with authority to spend up to $10 million to purchase the city of New Orleans and the Floridas from France. He also had access to $2 million on account in London for immediate payment of earnest money, if required. He had no explicit authority to offer more money, however, much less to bargain for all of the Louisiana Territory in place of the Floridas. True, Jefferson had made it clear to both Napoleon and Monroe that Monroe had full authority to act on his own without further instructions from the United States. On this account, it was really Napoleon's decision to sell all of Louisiana to the United States even before he actually had possession that made the deal possible. Completion of the deal apparently depended then on Monroe's willingness to commit another $5 million to France in payment while giving up part of his original charge, acquisition of the Floridas.

Napoleon had only the promise of Spain to relinquish Spanish title to all of what had been French Louisiana before 1763, as specified in a secret treaty signed with Spain on October 1, 1800 (Treaty of San Ildefenso). But that treaty also required France to commit part of Italy to the nephew of the Spanish king, rather than to one of Napoleon's relatives or favorites. It also required France not to part with any of the territory without the permission of Spain—which had not been given, or even asked for. Napoleon's willpower and the opportunism of the American negotiators overrode all these legal cavils.

Subsequent historians have argued the case for the success of the Louisiana Purchase, therefore, on grounds of the foresight, judgment, and decisiveness of the respective political authorities: Napoleon and Jefferson (Brecher 2006; Cerami 2002; De Conde 1976; Kukla 2003;

Roberts 2014; Tearle 2010; Van Meter 1977). A close reading of the archives of the two banking houses that carried out the financial arrangements to their conclusion, however, suggests rather that the foresight, judgment, and decisiveness of the bankers—Sir Francis Baring and Henry Hope in London, and Alexander Baring and Pierre Cesar Labouchere in Europe—were fundamental for the eventual success of the finance of the Louisiana Purchase.

References

Brecher, Frank W. 2006. *Negotiating the Louisiana Purchase: Robert Livingston's mission to France, 1801–1804*. Jefferson, N. C.: McFarland & Co.

Bordo, Michael, and Eugene N. White, 1991. "A Tale of Two Currencies: British and French Finance during the Napoleonic Wars." *The Journal of Economic History* 51 (2): 303–316.

Chernow, Ron. 2005. *Alexander Hamilton*. New York: Penguin Books.

Compton, Charles. 1833. *A Treatise on Tontine: In Which the Evils of the Old System are Exhibited, and an Equitable Plan Suggested for Rendering the Valuable Principle of Tontine more Beneficially Applicable to Life Tontines*. London: Effingham Wilson, Royal Exchange.

Cerami, Charrles A. 2003. *Jefferson's Great Gamble: the remarkable story of Jefferson, Napoleon and the men behind the Louisiana Purchase*. Naperville, IL: Sourcebooks.

De Conde, Alexander. 1976. *This Affair of Louisiana*. New York: Charles Scribner's Sons.

Ferguson, E. James. 1961. *The Power of the Purse: A History of American Public Finance, 1776–1790*. Chapel Hill, NC: University of North Carolina Press.

Jennings, Robert M., Donald F. Swanson, and Andrew P. Trout. 1988. "Alexander Hamilton's Tontine Proposal." *The William and Mary Quarterly*, 45 (1): 107–115.

Kukla, Jon. 2003. *A Wilderness so Immense: The Louisiana Purchase and the Destiny of America*. New York: Anchor Books.

Neal, Larry. 1990. *The Rise of Financial Capitalism: International Capital Markets in the Age of Reason*. New York: Cambridge University Press.

Neal, Larry. 2015. *From Babylon to Bernanke: A Concise History of International Finance*. Cambridge: Cambridge University Press.

Perkins, Edwin J. 2004. *American Public Finance and Financial Services, 1700–1815*. Columbus, OH: Ohio State University Press.

Quinn, Stephen, and William Roberds. 2024. *How a Ledger Became a Central Bank: A Monetary History of the Bank of Amsterdam*. Cambridge: Cambridge University Press.

Roberts, Andrew. 2014. *Napoleon: A Life*. New York: Viking.

Schama, Simon. 1992. *Patriots and Liberators: Revolution in the Netherlands, 1780–1813*. New York: Vintage Books.

Sylla, Richard. 2009. "Comparing the US and UK Financial Systems, 1790–1830." In *The Origin and Development of Financial Markets and Institutions*, edited by Jeremy Atack and Larry Neal. Cambridge: Cambridge University Press.

Sylla, Richard. 2011. "Financial Foundations: Public Credit, the National Bank, and Securities Markets. In *Founding Choices: American Economic Policy in the 1790s*, edited by Douglas A. Irwin and Richard Sylla. Chicago: University of Chicago Press.

Sylla, Richard. 2016. *Alexander Hamilton: The Illustrated Biography*. New York: Sterling.

Tearle, David. 2017. *Merchants of War: Barings Bank and William Bingham, Revolutionary Bankers from the War of Independence to the Louisiana Purchase*. Modbury, Devon, UK: The Incorporated History Press.

Van Meter, Suzanne R. 1977. "A Noble Bargain: The Louisiana Purchase." Unpublished Ph.D. Dissertation, Indiana University, Department of History.

Veru, Peter. 2021a. "Pieter Stadnitski Sharpens the Axe: A Revolutionary Research Report on American Sovereign Finance, 1797." *Research in Economic History*.

Veru, Peter. 2021b. "The French bonds: The Little-known Bidding War for France's Holding in American Debt, 1786–1790. *Financial History Review* 28 (2): 259–280.

Wright, Robert E. 2002a. *Hamilton Unbound: Finance and the Creation of the American Republic*. Westport, CT: Greenwood Press.

Wright, Robert E. 2002b. *The Wealth of Nations Rediscovered: Integration and Expansion in American Financial Markets, 1780–1850*. Cambridge: Cambridge University Press.

Wright, Robert E. 2008. *One Nation Under Debt: Hamilton, Jefferson, and the History of What We Owe*. New York: McGraw-Hill.

CHAPTER 4

Baring & Hope Anticipate Financing the Louisiana Purchase

The archival evidence at Barings has Pierre Cesar Labouchere as the designer of the financing scheme that enabled the Louisiana Purchase, although the initiative had been touted in various forms for months earlier. In his response to Alexander Baring, Labouchere asserted:

> Thus, the operation appears to me in a double point of view, and which induces me to blend the whole in trying it before our London friends [*Sir Francis Baring and Henry Hope*] for their acceptance or refusal.[1]

What Labouchere meant was that Alexander would make two separate proposals by the combined houses of Baring and Hope, one to the Americans for purchasing New Orleans with American bonds going to Baring & Hope and francs then paid to France; the other to France with French bonds taken by Baring & Hope and dollars then paid to the United States. Taking for granted that no American firm was present in Europe to take on such an operation, he went on to say:

> In an affair of the description of the present we can trust no Paris house. What our means connected with those of a few powerful friends can enable

[1] Baring Archive, NP1.A.4.3. [1803] 30 Jan. PC Labouchere to Alexander Baring.

L. Neal, *The Forgotten Financiers of the Louisiana Purchase*, Palgrave Studies in the History of Finance,
https://doi.org/10.1007/978-3-031-56277-8_4

> us to do, is impossible to any French house, they may undertake on cheaper and more altering terms, but must bring themselves and the house they serve to ruin. Money is scarce and will become more so. Debts of states are increasing and must still increase, all this is fatal to private credit, and to operations depending upon it.[2]

With the benefit of historians' hindsight, one sees both acuity and blind spots in Labouchere's appraisal of the times. His appraisal of French financiers was surely accurate. The work by Gilles Jacoud (1996), which focuses on the efforts by Napoleon's advisors to enact his desire to give the Banque de France the monopoly privilege of note issue in the first half of 1803 (an act finally accomplished by the law voted on April 14, 1803, just as the Louisiana negotiations began in Paris), concludes that the Banque de France was put into a state of crisis as it began to implement its privilege without the necessary access to financial resources.

As far as the joint capacity of Baring & Hope, Labouchere went on to mention the need to confirm their situation with respect to placing the new bonds of the Portuguese government. Labouchere had just returned from that country with freshly printed bonds for distribution to willing clients in both London and Amsterdam. The point of the Portuguese bonds was to finance a tribute to be paid by Portugal to France in order to maintain Portugal's neutrality in case of resumption of the war between France and England.

> Our first object at present must be to place our Portugal operation in such a train as to render us perfectly easy and which I am pretty well satisfied will be the case in the course of the present year provided political events do not take an untoward turn. The only cloud I perceive distinctly is the difference between England and Spain concerning the cutting of wood in the Bay of Honduras. I should not be surprised if France were to blow the flames and afterward make Spain pay the price of her active interference, [*Spain had recently joined with France in the war with England*] but from this I expect no war, nor do I immediately from the remaining differences between England & France concerning Malta and Egypt.[3]

Labouchere's appraisal of the chances of war resuming on the scale it actually did was sadly mistaken. Perhaps he was flushed with his success

[2] Ibid.

[3] Ibid.

in setting up the Portuguese loan in 1803, which was greatly aided by the resurgence of trade between Holland and England as a result of the Treaty of Amiens. When war resumed less than six months later, however, it focused at first on the West Indies, although it revolved around the attempt by France to regain control of St. Domingue rather than Spanish access to wood-cutting in Honduras. After Nelson destroyed the combined French-Spanish fleets off the Cape of Trafalgar and Napoleon defeated the armies of Austria and Prussia, war ended briefly with British domination of the seas (end of 1805) and French domination of Western Europe (end of 1806).

> With regard to French stocks therefore I consider them susceptible of little deviation save from an unexpected incident to B. [*Bonaparte*] and which though not likely must be guarded against. Respecting American stock I believe we have only to apprehend the further quantity that may come into the market in consequence of an arrangement with Spain for the remainder of Florida, a point which you are better able to appreciate than I am and taking for granted that a new levy or prolongation here [*Holland*] can equally be avoided next year here, by the operation now in question, I think the following proposal fair and satisfactory for all parties.
> (*Baring Archive*, NP1.A4.3)

While Labouchere's optimism about the prospects of peace was sadly mistaken, his appraisal that the value of French stocks depended on the military and personal fortunes of Napoleon has been echoed by all subsequent historians. René Stourm (1902) noted that even though Napoleon's reforms stabilized the domestic public finance of France during the Consulat, the price of French *rentes* debt never rose to the value of British Consols. Stourm suggests this was due to uncertainty over where Napoleon's search for glory would take French finances, an assessment more recently echoed by Pierre Branda.[4]

To Labouchere's credit, however, he left appraisal of the American stocks to the better-informed opinion of Alexander, who had recently returned from America after making a mutually profitable transaction with Albert Gallatin. This deal, considered a personal triumph by Alexander, had been to arrange both paying off the remaining foreign debt owed by the United States to Dutch investors, while also purchasing the remaining

[4] Branda (2007, Ch. XVI), *Bonaparte le gestionnaire*; cf. Bordo and White (1991).

stock of the Bank of the United States that was considered the debt owed to the Bank by the Federal government. Gallatin, in turn, was very pleased to make substantial progress in his goal to eliminate all traces of "Hamilton's mountain of debt" owed by the Federal government.[5]

How Alexander Baring Set the Ball Rolling

Alexander's original plan was likely conceived in cooperation with his father-in-law, William Bingham, who was with him in France at the time. The first part of their plan was for France to cede to the United States. the left (eastern) side of the Mississippi River and about half of the territory known then as West Florida. The total area included the strategic port of New Orleans, with access across Lake Pontchartrain as well as up the mouth of the Mississippi on the east side of the river to a line that is still the northern border of the state of Louisiana. The price for this grant of land, which would leave France in control of the Louisiana Territory west of the Mississippi and Spain in control of the eastern half of W. Florida (including the strategic port of Mobile Bay) as well as all of E. Florida, was to be $8 million. The second part of the plan was for France to pay the outstanding claims of U.S. merchants under the 1800 Treaty of Mortefontaine up to 18 million francs ($1,500,000).

For the purchase of New Orleans, the United States would create a stock of bonds paying 5% annually, but Alexander would purchase them at 80% of par (providing a yield of 6 ¼%) with interest payable in England. For settling the American claims, France would create a stock of 18 million livres in 5% *rentes* that the U.S. merchants would accept at par. Sir Francis (or his oldest son, Thomas Baring) noted that "B. (William Bingham) thinks the French stocks might be got with a profit of 25%."[6] As an additional *douceur* the United States would prohibit all intercourse with the blacks of St. Domingue, something that had been carried on surreptitiously during the Quasi-War and the administration

[5] Alexander had explained his side of the negotiation with Gallatin in his letters to his father in June 1802 (TBA, NP1.B11.1.1, Correspondence from Alexander Baring to his father, Sir Francis Baring, Negotiation for the purchase of Bank shares in America).

[6] *The Baring Archive*, NP1.A4.71, f. 1. "Note in hand of Sir Thomas Baring regarding Louisiana loan arrangements, undated." French *rentes* had risen to 50% of par under the monetary and fiscal reforms initiated by the Consulate.

of John Adams. Also, part of the American stock could be paid in provisions from America deliverable in St. Domingue to the French forces then deployed to restore the slave plantation system. Clearly, news of the defeat of the French army in St. Domingue and the death of General Leclerc in November 1802 had not reached Paris when Alexander wrote his letter of January 19, 1803.

Table 4.1 summarizes Alexander's plan, the first of the three plans developed by Baring and Hope over the next few months.

How would Barings make money from Alexander's plan? Most of it, presumably, would come from retailing the bonds created by the United States to wealthy and not-so-wealthy customers of Barings who had already invested in the stock of the Bank of the United States and in the 6% bonds of the U.S. Federal government that Alexander Hamilton as Secretary of the Treasury had created to replace existing state debts. Such sales might take some time, while the payments to France were clearly expected to take place quickly, even if spaced out over three or more years. In the meantime, to the extent that the U.S. payments to France could take the form of U.S. supplies to French forces in St. Domingue, Barings could earn more commissions.

Finally, if the French *rentes* would be accepted by the American claimants at par while Baring and Hope would purchase the equivalent sum of *rentes* at current market prices, then selling at 50% of par, the financiers would have another source of profit. In each financial transaction, Barings and Hope would act as the principal counterparty to one of

Table 4.1 Alexander Baring's Plan, January 19, 1803

[As summarized by Thomas Baring, oldest son of Sir Francis Baring; Alexander's letter no longer exists.]

From France to U.S.:

Cession of New Orleans + W. half of W. Florida

Up to 18 million *livres* in 5% *rentes* at par to settle U.S. merchant claims

From U.S. to France:

$8 million in U.S. 5% bonds, interest payable in England,
part paid in delivery of goods to French forces in St. Domingue

U.S. to cease supplies to Haitian rebels

Baring profits from buying U.S. bonds at 80% of par and French *rentes* at 75% of par, France to accept U.S. bonds at par and U.S. merchants to accept French *rentes* at par

Source: *The Baring Archive*, NP1.A4.71, Note in hand of Sir Thomas Baring regarding Louisiana loan arrangements, undated

the two nations, thus eliminating the possibility that some contractual dispute might lead to military hostilities. Instead, the aggrieved party, whether France or United States, could rely on its legal system to put matters right with either Baring or Hope.

Pierre Cesar Labouchere's Initial Plan

In response to Alexander's plan, Pierre Cesar accepted the terms of cessions and the amount to be paid by the United States to France and by France to the U.S. merchants. He modified it mainly by putting Baring and Hope explicitly as the principal counterparty to each country by making a separate contract with each country. In each case, the financial partners in the scheme would specify an overall commission of 8.5 to 9% for their services to the United States and France. He also suggested blending the two financing plans to some extent by providing that France would accept as part of its payments from the United States some of its own bonds (*rentes*) that it had created for its payments to the United States. From imagining the U.S. bonds could be sold quickly at a discount of 10% of face value, he increased the discount to 15% in his final "nut shell" description of the financing plan (Table 4.2).

Labouchere took several days to formulate the entire scheme before sending it off to Alexander when a trusted courier appeared to be available. At the same time, he sent a copy to Sir Francis Baring and Henry Hope in London for their assessment. Pierre Cesar also proposed that the United States. created a stock of $8 million, but in 6% bonds, arguing that these were more familiar to European investors who had taken up earlier issues of U.S. bonds. They would be delivered to the house of Baring and Hope at 90% of par, so with a face value of $8,888,888.89. These were not to be redeemable until 20 years, and then in the same manner as the United States was redeeming its existing 6% stock. (U.S. Secretary of the Treasury Albert Gallatin's rapid redemption program of existing U.S. debt, already well underway, was creating problems for European investors who wanted to count on long-term revenue streams.) Interest would start in favor of Baring and Hope from July 1, 1803.

Three months later, beginning September 30, 1803, Baring and Hope would start to pay France 1 million francs a month ending December 1806 (40 months in all). The three-month interval would give the financiers time to secure the first payment of interest from the United States and, perhaps, to sell some of the bonds to third-party customers.

Table 4.2 Plan by Pierre Cesar Labouchere, January 30, 1803

From France to U.S.:	
Cession of New Orleans + W. half of W. Florida	
To France (by Baring, Hope, Bingham, AB/PCL):	
Liv. 40,000,000 payable over 40 months, say 20 ½ in 5 pct. *Rentes*	
3,400,000 *[=8.5% of 40 million taken as commission]*	
36,600,000 @ 24 *{livres to the pound}* remit	£1,525,000
To U.S. (by Baring, Hope, Bingham, AB/PCL):	
cf 3,645,0000 @ *cf* 11 *{current guilders to pound}*	£ 331,363
	£1,856,363
To various agents of U.S. and France	
(*1 million liv. @ 24*)	43,637
disburse in all	£1,900,000
From the U.S. to (Baring, Hope, Bingham, AB/PCL):	
$8,888,888 88 8/9 in 6% bonds not redeemable for 20 years; sold in average at 85%	
will produce $7,555,555 @ 4/6	£ 1,700,000
From France to (Baring, Hope, Bingham, AB/PCL):	
18/m frs. French stock sold in average at 50%	
will produce frs. 9,000,000 @24 £375,000	£ 2,075,000
residue	£ 175,000
Deduct on the pay for America 9% *cf*120,000 @ 11	£ 10,000
profit	£ 185,000

Source: *The Baring Archive*, NP1.A4.71, Note in hand of Sir Thomas Baring regarding Louisiana loan arrangements, undated

To make these payments easier to cover by Baring and Hope, Pierre Cesar proposed that France would agree to receive at any time the monthly million francs in the form of their own 5% *rentes,* and continue to receive them up to the 18 million francs in face value they would have created to pay the American claims. Pierre Cesar also noted that Baring and Hope could buy these at their current market price, 45% of par, and make profit from having American claimants accept them at full price.

It appears that Labouchere already had in mind to deal for the French *rentes* in Amsterdam, where he had recently re-located to re-establish Hope and Co., as he calculated the gains from selling the French *rentes* at face value in terms of Dutch guilders. Further, if the Americans would approve being paid in guilders, receiving one-third of the French *rentes* in January of the next three years, Baring and Hope could take a further discount of 6%. As we saw above, in the final deal signed in May 1803, France did not create new *rentes* for the payments to the United

States in the actual agreement. Instead, the United States took on that responsibility directly. But we will see below that Pierre Cesar eventually persuaded Barbé-Marbois to accept existing *rentes* as part of the accelerated payments in exchange for an equivalent amount of the acceptances that Alexander had signed previously.

Pierre Cesar's letter goes on for another four manuscript pages to lay out in detail the reasons he would make the financing a double-sided transaction with specific suggestions on how to implement each phase of the financial operation. To begin, he asserts that, "in the times as they are now," both governments preferred to deal with private agents they knew and trusted rather than to deal directly with each other. Further, he asserted (correctly) that only the merchant banking firms of Hope and Company in Amsterdam and Sir Francis Baring and Company in London were capable of dealing effectively with both countries—Baring with the United States on one side of the transaction and Hope with France on the other side. Neither country would then have to deal directly with the other in terms of exchanging filthy lucre or even to establish formal diplomatic relations (which had not yet occurred).

Instead, each country would deal with a trusted private representative from the world of international finance. Essentially, these two young private individuals, Alexander Baring (age 28) and Pierre Cesar Labouchere (age 30), in their correspondence of January 1803 were proposing to take upon themselves complete responsibility for each side of the exchange—Alexander to assure the United States that it would receive the Louisiana territory and compensation for losses suffered by American merchants; Pierre Cesar to assure France that it would receive its full purchase price in a short period of time. Of course, these two young individuals also had to convince their senior backers in London that their plan was both feasible and profitable. This meant convincing Sir Francis Baring and Henry Hope in London, two of the wealthiest and best-established financiers in Europe, and both long-experienced in dealing with sovereign debts and international finance. Their approval ("brand") would ensure the success of the plan because they had proven their trustworthiness and capability for financing large-scale international projects for several decades already (cf. Ziegler 1988; Orbell 1985; Austin 2007; Flandreau and Flores 2009 for Barings; Buist 1974, Jonker and Sluyterman 2000 for Hope & Co.).

All in all, Pierre Cesar calculated that Hope and Baring would have to lay out a total of £1,900,000 over the period of 40 months he intended to stretch out the monthly payments to France. It is not clear in his letter whether the monthly payment would take the form of pre-accepted bills of exchange, as indicated in the U.S. records. Later correspondence in the Baring archives that deal with disputes over the division of the final gains from the financing, however, suggests that Pierre Cesar had in mind a single contract that would allow some contingencies, especially one that would commit France to accept back its own bonds in lieu of hard cash. The bulk of the £1,900,000 would be £1,666,666.67 for the 40 million francs, less an 8% commission to reduce the payment to France to £1,525,000. The magnitude of this financial arrangement was, in Labouchere's opinion, clearly beyond the capacity of any of the existing merchant banks in Paris.

It was not, however, beyond the capacity of the combined capital of Sir Francis Baring & Co. in London, Henry Hope & Co. also in London, and the newly re-established Hope & Co. in Amsterdam. While Labouchere was not a full partner yet in Hope & Co. in Amsterdam, he was surely aware of the capital accounts. In the June 30, 1803 accounts of Sir Francis Baring & Co., the total capital of all the partners was calculated to be: £384,993.18.10.[7] In addition, the account shows a total for Henry Hope & Co. of £216,120.5.4, which means that the two London houses combined had £601,114 capital available. The assets of Hope & Co. in Amsterdam, which were being restituted at the time, would have added another substantial sum, likely in the neighborhood of £200,000, making an approximate capital of £800,000. William Bingham, still the wealthiest man in America, and clearly intended to be part of the operation, was expected to take one-fourth of the initial outlay. If that proved to be the case (it didn't) the combined resources of the four partnerships would still have been only two-thirds of the total sum the combined partners would be committing to pay France over the next three plus years. A lot obviously depended on the market for U.S. bonds in London and Amsterdam (and the continued success of Hamilton's system under Gallatin's administration).

Pierre Cesar argued against Alexander's plan of overseeing U.S. or British supplies to the French forces in St. Domingue, as did Sir Francis. Both men emphasized the difficulty of monitoring the merchants who

[7] *The Baring Archive, AC.36, Day Book, 1802–1804.*

would be carrying the supplies. Further, Sir Francis was aware of the withdrawal of British forces from Haiti by a detailed report from General Maitland.[8] Pierre Cesar included another £331,363 that would be required to purchase the French *rentes* with a face value of 18 million francs but a market value of only 8 million francs. Pierre Cesar's final outlay was another £43,637, the equivalent of a million francs for what he termed as "grease for the wheels," and which the Barings termed as "*pots-de-vin*," or simply "*douceurs*." These were the bribes needed to get the officials on the American and French sides to turn the project over to the two banking houses without soliciting alternative sources of finance from competing firms.

Pierre Cesar divided the bribes up as 300,000 *livres* for Livingston and Parker on the American side; 300,000 for Talleyrand on the French side; 300,000 for an unnamed individual, who Sir Francis (or his son Sir Thomas Baring) later described as "the other party who set the business afloat." The remaining 100,000 *livres* were to go to the various bureaucrats responsible for the paperwork needed for the contracts. A puzzle remains why "Parker," obviously associated with the American Minister, Robert Livingston, was included among recipients of the "d*ouceurs*." Parker, however, turns out to be the same Daniel Parker who had introduced Sir Francis Baring into the profits to be made from Alexander Hamilton's financing of American debt. He would prove to be a key figure for arranging the financing of the Louisiana Purchase. The Baring Archives, moreover, refer to the same Daniel Parker, American merchant, who was in Paris representing the merchants who had suffered losses from his ship, the *Rosanna*, during the Quasi-War with France.[9] A "Parker" is also identified by James Monroe as the individual who informed him upon his arrival in Paris that Baring and Hope were prepared to back his offer

[8] *The Baring Archive*, NP1.A7.6.6 September 1799. "Memorandum by Sir Francis Baring, September 1799. Concerning General Maitland's report relating to St Dominga and Jamaica; Great Britain's foreign policy towards the West Indies."

[9] A Daniel Parker shows up as a principal investor in the *Rosanna*, receiving payment for losses paid out to investors in Philadelphia years later. He had been associated with Francis Baring in various ventures since 1789, as described above in connection with the tontine on U.S. debt. Reference: TBA HCOS.22, *Correspondence from Sir Francis Baring and Co with Daniel Parker, Nathaniel Sargent and others 1796–1803.*

to France for up to $10 million.[10] Parker's earlier and later adventures are worth describing in more detail below (Chapter 6).

More mysterious is the identity of "the other party who set the business afloat," clearly someone on the French side. Perhaps it was François Barbé-Marbois, "the man who sold Louisiana,"[11] but for various reasons this seems unlikely. The accounts of Barbé-Marbois, Livingston, and Monroe all have Barbé-Marbois asking the Americans who should handle the financing. Both Livingston and Monroe immediately recommended Baring and Hope. Given the limited extent of territory included in Alexander's first letter compared to the final cession of the entire Louisiana Territory, moreover, the "other party" was likely Pierre Samuel Du Pont de Nemours. In letters Du Pont wrote to Jefferson before he set sail to return to France from the United States in 1802, Du Pont urged Jefferson to offer to buy New Orleans and W. Florida from France rather than seize it by force, as was being urged by some members of Congress.[12]

After arriving in France and presenting a letter written by Jefferson to Robert Livingston, Du Pont wrote a letter to Jefferson on October 4, 1802 in which he spelled out a proposed treaty between the United States and France with just four succinct articles.[13] The first three were very similar to the three conventions actually signed on April 30, 1803, but the territory to be ceded by France was limited to New Orleans and W. Florida in Du Pont's' plan, just as in the initial plans of Alexander and Pierre Cesar. The fourth article in Du Pont's proposed treaty simply stated that the United States would pay France six million dollars, but this was just to be an opening, low-ball, offer by the United States, easily raised in further negotiations. Alexander and Pierre Cesar's initial offer of $8 million, agreed by Sir Francis, was therefore consistent with Du Pont's proposal. The other features of Alexander's plan concerning trade with St. Domingue and right of French trade with New Orleans were also features of Du Pont's earlier suggestions to Jefferson (Malone, pp. 46–79).

[10] Brown (2017, pp. 161–165). A full chapter, Chapter 6 below, must be devoted to Daniel Parker.

[11] Lyon (1942, repr. 1974), Deviosse (1989).

[12] Jefferson, *Correspondence between Thomas Jefferson and Pierre Samuel du Pont de Nemours, 1798–1817,* edited by Dumas Malone ..., pp. 61–67.

[13] Ibid., pp. 68–71.

The recent literature that deals with the precursors to the Louisiana Purchase emphasizes the letter carried by Du Pont from Jefferson to Livingston, dated April 15, 1802, not the letters between Jefferson and Du Pont (e.g., Brecher, Cerami, De Conde, Kukla, Winter). But from Du Pont's letters to Jefferson after Du Pont arrived in Paris, it appears that Livingston tried out versions of Du Pont's proposal with various French officials, including Barbé-Marbois, Talleyrand, and Joseph Napoleon, as well as Cambacérès and LeBrun, the Second and Third Consuls. Despite receiving positive verbal assurances, Livingston remained frustrated that he had no formal responses from any of the French officials.

Further, he was frustrated that he had no specific authorization from either Madison or Jefferson about what should be purchased, and how much should be offered (Brecher, Deviosse). These specific instructions, in fact, only came with James Monroe as "envoy extraordinary," who was urged by Jefferson to seal the deal in January 1803, the same time that Alexander Baring and Pierre Cesar Labouchere were deliberating just how to finance the proposal apparently "set afloat" by Du Pont. Monroe arrived in Paris on April 11, carrying with him Madison's instructions, dated March 2, 1803.

For 37 manuscript pages, Madison spelled out in detail the limits of negotiations that he and President Jefferson had determined, including a proposed treaty with seven articles that mimicked very closely the terms that Du Pont had suggested to Jefferson in his letter of October 1802. Indeed, Madison states that, "the overtures committed to you coincide in great measure with the ideas of the person thro' whom the letter from the President of April 30th 1802 was conveyed to Mr. Livingston, and who is presumed to have gained some insight into the present sentiments of the French cabinet."[14] Obviously unaware of the plans made by the Baring-Hope group to intercede between the two sovereign powers, however, Madison went into a number of contingencies he and Jefferson could foresee that might be points of objection to the cession of New Orleans by France. In each case, he laid out the fallback positions that Livingston and Monroe were permitted to concede if the French representatives insisted on a particular object. In light of the previous furor over the X, Y, Z affair, it is interesting that Madison allowed the American Ministers to pay the

[14] Madison's Instructions, f. 4, from: lcweb2.loc.gov/cgi-bin/map_item.pl?data=/service/gmd//gmd404m/g4042m/g4042lm/gklpooo4/msooo03.jps&style=klpma; accessed Feb. 19–20, 2019.

debt still claimed by the Beaumarchais family for the military supplies he had shipped to the American colonies during their Revolutionary War. But this would be allowed only if the French insisted on it (they didn't). Madison also allowed them to commit advance payment ahead of formal ratification of a treaty by both governments, which may be why Monroe was able to convince Sir Francis to make the advance insisted upon by Napoleon in September 1803.

Livingston and Monroe, however, could safely ignore Madison's instructions. First, because Madison and Jefferson presumed that while France would be reluctant to cede even New Orleans and part of West Florida to the United States, France surely would want to maintain control of the western part of the Louisiana Territory, they were completely unaware that Napoleon had decided to cede the entire Louisiana Territory to the United States. Second, because Alexander Baring had the approval from his father and partners to deal with the finances of the cession to the satisfaction of both countries. Clearly, the wheels had been greased sufficiently, thanks to Pierre Cesar's recommendations.

Calculating the "Financials" Ahead of Time

How would the financiers make money under Labouchere's plan? By adding the American bond sales to the French bond sales, Labouchere estimated the bankers would receive a total of £2,075,000. Subtracting the £1,900,000 they would disburse to the French government he estimated a residue of £175,000. Another £10,000 calculated as a 9% commission on American remittances of *cf* 120,000 then brought the expected profit to £185,000, a return of just under 10% over the three plus years of monthly payments to France.

This was not an exceptional rate of return for the time, given that even the British 3% Consol yielded roughly 5% throughout 1803. The sum, however, was large, and reflected the huge scale of the commitment undertaken by private banking houses, a scale out of the reach of their competitors, whether in Paris, Amsterdam, or London. Further, the risks they would bear at the time were increasingly uncertain. Pierre Cesar, from his vantage point in Amsterdam, stated that "Money is scarce and will become more so: debts of states are increasing and must still increase.

All this is fatal to private credit, and to operations depending upon it."[15] In fact, there was only a brief interlude of peace before war resumed on a larger scale than ever before between France and Great Britain, making risks of finance larger than before. This is likely why the commission demanded by Baring and Labouchere rose from 8 ½ - 9% to over 13% from January to May 1803.

One should note also that there are three distinct currencies in Alexander's plan and four in Labouchere's:

1. the newly defined French franc (*ff*);
2. the U.S. dollar ($), stable for the 10 years since its establishment by Alexander Hamilton;
3. the British pound (£), which had been floating since February 1797; and
4. the Dutch guilder (*cf*) with value uncertain under the recent Patriot revolution in Holland.

In each case, the financiers assumed all the risks of future changes in the exchange rates of the respective currencies. Sir Francis, in one of his responses, stated that the Spanish "piece of eight" would be taken as the standard for making any currency adjustments, perhaps anticipating the later role of Barings in the export of Mexican pesos to the United States and Europe (Chapter 9).

To get the $8 million committed, however, Labouchere proposed that America deliver to the houses of Barings and Hope, $8,888,888 8/9 of American 6% stock at 90% of par (to net the $8 million). Interest would begin on 1 July 1803. And the interest would, if possible, be payable in London, with the stock not redeemable till after a period of 20 years and then in the same way as existing U.S. 6% stock was being retired. All this, clearly, was to make the U.S. stock salable on the London market where the bonds would outperform the existing 3% Consols, even after Barings & Hope deducted ½ to 1% as their share of the interest.

On the French side, Labouchere continued:

> That France would engage to receive monthly payments of 1 million French livres at the rate of 4 s. British per livre up to the amount in

[15] Baring Archive, NP1.A4.3, "January 30, 1803. Letter by Labouchere to Alexander."

all of the FF 18,000,000 capital, which thus we should likewise take over at 4 s. (interest running in our favour from the beginning of An 12, say 22 Sept next), this last amount Fr. 8,100,000 fixed at the exchange of 5 livres per dollar we engage to pay by thirds – 1 Jan. 1804; 1 Jan. 1805; 1 Jan'y 1806 – or to satisfy the two last terms if agreeable to America, under discount at the rate of 6 per cent per annum."

I have thus reduced the whole transaction within a nutshell, and now for the presumptive result. I know how you must proceed and therefore allow one million livres money to grease the wheels and which I divide as follows:

Liv. 300m to Livingston & Parker
Liv. 300m to Tnd *[Talleyrand]*
Liv. 300m to the other party who has the bearing and to
Liv. 100m to further bureaus & other contingencies.
(*Baring Archive*, NP1.A4.3)

Labouchère added immediately, "nothing however to be paid till we are sure of what we hold." He continued to explain his overall scheme, "You perceive I make the whole a private transaction without loans etc., which must prove much more agreeable to both governments, and I believe they know they can depend on our disinterest and punctuality." To clinch Alexander's agreement, and really the agreement of the titular heads of the two firms, Sir Francis Baring and Henry Hope, Labouchere computed the profits that would result as £185,000 at the lowest and possibly as high as £200,000.[16] He then calculated that the probable disbursement at the beginning of each year at about £400,000, trusting that sales of the U.S. bonds would generate that easily for the first year, although if the United States were to give stock to Spain for the purchase (in addition to their debt already owed to Britain, the Netherlands, and France), he would have to drop another 5% off their price, down to 80% of face value. Nevertheless, the first funds could all be disposed of in the Netherlands in one or at best two years, and keeping a reserve right to give them to France at 45% "prevents in any event the possibility of a loss upon them" (*Barings Archives*, NP1.A4.3, f.4).

How should the profits be shared in such a complicated scheme requiring sustained commitment from the private investors, thinking in terms of four different currencies with varying exchange rates? Labouchere proposed:

[16] *Baring Archive*, NP1.A4.3, f.3.

4/16 at the disposal of Henry Hope Co. *[in London]*
4/16 at the disposal of F. Baring Co. *[in London]*
4/16 at the disposal of Wm. Bingham *[in Paris/London/Philadelphia]*
4/16 at our disposal *[Hope & Co. in Amsterdam]*
Each party shall furnish at the outset £10/m [10,000] for each sixteenth in the hands of F. Baring Co. & H. Hope Co. here who shall allow 4% interest upon the times and stand any further advances for which they shall be paid 5 pct. The above £10/m & sixteenths however must remain till the whole transaction is liquidated – which should be 1 July 1807 when the funds and American stock remaining should be divided in nature.
F. Baring Co. and Hope Co. to be allowed ½ pct. upon their transactions concerning the operating by job of American or French stocks, or remitting to Paris or Amsterdam. The risk of the remittances for account of the concern. And the houses of F. Baring & Hope Co. to be at liberty to act without control from the other concerned for the benefit of the whole.
(*Baring Archive*, NP1.A4.3, f.3)

Labouchere concluded, "This is the only method in which at the present moment I think the object practicable, but contrary to your idea I would not take the American without the first fund nor the latter without the proviso annexed, so raising the book value of U.S. stock to be issued." Nevertheless, he was sending a copy of this plan to London the next day and hoped that the heads of the two firms, Sir Francis Baring and Henry Hope, both residing in London, would agree. In any case, Alexander should keep Labouchere's proposal to himself until both had heard the reply from London. Sir Francis Baring and Henry Hope would approve or modify the proposal, and Alexander and Pierre Cesar would have to carry out their instructions.

The reply came to Labouchere from Sir Francis in a letter written on February 15, 1803:

> In a case of this description it is desirable to receive every communication & information, to sift every point to the bottom before we decide but in the present instance it is impossible: after we shall have exhausted our ideas in this letter, we must drop every thought of correspondence &

leave the decision altogether to A. B. [*Alexander Baring*] who must be governed by circumstances, his own prudence & judgment.
(*Baring Archive*, NP1.A4.4)

Sir Francis had discussed his response with Henry Hope, he makes clear, and then divides his response into a judgment about the political circumstances of the time and then about the powers of the two firms to undertake the joint financing obligations. On the political front, he concludes, "that peace is more likely to continue than to be disturbed, between this, & the Spring of 1804. Further this deponent sayeth not" (ibid.). But on the "question of powers," he raises considerable doubt and ambiguity, "which arise altogether from the predicament in which we stand with the PL. *[Portuguese Loan]*. We are choked with it, & although fully competent to cover the whole, yet, when it adds so materially to further large masses, it needs to undergo a previous discussion. My participation is reduced to ¼ of 8 million. I am desirous to remain with ¼ of 4 million but I must have reasonable prospect of reducing it to that sum, before I engage to any extent for the whole of both the new objects" (ibid.).

If the Portuguese Loan could be re-allocated, however, then both the French and American projects could go forward, although "our friend" *[Henry Hope]* did not care so much for the French part of the proposal, as it had the most risk. Sir Francis, however, felt they could not get the American contract without doing the French contract at the same time. He concluded, "My opinion is, that risk attends every part, but that, if peace continues [in] 12 months we shall have the means & greater facilities of liquidation for the F [*French*] provided the delivery *[of the A]* is made within a reasonable time, I mean that it is in our names & at our disposal in a few months" (ibid).

Sir Francis discussed at length how the American bonds should be divided up between England and Holland. In England, the recent failure of the firm handling American government remittances, Savage, Bird and Bird, had softened the market for American securities generally, which were already weak except for bonds that could be sent immediately to the United States for redemption. In Holland, it was uncertain how long the prolongation of payments on Netherlands sovereign debt would continue. But his general feeling was that the American part of the proposal could be divided in equal portions, leaving it up to Alexander Baring to make the final determination.

Further, Sir Francis added that "T. [Talleyrand] ought to make a more conspicuous figure, say 400,000 & which may soften his feelings about the P (Portugal) business, a most important omission at the time & which cannot otherwise be retrieved" [ibid]. He also advised Labouchere that "You must ask P about L" [probably Daniel Parker about Livingston, see Chapter 6].

Sir Francis made it explicit then that the division should be half for the house of Hope and half for the house of Baring. Alexander Baring would be given a proportion under Sir Francis' direction, and Pierre Cesar Labouchere's compensation would "depend on future circumstances" (ibid.). Further, the chance of war breaking out again before all the arrangements could be completed would make sales of the American bonds more difficult, so "perhaps in the body of the arrangement it may be stipulated that the party shall deliver forthwith 10 of dollars in a 5 pct. at par, the other 18 of francs also at par which will leave the public wholly in the dark about terms, or it may be referred to a subordinate condition, or a margin in which AB may sign in his own name, [as attorney to H & Co. & to F. B. & Co.] as a third party" [ibid.]. Also, Bingham should intimate to Livingston that the vessel which carries out the agreement should also bring back all 5071 of the certificates, "without which the expectations raised on the occasion cannot be gratified" (ibid.).

The letter continues on the next folio with the words, "a subsequent consultation with my pillow, & again amongst ourselves, has induced us to form a new, & in some measure a different opinion. — The operation for the F to remain as before. But we all tremble about the magnitude of that for the A account" (*Baring Archive*, NP1.A4.4). Nevertheless, Sir Francis proposed to contract for five, or at most six parts in ten of the whole bond issue for the United States, "provided that America would engage to pay the interest in London or at Amsterdam at one of our houses" (ibid.). He then proposed a staggered payment schedule for the French, consisting of 16 monthly payments adding up to 25 million francs, presumably the remainder of the 40 million suggested by Labouchere after the initial payment of FF15 million.

The matter was clearly still inconclusive for Sir Francis, because he then added another two pages of instructions, based on conversations with Henry Hope, who had been looking at the same letters sent from Paris and Amsterdam as Sir Francis over the past several days.

The result is that we are precisely of the same opinion. We have considerable apprehension about the time which will elapse before we have possession of the documents with which alone we can act. If we calculate on 12 or 14 months of peace, & that 4 or 5 months elapse, before we get the documents, the interval will be short, but although it ought to weigh in the scale, yet it is not of itself decisive.

The most important is the **P** *(Portugal)* account, which if stagnant, will absorb too much of our means to enable us to accomplish the rest. You must, therefore, be satisfied, either in consequence of permission being granted for the circulation with you; or that, when new manufactured as proposed, that you will be able to dispose of at least one third, but rather a moiety of the whole in the course of the year 1803 & this point we consider as indispensable to enable us to undertake the **A** *[American]* operation.

We have no objection to the operation for the **F** *[French]* separate & distinct without combining it with your sales of the **P** *[Portugal]*, even if you retain the whole of the **P** *(Portugal)* on your hands.

But we must decline absolutely the **A** *(American)* either separately, or united with the **F** *(French)* unless you can satisfy yourselves, about making progress with the **P** *(Portugal)* for unless we can rely upon receiving assistance from that source, we do not choose to expose ourselves to the consequences. Of course, if you can rely on resources from that object, in the manner described, you may engage for the **F** *(French)* or for the **A** *(American)* both, or either, according to circumstances.

Clearly, Sir Francis was juggling with a confusing variety of financial products available on the London Stock Exchange for investors of all kinds, but especially those he may have persuaded to purchase shares in the United States liquidated debts earlier, and in shares of the Bank of the United States most recently in 1802. The market for U.S. securities was shaken at the time, given the recent failure of Bird, Bird, and Savage, the American firm most responsible for handling the U.S. government's accounts in Europe. His clients were not taking up the offer of the newly created Portuguese government bonds as quickly as he had hoped. Nevertheless, he had a clear picture of the range of securities that his customers for the American securities would take up willingly.

What I have mentioned in this sheet as subsequent to our meeting is the result of our judgment, & on which you can act. If we succeed I must give you further ideas with regard to our future conduct, which will require much management, for I am persuaded that in any other hands but ours, the A will not be worth more than 75 to 78. In recollection it would be very desirable that the certificates should be sent direct to the confidential person of A in their place, on the receipt of which the first payment shall be instantly made at Paris, & the second on the 31 October for as there are no duplicates, it would be too hazardous to get them from Paris here, de novo, which will require much management. The certificates for every 100m should be nearly as follows: 10 of 500…5000; 10 of 2000…20,000; 5 of 4,000…20,000; 20 of 1000…20,000; 10 of 3000…30,000; 1 of 5,000…5,000, to make 100/m

I must request that no calculation may be made, these sent to AB should be burnt & even this letter after extracting such notes you may think useful. My nerves are equal to the operation, but not so, to the imprudencies which I see committed to paper, knowing that the paper is carefully preserved… I can say no more.

(*Baring Archive*, NP1.A4.)

At this point, Sir Francis' nerves were such that he simply had to rely on the judgment of his second son, Alexander, who was on the scene in Paris, to take on board all the points being raised in London and Amsterdam regarding the feasibility of the financial operation required for the Louisiana Purchase. The next lengthy letter to Labouchere was written on February 24, 1803 and raised the possibility of placing 18 million livres worth of French bonds among six different agents with 3 million each. One agent would be Pierre Cesar Labouchere, another Charles Wall, junior partner of Sir Francis Baring, and the other four Parisian bankers who had been part of the Portuguese loan earlier: Babut, Hottinguer, Insinger, and Baguenault.

First mention is made of another Dutch banker, de Smeth, who would play a major role in the final distribution of American bonds in Europe. Taking advantage of the period of peace created by the Treaty of Amiens, de Smeth visited Sir Francis Baring in London, telling him that he then planned to go to Paris where he would meet Alexander Baring. "but we are agreed he (Alexander) is never to mention the subject unless hinted at by the latter, so he will be at liberty to act as he thinks proper, and I doubt whether De S would trust any of his correspondents but [3rd illegible, but likely Willink]" (NP1.A.4.5).

On March 1, 1803, the terms of the contracts appear to have been set in Paris by Alexander Baring, given the response to Labouchere by Sir Francis.

The only point which we seem to view differently is the extent of the immediate advance. Whilst even AB's to you confirm me that we might obtain a great deal in the same manner as we fetched for P & the additional security which it attaches to the transaction is what makes me think it so desirable. However, I agree with you & our friend that AB understands the subject perfectly & that he should have carte blanche. He may expect one more letter from you perhaps after our dispatches, but then he must be left entirely to his own judgment." (NP1.A4.5)

The next letter, sent on March 2, 1803 to Alexander by Pierre Cesar, gives further instructions to Alexander, while also leaving "the matter totally to your management making such modification in our plans as the nature of the case will admit of, & considering that this is not our only object to attend to or require." But,

With regard to the choice of the stock I must assert that here we can dispose of nothing which is not payable here [Amsterdam] or in London & if we could obtain a certain number of capital obligations, say 10 of one million dollars each to be made in blank & susceptible of being subdivided in shares to bearer, at a fixed rate of exchange for payment of interest & reimbursement of capital, this would prove by far the most easy method & most consonant with the ideas of our monied people. You should avoid however every thing which requires notarial or ministerial signatures here or in London, as we might otherwise come in the same scrape as we have with Portugal, which although ultimately of advantage to us occasioned a great deal of reaction & trouble. (*TBA*, NP1.A4.6)

Labouchere goes on in great detail about the assessments made by Sir Francis of the reliability of the several Parisian bankers, arguing in favor of Baguenault and against Perregaux. "I dread his envious disposition, which would never let him rest satisfied under a division & for the whole I would not trust him so well as we do the other." (Perregaux was then the lead regent of the newly formed Banque de France, a position he owed, no doubt, to being the first Parisian banker to advance funds to Napoleon after his coup of 18 Brumaire.) There follow concerns about the reliability of various merchants trading from the West Indies, who could be relied on to turn accepted bills of exchange to good account, repaying Barings and Hope with profit from the sales of imported goods. The Portuguese account is still a matter of concern.

On the 21st of April, a letter appears to be from Sir Francis to Alexander in Paris, then in the throes of the final negotiations for the financial details. Sir Francis was equally immersed in the complexities of the deal and the state of the market for securities in London, especially for American securities.

> The credit of a foreign country is affected in an other, generally, altho the failure has been only partial, their American land & stocks suffer because a large sum of commercial bills have been protested. The object to be looked to, after the cause has been ascertained, is the probable condition, & here we are again at a loss, for we must consider the credit of America generally & the revival of confidence on some abstract questions & the probability of peace or war. I can perceive many favorable circumstances & expedients which are probable at the same time, it must be admitted, that there is a sort of mist, which hangs over the whole of the business, that is impenetrable.
>
> (*BA*, NP1.A4.7: Sir Francis Baring to P C Labouchere and Alexander Baring).

Nevertheless, Sir Francis had a few more suggestions to make, perhaps assisting B (probably Bonaparte), by announcing a payment of 500 thousand guilders on June 19 for payment in three months. But this might require confirmation with the Dutch merchant banker De Smeth. The delay of the certificates from the United States until after the matter has been confirmed by Congress is "a very great objection but I fear an insuperable one." In any case "We must endeavor to issue the certificates themselves and whatever operating may be afterwards contrived must be the result of circumstances" (ibid.).

The "Final Plan" Agreed by Sir Francis Baring and Henry Hope

The third and final plan proposed by Sir Francis in his letter of 15 February 1803 in collaboration with Henry Hope also had four currencies (NP1.A4.4). Essentially, it accepted Labouchere's plan with provisos that the Amsterdam house would take on more of the outstanding Portuguese bonds that were still not fully sold from the 1802 arrangement with France and Portugal. This would reduce Sir Francis' share of the Portuguese bonds from £2 million to £1 million. Henry Hope still remained queasy about the extent of the American commitment but was reassured that, with the renewed connections with Dutch bankers that Pierre Cesar was establishing, he could make a profit on the French *rentes*. Moreover, with guarantee of the Brazilian diamonds backing the Portuguese bonds, Hope's renewed connections in Amsterdam made him (or his *entrepreneurs* there) willing to absorb another £1 million.[17]

Indeed, Sir Francis' letter to Labouchere, 21 April 1803, bubbles over with enthusiasm for the deal finally struck by Alexander with the three political agents in Paris. He begins, "I view the plan in the first instance upon this principle, that it cannot be had, to the extent of our powers, to keep or retain *without* [author emphasis] sales." He goes on to compare the Portuguese bonds with the American bonds, calculating that with their commissions on each set of bonds both will yield a 5% return. "Ergo (although both are good) yet the last (American) is the best with regard to security; you prefer the first (Portuguese); I prefer the last. These opinions will facilitate an arrangement between us at the conclusion, for I shall be ready to keep as much of the last as my powers are equal to; and at all events to exchange whatever I may have in the P. O. (Portuguese) against the other, and so vice versa, as it regards yourselves" (*BA*, NP1.A4.7).

Sir Francis then reports that American stocks seem to be rising in general, due to political factors alone, which augurs well, as long as America remains neutral (and continues to reap high customs revenues as a result). "If we remain at peace the ball will be at our foot. In case of war we shall at least have a good margin in the price, and at all events a good interest on that part which we shall retain for the necessity on the disposal of a considerable part of the price be it what it may." Nevertheless, he hopes that Bingham, who had obviously been kept very much in touch with the negotiations ongoing between Alexander and the political agents of France and the United States, will be able to guarantee that the remittances of interest payments in U.S. dollars will retain their existing rate of exchange, namely on a par with the Mexican dollar. The letter to Alexander concludes, nevertheless,

> Although I am aware that you must have a variety of plans & considerations, all of which must tend to facilitate & ameliorate our plans, yet I have stated what occurs to me without adverting to any circumstances of that description, but after have done so, I must again add, that we trust entirely

[17] Buist, p. 513, Appendix E-IV, shows a number of the Portugal bonds redeemed and a sharp increase in the number taken by Borski and associates in 1804.

> to your discretion & judgment, which I think will embrace everything that is material for our general contract & you will no doubt consider with the time when we can begin to operate (which is the true period on which we must speculate) & allow, or at least give as much notice as you can that we may prepare our funds, which cannot be collected & applied at very short notice. The manner etc. of communication I leave altogether to yourself.
> (*Baring Archive*, NP1.A4.7)

Another, more detailed, letter from Labouchere in Amsterdam, dated April 28, 1803, to Alexander in Paris is copied to Sir Francis. In it, Labouchere tries to reassure both Alexander and Sir Francis that the situation with the Portuguese bonds remains sound, both in Lisbon and Amsterdam, but he also agrees with Sir Francis that the London share of the American bonds can be 6 parts and the remaining 4 in Amsterdam. The implication is that Henry Hope in England will take up a reasonable portion of the American bonds, as well as continue to hold a substantial part of the Portuguese bonds. Left unsaid is that Pierre Cesar had arranged with the established Dutch bankers for the American government debt, the Willink brothers, as well as another Amsterdam firm, the De Smeth brothers, to take on a substantial part of the American bonds. Again, however, he concludes that Alexander must make the final determinations on the spot in Paris (*Baring Archive*, NP1.A4.8).

Table 4.3 summarizes the actual treaty formulated by the French and U.S. representatives on April 30, 1803. Using the same calculations of exchange rates and market price of the U.S. bonds to be issued that Pierre Cesar used in the earlier plans, but substituting $15 million in place of $8 million + 18 million *livres*, Pierre Cesar would have calculated Baring and Hope would realize a loss of nearly £10,000, rather than gains of £175–185,000. True, the final deal was for the entire Louisiana Territory including New Orleans, not just New Orleans, but the critical factor appears to be that the U.S. bonds proved to be much more highly priced in 1804 than could be foreseen in early 1803.

This may explain in part why Pierre Cesar in later correspondence claimed that had he been the agent in charge of the negotiation in Paris, he never would have signed it. Nevertheless, Alexander Baring, who was in Paris, used the power of attorney given him by both Sir Francis and by Henry Hope to sign off on 92 separate bills of exchange for the eventual payment to France of 52,000,000 French francs. Clearly, Alexander took

Table 4.3 Counterfactual estimate of profit from actual arrangement, with initial assumptions of Baring & Hope

Cession of Louisiana Territory (including New Orleans, but not Florida)	
To France (by Sir F. Baring & Henry Hope)	
Liv. 60,000,000 payable over 40 months, 6 million when treaty ratified, ½ million weekly thereafter in accepted bills of exchange	
5,100,000 *[=8.5% of 60 million taken as commission]*	
remit 54,900,000 @ 24 *{livres to the pound}*	£2,287,500
From the U.S. to (Sir F. Baring & H. Hope)	
$11,250,000 in 15 yr. unredeemable bonds 6% sold on average at 90%	
will produce $10,125,000 @ 4s.6d/$	£2,278,150
profit	–£ 9350

Source: *The Baring Archive*, NP1.A4.71, Note in hand of Sir Thomas Baring regarding Louisiana loan arrangements, undated

seriously the authority granted him by both his father and his brother-in-law to make the final agreement in Paris.[18] Events had transpired to make feasible a dramatic change in scale of the financing, as well as a change in the role of the private agents responsible for the financing.

What Happened in the Meantime?

News traveled by sailing ship across the Atlantic, usually in three different ships to assure arrival of at least one important document, such as a standard commercial bill of exchange, and sometimes in four. The delay could vary from three weeks to two months. So, while General Charles Leclerc, head of the French forces sent by Napoleon to seize control of the sugar plantations of St. Domingue from the slaves led in revolt by Toussaint L'Ouverture, died of yellow fever in November 1802, Napoleon only learned of it in late March 1803. Earlier in March, as yet unaware of the disastrous turn of events in Haiti, Napoleon had dispatched Pierre-Clément Laussat to take control of the Louisiana Territory from its Spanish governor. In the United States, Thomas Jefferson had learned that the Spanish governor had closed off American merchants from their right to deposit their goods in New Orleans starting in October 1802.

[18] No copy of that agreement, however, appears in the Baring Archive!

Only in January 1803 did Jefferson summon his protégé, James Monroe, to go to France to negotiate the purchase of New Orleans and W. Florida, just as his friend, Pierre Samuel Du Pont de Nemours, had advised him to do earlier in 1802. Monroe did not depart New York for France, however, until March of 1803, sailing to France just as Laussat was sailing from France to New Orleans. Monroe only arrived in Paris on April 11, 1803. (See above the "Time Line of the Financing of the Louisiana Purchase," to keep track.)

These two events, the death of Leclerc and the outrage in the United States from the arbitrary closing of New Orleans to American traders, combined with the rising expenses of maintaining the French forces being assembled in Holland to reinforce Leclerc in St. Domingue and to assist Laussat in taking control of Louisiana from Spain, surely explain why Napoleon made the sudden and complete reversal of his plans for an overseas empire. Instead of challenging British naval superiority in the West and East Indies, he would focus thereafter on creating a continental European empire.

For the financiers, however, the letters in the Baring Archive do not cover explicitly what enabled the two firms to respond effectively on such short notice to the greatly enlarged scale of the transaction. At the close of Sir Francis' letter of February 15, 1803, he urged both Alexander and Pierre Cesar to burn all his letters after digesting them, and presumably he burned their letters that he received afterward. All three correspondents were concerned to send letters only with trusted agents, supposing that any mail sent through government services would be read by either the British or French intelligence services. Nevertheless, the correspondence that makes up most of the remainder of the Louisiana Purchase folder deals with a prolonged dispute over how the profits from the financing should be shared between the two houses, Hope and Co. in Amsterdam and Baring and Co. in London. These allow us to infer what two events occurred that reassured both houses to proceed confidently and on an even larger scale than originally contemplated.

The first event was the reassurance to Sir Francis about the marketability of the U.S. bonds that would be created. Initially, in mid-February 1803, he was not sure how his London investors would respond to the purchase of U.S. bonds given the recent failure of the firm of Bird, Savage, and Bird, the American firm responsible for making payments to British correspondents. Not mentioned in his subsequent letters is that Sir Francis had assumed those responsibilities for the U.S. government in place of Bird, Savage, and Bird. Nevertheless, on February 11, 1803 Sir Francis wrote a long letter to Rufus King, the American Envoy to the Court of St. James, assuring him "we shall esteem ourselves highly flattered with the employ [of the agency of the Treasury of the United States for their pecuniary transactions in this place] & ready at all times to obey the commands of the Treasury or any branch of the executive administration of the Government of the United States."[19] Also not mentioned in the correspondence is the success of Alexander's arrangement made in March 1802 to assume responsibility for paying off the remainder of American debt to Dutch creditors, as well as to purchase the remaining shares of the Bank of the United States owned by the Federal government. The combination of these events made it clear that Barings would thereafter be the primary financial intermediary in Europe for U.S. public funds (Hidy, 1949).

With the marketing design set for the American securities by the joint judgment of Sir Francis Baring and Henry Hope, the second event, which has to be inferred from the later dispute over the split of the profits between Amsterdam and London, must have been the arrangement made by Pierre Cesar to associate two well-known Dutch banking houses in the finance of the American bonds. Presumably, he had already thought of using these Dutch intermediaries to assist in his financing of the French *rentes* that were considered an essential part of the original negotiations. When they showed an eagerness to take up the U.S. bonds as well, however, Labouchere initiated a formal partnership with the two firms of R. and G. de Smeth and Wm. and G. Willink in Amsterdam. Later, Sir Francis presented the formal arrangement that had been made among the three firms to make the case to the British Prime Minister, Henry Addington, that helping the Americans acquire New Orleans was a strategic benefit to Britain as well (*The Baring Archive*, NP1.A4.30). The joint venture in Amsterdam, by which the three firms would receive nearly the whole of the American debt to be paid off, would re-package the obligations as shares in a 15-year investment fund paying 5% interest in guilders to any investor wanting to receive payment in Amsterdam. (See Appendix E for the Dutch plan.)

An additional third event that enabled Baring and Hope to take on the obligation of paying 60 million, in place of 40 million, francs to France

[19] LOC, Baring Mss., MMC 2475, Copies of letters addressed to the Treasury department of the United States of America by Sir Francis Baring & Co., p. 1.

within three years was the suggestion, apparently made by Alexander during the negotiations in the last two weeks of April 1803, that the outstanding claims of the American merchants would be handled directly by the U.S. Treasury, up to a further limit of 20 million francs. This was an increase of 2 million francs that the merchants would be eligible to receive, but now it would be in U.S. dollars paid out in Washington, rather than in French *rentes* that would be worth much less than their face value when sold and exchanged for dollars. Maintaining the same exchange rate between the French franc and the U.S. dollar for the claims, however, meant that the United States would have to come up with another $3.75 million, independently of the services of Baring and Hope, and might have to pay these sums within a year or two. The claims already submitted on behalf of American shippers had amounted to 18 million francs and their payment would depend only on verification by American commissioners.

For France, however, this arrangement enabled Barbé-Marbois to convince Napoleon that he had extracted a price of 80 million francs, well above Napoleon's initial minimum asking price of 50 million. (American histories are correct to give $15 million as the agreed purchase price, with only $11.25 million owed to Baring & Hope, but one should recall that Alexander had already arranged to reduce U.S. Federal government debt by paying off the remainder of the Dutch loan and purchasing the government's stock in the Bank of the United States back in Summer of 1802.) Best of all for the concerns of Baring and Hope, the financiers would be relieved of the task of monitoring the individual payments to various merchants, and of distributing the French *rentes* among individual entrepreneurs.

To summarize, two geo-political events changed Napoleon's mind about Louisiana; (1) the failure of Le Clerc's expedition to regain control of St. Domingue, and (2) the failure of the French armed forces to leave port in Holland in time to establish control of New Orleans, due to unfavorable weather conditions in the North Sea. The French army could, however, be diverted toward Austria instead, but that would require fresh financing for France forces on foreign soil. Then, two financial events changed the minds of Sir Francis Baring and Henry Hope about the possibilities for financing the Louisiana Purchase: (1) renewed confidence in U.S. finances by Sir Francis Baring, and, (2) renewed partnership with Dutch financiers in Amsterdam by Pierre Cesar Labouchere. As geo-political events persuaded Napoleon to give up all of Louisiana, financial market developments persuaded the Baring-Hope partnership to raise their money offers as well, especially once the complication of marketing the French securities and then making individual payments to American merchants had been removed from the deal.

In June 1803, Alexander Baring left Paris for London to receive final instructions from his father, Sir Francis Baring. From London he then sailed in August to Washington, D.C., where he arrived in September to oversee printing the 5071 certificates. After the U.S. Senate approved the purchase on October 20 and the House of Representatives approved the issuance of the debt required, the bonds were printed to the specifications required by the banking firms of Baring and Hope, with the names of the two other Dutch firms as arranged by Pierre Cesar in Amsterdam. These were the two firms of Raymond and Theodore de Smeth, and William and John Willink (Appendix C). Alexander, however, refused to accept them from the printer, despite Gallatin's urging on behalf of the U.S. government, until he had himself received official notice that the Louisiana Territory had been officially transferred, first from Spain to France, and then, from France to the United States.

In fact, the transfer from Spain to France occurred on November 30, 1803 and the subsequent cession from France to the United States took place on December 20, 1803. News of this success did not arrive in Washington for another 10 days, however, despite the urgency of getting official notification to the officials in Washington. Only on January 10, 1804, was Alexander willing to receive his 1/3 share of the bonds to take back to London, and sign off for the remaining bonds to be taken on a U.S. naval vessel, which left New York on February 13, 1804. That vessel did arrive safely and the remaining 2/3 of the bonds were received by Robert R. Livingston in Paris on April 25, 1804. Livingston then allowed the accepted bills of exchange to be dated seriatim for the remaining payments to France, on the approval of Pierre Cesar, who then took the bonds back to Amsterdam for distribution to his partners. The sustained efforts of the two brothers-in-law over the 15 months following Alexander's original letter to Pierre Cesar finally paid off, and the Louisiana Purchase had been successfully financed.

Why then, have their heroic efforts been ignored to date in the historical literature? Their names do not come up in the historiography, even though they were essential for completing the Louisiana Purchase in the first place by arranging, and then implementing precisely, the terms needed for its finance. Instead, the political decision-makers are given all the credit for initiating and completing the deal. If so, why should it have been necessary for Baring and Hope to "grease the wheels" in the first place? Surely, all the players in the deal, whether acting as principals or agents, as politicians or financiers, whether American, French, British, or Dutch were important. They all deserve a closer look, especially the *financial* principals, agents, and promoters.

References

Austin, Peter E. 2007. *Baring Brothers and the Birth of Modern Finance*. London: Pickering & Chatto.

Bordo, Michael, and Eugene N. White, 1991. "A Tale of Two Currencies: British and French Finance during the Napoleonic Wars." *The Journal of Economic History* 51 (2): 303–316.

Branda, Pierre. 2007. *Le Prix de la Gloire: Napoléon et l'Argent (Divers Histoire)*. Paris: Librairie Arthème Fayard.

Brown, Stuart Gerry. 2017. *The Autobiography of James Monroe*. Syracuse, NY: Syracuse University Press.

Buist, Marten G. 1974. *At Spes Non Fracta: Hope & Co. 1779–1815*. Amsterdam: Bank Mees & Hope NV.

Deviosse, Jean. 1989. *L'homme qui vendit la Louisiane, récit*. Paris: Olivier Orban.

Flandreau, Marc, and Juan H. Flores. 2009. "Bonds and Brands: Foundations of Sovereign Debt Markets, 1820–1830." *Journal of Economic History* 69 (3): 646–684.

Hidy, Ralph W. 1949. *The House of Baring in American Trade and Finance: English Merchant Bankers at Work, 1763–1861*. Cambridge, MA: Harvard University Press.

Jacoud, Gilles. 1996. *Le billet de banque en France (1796–1803), de la diversité au monopole*. Paris: Éditions L'Harmattan.

Jonker, Joost, and Keetie Sluyterman. 2000. *At home on the world markets: Dutch international trading companies from the 16th century to the present*. The Hague: Sdu Uitgevers.

Lyon, E. Wilson (1942, 2nd printing 1974). *The Man Who Sold Louisiana*. Norman, OK: University of Oklahoma Press.

Orbell, John. 1985. *A History of Baring Brothers to 1939*. London: Baring Brothers & Co., Limited.

Stourm, René. 1902. *Les Finances du Consulat*. Paris: Guillaumin et Cie.

Ziegler, Philip. 1988. *The Sixth Great Power: A history of one of the greatest of all banking families, the House of Barings, 1762–1929*. New York: Alfred A. Knopf.

CHAPTER 5

All the Players Were Important

While Alexander Baring and Pierre Cesar Labouchere were acquiring their knowledge of the changing world of the North Atlantic and the new challenges presented for international finance during the upheavals caused by the American and French Revolutions, François Barbé-Marbois was living through all of them as a first-hand observer (and prolific author). Born on January 31, 1745 in Metz, France, where his father was the director of the local mint, he proved to be a child prodigy, absorbing all the classics in Latin and Greek from his Jesuit instructors. At age 20, he was in Paris studying the law, but catching the attention of various members of the nobility with his erudition and facility with language, began a career in French public service as a junior diplomat for Louis XV. Serving with distinction in the courts of Regensburg, Vienna and Dresden, his diplomatic career appeared over when the Austrian court learned he had backed the Prussian contender to become the new Elector of Bavaria in 1778. It was a fluke that one of his young friends in the diplomatic corps was appointed to be the minister plenipotentiary to the American colonies in revolt. The Chevalier de la Luzerne, having the privilege of selecting his secretary and *chargé d'affaires*, picked Barbé-Marbois. Sailing in convoy escorted by French frigates from Lorient in June 1779, Luzerne and Barbé-Marbois arrived at Boston on August 3. By chance, John Adams and his precocious son, John Quincy, had also

L. Neal, *The Forgotten Financiers of the Louisiana Purchase*, Palgrave Studies in the History of Finance,
https://doi.org/10.1007/978-3-031-56277-8_5

Fig. 5.1 François Barbé-Marbois (*Source* https://en.wikipedia.org/wiki/François_Barbé-Marbois#In_the_Revolution)

been passengers on the French frigate *Sensible* with Barbé-Marbois and Luzerne. They only met, however, when disembarking in Boston. Immediately, however, Barbé-Marbois and both Adams struck up a friendship that would carry through the years to come. Barbé-Marbois and John Quincy struck a bargain to teach each other their mother tongues. Only later did Barbé-Marbois discover that the English taught him by John Quincy was better as a roustabout in New England's seaports than in diplomatic circles![1] (Fig. 5.1).

When Luzerne was recalled to enter the Ministry of the Marine in France in 1782, Barbé-Marbois continued as the French Consul-General based in Philadelphia. In charge of the French delegation while a new

[1] Deviosse, p. 66. "Sous pretexte d'apprendre à son élève la langue qui se pratique *vraiment* en Amérique, il lui avait enseigné le slang."

ambassador was being sent from Paris, Barbé-Marbois was part of the post-revolutionary process in America, the "critical period" of 1784–1789. In addition to being received into the highest levels of American politics, he was also welcome among the Philadelphia elite, thanks to his marriage on June 17, 1784 to Elizabeth Moore. Her father, in addition to being a wealthy merchant, was a powerful figure in Pennsylvania politics, having served as president of the Pennsylvania legislature. François Barbé-Marbois then set up French trade consuls at each American port after independence was acknowledged by both France and Britain in 1783. He made it a point to learn the commercial possibilities of each colony, even encouraging Thomas Jefferson to put his "Notes on Virginia" into publishable form.[2]

François, however, still lacked the necessary quality of nobility needed for representing Louis XVI, despite having added "Marbois" to his surname when he was a student in Paris. A new ambassador was appointed over Barbé-Marbois despite the recommendation of the former ambassador. As a recognition of his ability and service to the Crown, however, he was appointed as the Intendant of the most prosperous colony of France, Saint-Domingue. This position meant that he was in charge of the civilian governance of the colony, while the military power was exercised by a Governor. Initially, the new governor, Count Lefèvre de La Luzerne, the younger brother of the Chevalier de la Luzerne, welcomed Barbé-Marbois, knowing what high regard he had with both his brother and de Castries, the minister of the French navy. With the governor's support, Barbé-Marbois took seriously the task of restoring Saint-Domingue's economic value to the mother country. In the course of expanding the access to the southern part of the modern Haiti and introducing new crops throughout the French portion of Hispaniola, however, he managed to earn the intense dislike of the major sugar barons. Most likely this arose from his insistence that they conform to the mercantile rules of the mother country, France, but his position became fraught when a new Governor appeared, replacing Luzerne, who had been recalled to

[2] Jefferson first published his only book in Paris, while he was serving as the Trade Representative of the United States in 1785, then a French translation in 1787 and the English version in London in 1787. An early book translated Barbé-Marbois's personal journal recounting his adventures as a senior diplomat representing French interests to the revolutionary United States, *Our Revolutionary Forefathers*, in 1929.

France to become the new minister of the Marine, part of the constant re-shuffling of ministers under Louis XVI.

The new governor sought the support of the local planters by undercutting Barbé-Marbois at every opportunity. Life became increasingly unpleasant for a conscientious intendant, who found his every initiative undercut by the refusal of the new governor to allow enforcement of Barbé-Marbois' orders, such as completing a road from Port-au-Prince to Cayes on the southern peninsula of Haiti. Pleading to Count Vergennes to be recalled on the grounds that his absence from France was now approaching 10 years and he wanted to return to his natal home in Lorraine, his wish was finally granted, no doubt with the support of his friend in Versailles, de la Luzerne. His recall to France occurred just in time to avoid being attacked by a mob, who burned his residence while he and his family looked back from the ship that had been assigned to take him back to France—just as the revolution there was beginning.

Nevertheless, he managed to avoid the perils of the Terror in the early years of the French Revolution by devoting himself to the city of Metz, where his family was long-established. He stayed in Paris just long enough to defend his handling of finances in St. Domingue from the accusations of the white planters who had come to Paris to make their case to elevate their status from colony to department. He remained committed to bring his American wife and two small daughters to his home in Metz, turning down the offer to be the intendant in charge of the King's Civil List. He would have accepted the position, but only on condition that he administer it strictly as mandated in law, without dispensing favors to journalists or royalist supporters in the National Assembly. The offer was withdrawn, fortunately for him, as the later occupants of that office were either guillotined or forced to flee for their lives (e.g. Amer Talon, discussed below). In January 1792, however, he accepted the position to be special envoy to the German Diet meeting in Ratisbon and then as ambassador to the imperial court of Austria in Vienna. Again, he was fortunate to be sent away from Paris before the outbreak of the Terror. He was able to return to his home in Lorraine instead of Paris during the Terror.

In the interval, however, his wife Elizabeth had to be protected from the grasp of the Terror when she attempted to leave France to visit her dying father in Philadelphia in 1792. Only repeated interventions by the American ministers to France, Gouverneur Morris and then James Monroe, who assured the Committee for Public Safety that Elizabeth was an American, not an émigré, eventually eased their fears so that she could re-emerge from hiding. James Monroe and wife actually visited Barbé-Marbois in Metz before Monroe was recalled as the American representative in 1796. When the Terror in Paris ended, François had the courage to return to Paris in 1795 to serve in the newly formed Conseil des Anciens as the representative for the region of Lorraine.

As a moderate member of the Conseil des Anciens and a leading member of the Club de Clichy, he served as president from 20 May 1797 to 19 June 1797. His trenchant criticisms of the corruption rampant under the executive powers exercised by the 5-member Directory, however, earned him arrest in the coup of 18 Fructidor, Year V (September 4, 1797) and two years of exile to French Guiana. Barbé-Marbois returned to France under the terms of the Consulat created to replace the Directory after the subsequent coup of 18 Brumaire, Year VIII (November 8, 1799). Back in France, and reunited with his wife, he rose in favor with Napoleon due to his diligent work habits and probity. Further, he stood out as determined to eliminate corruption throughout the French civil service, all the while maintaining unfailing sycophancy to the rising star of Napoleon. His services in managing the sale of Louisiana were rewarded by Napoleon's generous payment of *f*192,000 (Stourm, p. 25), which enabled him to purchase the Chateau Noyers in Normandy at the price of *f*273,500 (Deviosse, p. 389).

This gesture by Napoleon does add credibility to Barbé-Marbois's recount of his arguments to Napoleon on the eve of the arrival of Monroe in Paris that favored accepting the loss of Haiti and therefore ceding the entire Louisiana territory to the United States. Countering the arguments of the Minister of the French Navy, Desmaretz, who argued in favor of maintaining control over the West Indies, Barbé-Marbois favored replacing the lost sugar trade with Haiti with an expanding trade with the ever-growing and prospering United States. This suggests that Napoleon valued Barbé-Marbois's experience in the United States as Consul-General, 1781–1784, over his record of civilian administration in Saint-Domingue, 1785–1789. There is no mention of Napoleon asking advice from Barbé-Marbois before he launched the ill-fated invasion of Haiti, however, probably because he was aware of the rancor against Barbé-Marbois by the proprietors of the largest sugar plantations, who had hastened his departure from the island in 1789. If Napoleon did ask Barbé-Marbois for advice about dealing with Toussaint L'Ouverture, however, he probably advised Napoleon to accept L'Ouverture's attempts to restore production of the expropriated plantations by freed blacks as part of their military obligation, something he had suggested earlier would be required to make the transition from slavery to full emancipation.[3]

The French historian Stourm discounts Barbé-Marbois's ability as an expert in finance, however. He notes that Napoleon's letters to Barbé-Marbois were often angry and disparaging, while they always had a respectful tone to his other two major financial advisors—Mollien and Gaudin (Stourm, p. 23). Nonetheless, the work by Barbé-Marbois when he was advising Napoleon on the merits and dangers of giving the newly established Banque de France the monopoly of note issue for France (at the same time Livingston was frustrated by losing touch with his best contact in the French administration) shows that his efforts were by and large accepted by Napoleon.[4] Further, Napoleon later appointed him in September 1807 as the first president of the re-established *Cour des Comptes*. Noted for his meticulous accounts and scrupulous auditing, especially after the affair with the *Négociants Réunis*, he was ideal for this position. Indeed, after a brief period as Minister of Justice under Louis XVIII, he continued to preside over the government accounts under the successive constitutional monarchs who followed Napoleon. He surely deserves an honored place in French history as that nation's longest-lived public servant, dying at age 91 in 1837 (Fig. 5.2).

Although overlooked in most histories of the Louisiana Purchase, Albert Gallatin as Secretary of the Treasury was the American counterpart to the French Minister of Finance, François Barbé-Marbois.[5] Both men were born in Europe: Barbé-Marbois in Metz, Lorraine and Gallatin in Geneva, Switzerland. Both came to the United States as young men within one year of each other, Barbé-Marbois in 1779 and Gallatin in 1780. Nevertheless, there is no evidence that they ever met personally during the next few years while both men explored possibilities for their personal futures in the newly formed United States of America. Barbé-Marbois was fully engaged in diplomacy with the new U.S. government based in Philadelphia, although he also visited the sea ports where

[3] Barbé-Marbois (1796).

[4] Jacoud (1996), highlights the support given by Barbé-Marbois to Napoleon's effort to give the new Banque de France national monopoly of note issues.

[5] More recently, enthusiastic biographies have appeared to supplement the early works of Adams (1879), Ferguson (1971), Walters (1957). See especially Dungan (2010), May (2018), McCraw (2012), Wright and Cowen (2006).

Fig. 5.2 Albert Gallatin (Portrait by Gilbert Stuart, 1803. https://upload.wikimedia.org/wikipedia/commons/b/b6/Albert_Gallatin_%28by_Gilbert_Stuart%29.jpg)

French consuls could be appointed. At the end of his stay in America, Barbé-Marbois did accompany James Madison and LaFayette to a postwar settlement with the Iroquois in upstate New York,[6] but that was his only venture into the wilderness of the frontier areas of the new country. Gallatin, by contrast, was determined to make his fortune by settling on a promising section of land on one of the new frontiers created by the treaty of Paris in 1783. Even later, when setting up the financial arrangements for the Louisiana Purchase, Gallatin only mentions perfunctorily that he

[6] The Treaty of Fort Stanwix (1784) as described in Deviosse, Ch. IX, Les Peintures de Paix.

had received a short note from Barbé-Marbois regarding the treaty in Paris. Even then, that note only expressed the desire on the part of France that the American side move quickly to ratify the treaty and fulfill the financial requirements. Much more detailed and personal was the letter he received from Alexander, which contained the specifics of the agreement that Alexander had made with the signatories in Paris, although not the orders Alexander had obtained from his father and Henry Hope.

After exploring the wilderness of northern Maine at the recommendation of another Swiss emigré, Gallatin returned to Boston, spent a brief spell teaching French at Harvard, but resumed his search for a suitable frontier settlement when he met a Frenchman, Jean Savary de Valcoulon, in 1783. Savary had arrived in Boston as the agent of a Frenchman who now wanted the state of Virginia to repay him for money and material he had loaned to Virginia during the war. Over the next three years, the two European adventurers surveyed the possibilities for land that might become profitable to the west of the Allegheny Mountains. Eventually, they found a likely location along the Monongahela River in the farthest west of land still claimed by Virginia, where Gallatin and Savary staked a joint claim. This enabled Gallatin to become a citizen of the state of Virginia in October 1785. When Gallatin reached the age of twenty-five in February 1786, moreover, he could now take possession of his inheritance from grandparents in Geneva. This he used to buy more land upstream in the far southwestern corner of the state of Pennsylvania. Now he would be involved in the state politics of Pennsylvania, not Virginia.[7] He became one of the few well-educated and knowledgeable settlers in the western edge of the United States at the time. His efforts to expand roads and navigable rivers to the west would take him eventually to Philadelphia and into the halls of power of the new Federal government. He proved much more successful as an elected legislator from one of the most lightly populated parts of Pennsylvania than as either a business man or estate owner. (A glass-works that he started at New Geneva never made a profit, and Friendship Hill would have required slave labor to make it profitable, although Gallatin's house had a magnificent view.)

While representing his fellow pioneers in the wildernesses of western Pennsylvania in the Pennsylvania House of Representatives (1790–1792), however, he won the appreciation of William Bingham. Bingham, already

[7] Today, his home at Friendship Hill is a National Historic Site operated by the U.S. National Park Service, but only lightly visited.

renowned as one of the richest men in America, presided over Philadelphia society in his magnificent residence, Mansion House, with his beautiful wife, Ann Willing, while also presiding over the Pennsylvania House of Representatives. As Speaker of the House, Bingham appointed Gallatin "to no fewer than forty committees, most of which relied on their new member to draw up their bills and prepare their reports."[8] Gallatin also supported Bingham in promoting the construction of the Lancaster Turnpike, which opened more of western Pennsylvania to potential settlement when it was completed in 1795. Begun in 1792, this privately financed and constructed paved road was the country's first engineered road. Gallatin's later proposals for Federal financing of infrastructure projects to connect all of the regions of the United States were clearly grounded in this early highway, which made Friendship Hill more accessible to visitors from Philadelphia or New York. He also drew up the charter for establishing the Bank of Pennsylvania in 1793, with branches to serve Pittsburgh, Harrisburg, Lancaster, Reading, and Easton, which foreshadowed the rapid development of state-chartered banks with branches in response to Hamilton's Bank of the United States.[9]

So well-regarded was Gallatin for his workaholic efforts in the Pennsylvania House that the members voted him to become Pennsylvania's Senator to replace the retiring William MacLay. His election was despite Gallatin already becoming known as a Jefferson supporter while the majority of the House were, like Bingham, Federalists. In the U.S. Senate, however, the majority of Federalists took exception to Gallatin's presence and they raised the issue of whether he was really eligible for office. The Constitution required officials elected to Congress to have been citizens of the United States for at least nine years. Gallatin's declaration of citizenship in remote West Virginia in October 1785, apparently did not pass scrutiny, so the existing members of the U.S. Senate, including the other Pennsylvania Senator, Robert Morris, voted to remove him when the new session began in February 1795. His brief term of office as Senator (December 2, 1793 to February 28, 1794), however, made him a devoted member of the Madison-Jefferson party, the Democrat-Republican. Accordingly, he became outspoken (and effective) speaker

[8] Alberts, p. 238.

[9] Knodell (2017).

against the ruling Federalist party when he became a duly elected member of the U.S. House of Representatives in 1795.

Gallatin became the effective leader of the Republican minority in the House when he began his term in March 1795, as both Jefferson and Madison had left Philadelphia to return to their respective estates in Virginia. Like Hamilton, Gallatin was enthusiastic about the writings of Jacques Necker, the Swiss financier who tried, unsuccessfully, to restore the finances of the French monarchy under Louis XVI. He was not enthusiastic, however, about Hamilton's reluctance to provide annual Treasury reports to the House of Representatives. Lacking even annual totals of Federal revenues and expenses for the first term of the new government, Gallatin produced his own estimates and assessments in 1796 with his first major publication, *A Sketch of the Finances of the United States.* This work effectively established Gallatin as the financial authority for the Republican-Democrat party that emerged under the leadership of Jefferson and Madison, during the tumultuous term of John Adams. His point-by-point criticism of Hamilton's efforts to consolidate the state and Federal debts into a marketable set of three new issues of Federal debts was likely colored by his reaction to the lavish display of mansions and hospitality by Bingham and Morris in Philadelphia, both of whom had profited spectacularly from Hamilton's re-financing of the Revolutionary War debts.[10]

When, however, he became Secretary of the Treasury himself after Jefferson's election in 1800, and then had to deal with the financial implications of the policies of Jefferson and Madison, he became much more appreciative of the system left in place by Hamilton. He appreciated especially the usefulness of the Bank of the United States with its branches located in the country's main seaports where most of the government's revenue was collected by the Federal customs officials installed by Hamilton and his successors. The main difference, perhaps, lay in their attitudes toward the marketing of the national debt, which Gallatin was determined to pay off as quickly as possible. Hamilton, in Gallatin's opinion, had dithered and seemed willing to increase the Federal debt, if that was required to build up and maintain the military

[10] Sylla (2011) compares Gallatin's work with a nearly contemporaneous, but unpublished, work by Hamilton to assess the philosophical differences, which he finds were less than the mutual vituperation between the two pre-eminent Secretaries of the Treasury at the time led later historians to believe.

and naval strength of the new country. Gallatin did regret Jefferson's elimination of all Federal excise taxes that Hamilton had initiated, but hoped that land sales might replace the revenue lost as a result. Consequently, Gallatin was very supportive of westward settlements, and as Treasury Secretary he facilitated them by establishing regional land offices as new areas opened up. Moreover, he continued to provide effective financial terms to yeoman farmers, not land speculators like Bingham or Morris!

Therefore, when Jefferson finally decided to put forward a financial offer to Napoleon for purchasing outright the port of New Orleans in January 1803, Gallatin was very supportive. Indeed, he may have been the most determined of any member of the Jefferson administration to see the deal through, even when it became so much larger to include the entire Louisiana Territory as well as New Orleans. Early on, Levi Lincoln, Jefferson's Attorney General, raised the possibility that buying New Orleans outright by the Federal government might not be allowed under the terms of the Constitution. He suggested, therefore, that it might be expedient to have New Orleans acquired by an existing state, perhaps Georgia, or even to have the Constitution amended to permit direct acquisition by the Federal government. Gallatin immediately rejected Lincoln's arguments as specious, and argued strenuously that the Constitution implied the sovereign authority of the Federal government to take whatever measures might be needed to acquire new territory. (This was the same argument (implied powers of a sovereign state) that Hamilton had used to persuade Congress to establish the Bank of the United States in 1790.) Further, he gave explicit instructions to Monroe to have the French government accept U.S. Treasury bills as payment for New Orleans. When the full extent of the Louisiana Purchase became known in July 1803, Gallatin exceeded his nominal authority as a Secretary of the Treasury by urging the governors of the states of Kentucky and Tennessee and the Territory of Mississippi to mobilize their respective militias to take New Orleans by force in case the Spanish resisted.[11]

Nevertheless, the actual terms of the finance of the Louisiana Purchase were not made explicit even for Gallatin until Alexander showed up with his powers of attorney from Sir Francis Baring and Henry Hope. It remains unrecorded just how and why Gallatin acceded to the demands of Alexander for complicating matters by printing up 5071 instead of 1125

[11] Alberts, pp. 178–180.

bond certificates, specifying 13 different denominations instead of one, and splitting them into 6 separate packets instead of one or two destined for Amsterdam or London. Alexander reported to his father that it was fortunate they had set the terms of the financing in Paris and not in Washington, as the Americans had a greatly inflated idea of the value of their debt. He went on to assert that it was his personal presence that enabled the bonds to be printed out as desired and he doubted that anyone else could have prevailed. From our perspective, it appears that the success of Alexander in dealing with the earlier transaction in Spring 1802, described above, set Alexander's reputation with Gallatin. Their mutual respect for each other would endure to the end of their lives. But it had to be Gallatin's innate enthusiasm for westward expansion that kept him cooperating with the specific demands of Alexander (Fig. 5.3).

After arriving at Boston in November 1795, Alexander ended up staying in America for another six years. In the meantime, he arranged to purchase half of the lands offered by Bingham (and Bingham's partner, Henry Knox) in February 1796, married Bingham's oldest daughter, Ann Louisa, in August 1798, fathered two sons, and made himself well-known among the American elite. It was during this period also that he met Charles Maurice Talleyrand, who was often a guest of Bingham while serving his self-imposed exile from revolutionary France (April 1794–June 1796). Alexander reported to his father that while he agreed "perfectly in his [Talleyrand's] arguments, and thought highly of his personal abilities but I should have some scruples in trusting to his integrity." With careful calculation Alexander reckoned, "he [Talleyrand] may perhaps be useful hereafter."[12]

Actually, Talleyrand was useful immediately as he shared with Alexander the notes he had made himself when he and Théophile Cazenove had visited the Maine lands held by Bingham and Henry Knox in the summer of 1794 (Furstenberg, p. 90; Poniatowski, Ch. III). Alexander's own trip of exploration to Maine took place two years later in the summer of 1796. Perhaps relying more on Talleyrand's notes than his own observations, Alexander was accompanied by William Bingham, the Bingham ladies—Mrs. William Bingham, née Anne Willing; her yet unwed younger sister, Abigail Willing (almost 20 years old); and her two delightful daughters, Ann Louisa (14) and Maria Matilda (13).

[12] Orbell, ODNB, citing Baring Archive, DEP3.5.27) "Transcription of correspondence in regard to the Maine Lands, 1792–1836, Volume 1."

Fig. 5.3 *Alexander Baring* (*Source* https://baringarchive.org.uk/exhibition/baring-portraits/)

Adding luster to the party was the Vicomte de Noailles, who had become established as a member of the Bingham household since his arrival in Philadelphia in 1794 with another young French émigré of means, Antoine Omer Talon (Alberts, p. 286).

With the advice of both Robert Morris and William Bingham, the two distinguished French emigrés had already invested in land north of Philadelphia to establish an idyllic asylum for royalists fleeing revolutionary France. Misspelled as *Azilum*, the village failed to prosper despite a magnificent hotel, rumored to be intended as the residence for Marie Antoinette and built before Noailles and Talon learned of her execution in France. Talleyrand's dismissal of Azilum's prospects when he had visited it during his return from exploring the lands in Maine may have persuaded

Alexander of the need to induce yeoman settlers to the lands in Maine in preference to French artisans and nobility with their servants.

After the due diligence of the Maine lands, Alexander took the better half of the lands offered by Bingham and Knox (the half most accessible by sea), and left further management of the real estate to an agent employed by Hope and Company. Thereafter, Alexander found the financial opportunities in Philadelphia and New York much more interesting than land speculation in a country still lightly populated by European settlers, who found themselves always in conflict with the asserted property rights of Native American tribes. (A similar conviction must have motivated Antoine Omer Talon to return to France, leaving behind his implanted French colonists from St. Domingue and Paris.) Alexander never visited Maine again until many years later, when as Lord Ashburton he came to sign the official treaty that fixed the northern boundary of Maine in 1842. When the portion bought by Alexander was sold in 1834, it proved to have been one of the few loss-making land speculations for Barings. The Louisiana Purchase, by opening access to overseas markets for American settlers in the fertile lands of the upper Midwest, diverted migrants from New England generally, and especially from Maine.

Back in Philadelphia after the purchase of the lands in Maine, Alexander surely monitored the course of Hamilton's "financial revolution" in American public finance. Even in 1790, when Hamilton had published his First Report on the Public Credit, Sir Francis Baring had taken a substantial position in the success of Hamilton's plan for paying off the debts accumulated by the individual states and the Continental Congress during the War of the American Revolution. (As described above in Chapter 3.) In 1798, as Hamilton's plan was succeeding even without Hamilton in office, Alexander arranged a $5 million loan for the Adams administration in the United States, then engaged in the Quasi-War with France (1798–1800) as American merchants attempted to continue their profitable trade with the West Indies. The year 1798 was also when Sir Francis and Daniel Parker collaborated on an ill-fated expedition to Surinam using an American ship, the *Rosanna*, to take advantage of the neutral status of American shipping at the time (and when François Barbé-Marbois was serving time as an exile in adjacent Sinnamary, French Guiana).

Alexander would return to the United States in June 1802, moreover, to arrange a further repayment of the outstanding debt of the United States to their Dutch bankers. According to Alexander's letter to his father to explain this speculation, undertaken strictly on Alexander's initiative, he had, unexpectedly, developed a very cordial and mutually agreeable relationship with the new administration's Secretary of the Treasury, Albert Gallatin. Originally, Alexander had sent Gallatin a polite letter to remind him that his father's firm was still the principal banking house handling American government remittances to Europe, but then he received an invitation from Gallatin to help with the next payments for redeeming the Dutch loan. Alexander, knowing that his father already had a favorable view of the stock of the Bank of the United States, holding 147 shares already either in his name or for others, and learning that Gallatin also wished very much to pay off this debt owed to the Bank of the United States, made Gallatin the offer that he took pains to explain to his father would work out very well for Barings.[13] Gallatin's letters to Alexander, enclosed with Alexander's letter to his father, made clear that Gallatin was very enthusiastic about the proposed deal, and only wanted to convince first, President Jefferson, and then, the members of the Commission for the Sinking Fund, to get their approval in order to conform to the legal requirements of the Federal government. This arrangement was jointly approved by James Madison, Secretary of State; Levi Lincoln, Attorney General; and Albert Gallatin, Secretary of the Treasury, who met as the official commissioners of the sinking fund for retiring U.S. Federal government debt. Their approval of Alexander's proposal came after the Bank of the United States refused to enter into the repayment to the Dutch. A competing offer from the Manhattan Company in New York, Aaron Burr's attempt to compete with Alexander Hamilton's Bank of New York, had a less favorable rate of exchange for the U.S. dollar with the Dutch guilder.[14]

Clearly, Alexander had established cordial relations with the highest officials of the Jefferson administration, despite being the son-in-law of the former de facto head of the Federalist Party, William Bingham. One presumes also that Alexander was able to take advantage of Pierre Cesar Labouchere's renewed presence in Amsterdam. Pierre Cesar had returned, briefly, to Amsterdam in late 1801, and arrangements had been made with the Dutch government to restitute the Hope property that had been

[13] *Baring Archive,* NP1.B11.1, Correspondence from Alexander Baring to his father, Sir Francis, Philadelphia, 1st June 1802.

[14] U.S., *Report of the Treasury, 1802*, pp. 269–270.

confiscated by the previous Patriot government (Buist, p. 55). Along with arranging the final payment of the U.S. debt to the Dutch, Alexander also purchased the remaining shares of the Federal government in the Bank of the United States, much to the satisfaction of Albert Gallatin, who felt that the price offered by Alexander was better than if the stock had been sold on the U.S. market. (He would have a different opinion on Alexander's pricing of U.S. debt in 1803.)[15]

In 1801, Alexander had returned to London with his wife and two infant sons, Bingham and Francis, determined to raise his children in a more civilized and cultured environment. He was accompanied by his father-in-law, William Bingham, as well. Bingham's wife, née Ann Willing, had fallen ill, probably with pneumonia, in winter of 1801 and died shipboard, May 11, 1801, while Bingham was trying to get her to a healthier environment in Madeira. He had her buried in Georgetown, the Bahamas. Bingham then returned to Philadelphia and, grieving from the death of his wife, decided to join Alexander and his family as they carried out their long-standing plan to return to London.

After settling in London with Alexander, his two daughters (Ann's younger sister, Maria, had made the voyage as well), and his two grandsons, Bingham had recovered enough to want to revisit Paris when that opportunity opened up with the Peace of Amiens, signed in March 1802. It appears that Bingham and his daughters were in Paris in mid-summer 1802, when Pierre Samuel Du Pont de Nemours showed up to give Robert R. Livingston his proposal, approved by Jefferson, to purchase New Orleans from France. There is record of Bingham renewing his friendship with Livingston while in Paris, as well as visiting Talleyrand, who had been a frequent guest of Bingham's while in temporary exile in America. Alexander could have also been with the family in Paris in late summer after returning from the United States in the early summer of 1802, and he was certainly with them in Paris over the Christmas holidays in 1802. The circumstances all combined to put both William Bingham and Alexander Baring in contact with Talleyrand, Livingston, and Du Pont de Nemours in the period of formal Peace of Amiens, March 1802–May 1803, exactly when the idea of a Louisiana Purchase was brewing (Fig. 5.4).

[15] U.S. Treasury Report (1802, pp. 269–270).

Fig. 5.4 Pierre Cesar Labouchere (*Source* https://www.wikitree.com/photo/jpg/Labouchere-1)

While Alexander was abroad in the United States and getting married to the eldest daughter of the richest man in America, Pierre Cesar was making himself useful to Henry Hope in London. He also managed to make a worthy marriage himself in 1796, to Dorothy Elizabeth Baring, the third daughter of Sir Francis Baring. A repeated story about Pierre Cesar's negotiating skills recounts that when he first asked Sir Francis for permission to court Dorothy Elizabeth, Sir Francis refused. So, Pierre Cesar asked, presumably after reflection, if it would make a difference if he were a partner with Henry Hope, not just a senior clerk. And Sir Francis had to agree that it would. That prompted Pierre Cesar to ask Henry Hope if he could become a partner if he were married to the daughter of Sir Francis, and Henry Hope agreed![16] The marriage took place on November 26, 1796, and two sons quickly followed: Henry was born on August 15, 1797 and John Peter was born on August 14, 1798, both at Broome Hall in Surrey. Later, Henry became a Member of Parliament and distinguished himself by introducing the bill to end the British Navigation Acts in 1848.

The Laboucheres descended from a distinguished family of Huguenot cloth merchants in Orthez, a picturesque town on the river Gave de Pau in southwestern France. As well as being the ancient capital of Béarn, Orthez was a major center of French Protestantism and today has a major museum devoted to Huguenot history. The Revocation of the Edict of Nantes in 1685 by Louis XIV was enforced in Béarn by the *dragonnades* that removed individuals from their homes, farms, and businesses and culminated with exile if they did not renounce their faith. The Labouchere family, with their commercial connections in the cloth trade, gradually dispersed over time as well in common with many of the more prosperous Huguenots. Pierre Cesar's father, for example, was smuggled to England at the age of 14 in 1735 to be educated by his cousin, Jean Jacques de Majendie, then vicar of St. Martin Orgars and later court chaplain. In 1740, his education complete, he moved to Holland, where he continued his family's trade as a cloth merchant in The Hague, where Pierre Cesar was born in 1772.[17] Meanwhile, his uncle, Pierre de Labouchere, had become a successful merchant in Nantes, perhaps the most prosperous port in France at the time, thanks to the booming trade with the West Indies. Pierre Cesar went to his uncle's firm in Nantes in 1785 to receive training in international merchant trade and finance. (Vincent Nolte, who would appear later as the agent of Baring and Hope in New Orleans, was also sent to the Labouchere firm in Nantes for further training in 1804. By that time the leadership of the firm had passed to Pierre Cesar's younger brother, A. M. Labouchere, who, after serving as well as a clerk first with Hope and Co. in Amsterdam and then with John and Francis Baring in London, returned to Nantes in 1803 to establish his own firm.)

[16] The story is, no doubt, too good to be true, but the biographer of Henry Labouchere, Pierre Cesar's grandson, claims he got it from a member of the Baring family, a Rev. Alexander Baring, many years later (Thorold, p. 2).

[17] These details supplied to me in a personal e-mail by Mr. Joan Labouchere, the family genealogist, December 2022.

Pierre Cesar's uncle was only too pleased to establish a further connection with the house of Hope and Co. by sending his nephew to Henry Hope's firm in 1789. Pierre Cesar was slated to become the specialist for French affairs of the House of Hope that year, just as everything was becoming much more interesting for everyone dealing in international trade and finance, especially in France and Holland. When his three-year term of service with Henry Hope was coming to an end in 1794, Pierre Cesar suggested to Henry Hope that he might continue if he could have a modest raise in his fixed salary. The story, related by Vincent Nolte, is that Hope told him to come in the next morning, whereupon he was given power of procuration, entrusted with the signature of the house at the age of twenty-two.[18] After the French invasion the Hopes fled to London leaving Pierre Cesar to run the merchant bank in Amsterdam, with the help of Alexander Baring. Only in 1802 was he signed on as a permanent member of the firm, with "a suitable share in the profits," so it appears that the power of procuration preceded his wedding, and the wedding preceded the partnership.[19]

Two years after Pierre Cesar had joined Hope and Co. in Amsterdam, Alexander Baring appeared in Amsterdam to learn the business of international finance as practiced by the leading firm in Europe, Hope and Company. Alexander clearly came to respect the ability of the chief clerk in Hope and Company, the man who would soon become his brother-in-law, and later, his partner in major operations in international finance, including, but not limited to, the Louisiana Purchase. Shortly after Alexander appeared, Henry Hope, the leading partner, moved permanently to England, leaving behind Pierre Cesar and Alexander to settle up the accounts of the firm before they, too, had to leave for England in the face of the arrival of the French army in Amsterdam. While Alexander was shortly sent off to check on the prospects of land purchases in the United States, Pierre Cesar remained in London. In addition to marrying Alexander's older sister in 1796, he assisted Henry Hope by maintaining that firm's correspondence with its affiliates on the continent.

[18] Nolte, p. 51, infers that Labouchere became a partner at this time, although Buist finds that partnership was withheld until Labouchere was sent back to Amsterdam in 1802 to re-establish the firm while Henry Hope remained in England.

[19] Joan Labouchere, current descendant of Pierre Cesar, insists this is the correct sequence for Pierre Cesar's career and marriage (e-mail, 2023).

Even though Madame Labouchere was bearing her second son in 1798, Henry Hope sent Pierre Cesar to Hamburg in June 1798 to deal with Hope's affairs with the firm of Martin Dorner, whose death in April 1798 caused that firm to suspend payments. In the few months Pierre Cesar was in Hamburg he managed to expedite the settlement of Dorner's affairs, put Hope's claims on an equal status with those of local creditors, and set up a replacement firm, Matthiesen and Sillem , to continue the intermediation of Baltic trade with Amsterdam through Hamburg.[20] While in Hamburg to determine which firm should replace Dorner, moreover, Pierre Cesar made a striking impression upon the son of Johann Heinrich Nolte, one of the many Hamburg merchants engaged in foreign trade that Labouchere had rejected as possible replacements for Doerner. Vincent Nolte, Johann's son, however, would become a representative of Baring & Hope in New Orleans after its acquisition by the U.S. Nolte's presence in New Orleans as a cotton factor would help make the financing of the Louisiana Purchase even more profitable for the two firms. That business would come later, but another profitable enterprise may have come to Pierre Cesar's attention while he was in Hamburg, one that was to send him to the Dutch colony of Surinam in 1799.

The background to this adventure is not clear, overshadowed as it was by the general disruption of trade in the West Indies and the increasing difficulties for European powers to sustain their economic privileges among the scattered islands and coastal plains. Slave revolts spread throughout the West Indies and the southern United States with renewed intensity after August 1791 when news of the uprisings in the French colony of St. Domingue spread throughout the Atlantic trading world. The example of U.S. independence from the most powerful naval force in Europe made the hold of the other European powers—Denmark, France, the Netherlands, Portugal, and Spain—on their American colonies increasingly tenuous (Liss, 1983). So it was that the Dutch colony of Surinam, bordered to the south by French Guiana and to the north by Spanish Venezuela, came into the hands of the British in 1799, if only temporarily. (Surinam would return to the Kingdom of the Netherlands as a colony after the Congress of Vienna in 1815, only becoming the independent Republic of Suriname in 1975.)

[20] Buist, pp. 173–182.

The impetus for Pierre Cesar's voyage to Surinam in 1799 and for Britain's seizure of the Dutch colony occurred at the instigation of the French émigré, Antoine Omer Talon, who had earlier caught the attention of Alexander Baring as another European speculator in American lands. Talon appeared in Hamburg in 1798 to inform the British consul that the governor of Surinam, M. Frederici, frustrated by the ongoing disruption to trade in the Caribbean that had paralyzed the Surinam economy, was willing to turn the colony over to the British, but under the guidance of Talon. All that was required by Frederici was a significant show of force by the British Navy, a substantial payment to Frederici, and permission for Talon to secure shipment in neutral ships of a vast accumulation of tropical goods that had accumulated on the wharves of the Suriname River to Hamburg. These goods, when brought to market in Hamburg, would fully compensate the payments by the British government to Frederici, Talon, and the British invasion force.[21]

The details of the merchandize lying in Surinam that Talon gave: 70,000 barrels of sugar, 20 million pounds of coffee, 20 million pounds of cocoa, and three million pounds of cotton in the colony's warehouses, were clearly intended to interest merchants such as Baring and Hope.[22] In fact, Sir Francis gave very similar details to Pierre Cesar Labouchere and William Gordon Coesvelt, a Danish merchant in St. Croix who had previously served Hope and Co. in Amsterdam by monitoring the performance of plantations in the Dutch West Indies (including Surinam, Curacao, Aruba, and Sint Maarten). In the letter of instructions that Sir Francis sent to Coesvelt and copied to Labouchere on 15 June 1799, Coesvelt was authorized to purchase any part or all of the products Talon had told Baring & Hope might be available in Surinam: 25,000,000 pounds of coffee; 3,000,000 of cotton; 2,000,000 of cocoa; 60,000 hogsheads of sugar; subject only to conditions of marketable quality and the maximum prices to be paid in Dutch currency.[23] (Coesvelt would eventually become a partner of Hope and Co. at Labouchere's insistence when Alexander Baring absorbed it into Barings in 1815.) Coesvelt was further instructed that the risks (and profits) of the purchases were to be shared 1/5 with

[21] Duffy, pp. 313–316, describes the military & naval part of the action that followed, in which Talon played a major role, for which he was amply compensated.

[22] Griffith, 2017.

[23] Baring Archive, NP1.A7.6.3.

the Dutch Governor Frederici and his commander, Coehoorn; 1/5 with Coesvelt himself; and 3/5 for Baring Bros (John and Francis).

Labouchere's instructions follow with copies of the very detailed instructions given to Coesvelt as well as letters commissioning the captains of the two ships, the *Queen Charlotte* and the *Eurydice*, which were to proceed to Barbados with Labouchere and another agent of Hope and Co. from Amsterdam, M. Couderc. Coesvelt apparently voyaged ahead of Labouchere to Barbados, where he was to leave instructions for Labouchere while he went on with Talon, Coehoorn, and the British navy to occupy Surinam and pay off the Dutch governor, M. de Frederici. It is clear from the accounts of the military operation in the British national archives that the speculative enterprise suggested to Baring by Coesvelt proved to be very profitable indeed. M. Talon, who initiated the project in Hamburg, was paid £70,000 by William Huskisson, the Under-Secretary of War at the time, in gratitude for this windfall for the British forces, which until then had concentrated on cleaning out French and Spanish possessions in the Caribbean while keeping American merchant ships out of the British possessions (Duffy, 1987).

Antoine Omer Talon, however, remains a mysterious figure. A royalist sympathizer in the early stages of the French Revolution with his uncle, Maximilien Radix de Sainte-Foix, he became a prosperous financier and politically well-connected enough to become a member of the Constituent Assembly in 1789. There, he reputedly disbursed sums of money to delegates in the Constituent Assembly on behalf of Louis XVI as a possible constitutional monarch, a goal held by many of the nobility at the time, including Barbé-Marbois, Du Pont de Nemours, and, probably, Talleyrand. Unlike Talleyrand, however, Talon was not able to conceal his ideology and had to flee for his life in September 1792, narrowly avoiding the massacres of royalists that month. One source claims he was concealed in a fish barrel while being sailed across the Channel in a fishing boat, but arrived safely in London. There, he resided for a time with William Huskisson, who had been part of the British embassy staff in Paris during the revolution. Huskisson was about to become the British spy-master for William Pitt and it seems that Talon would have been a perfect spy for Britain. Nevertheless, he passed up the opportunity to return to France in disguise, at least for the time being, and did not return until 1800 when Napoleon as First Consul encouraged a number of *emigrés* to return.

Instead, when the Alien Bill was passed in Britain following the execution of Louis XVI in January 1793, Talon, like Talleyrand , felt obliged to leave England for the United States in February 1793.

With the Vicomte de Noailles (Lafayette's brother-in-law), he reached Philadelphia in February 1793 and the two French royalists met briefly with President Washington, much to the disgust of Citizen Gênet, whose exhortations for the Americans to come to the aid of the French revolutionaries were also rebuffed by the Washington administration. While in the United States, Talon became a leader of the French expatriate community along with Noailles, using his connections with Gouverneur Morris while in Paris to elicit support for purchasing land from Robert Morris. With Morris' support and advice, Talon established a settlement for French emigres, *Azilum*, located some thirty miles north of Philadelphia at a bend of the Susquehanna River. *Azilum* lasted as a possible refuge for French royalists for a few years, although Talleyrand observed (before he returned to France) that the settlement had more agents trying to lure French buyers than actual settlers. (Talleyrand had passed through Azilum on his foray to evaluate the prospects for the lands in Maine that William Bingham had acquired from William Duer.)

Nevertheless, Talon's efforts to attract French settlers to yet unsettled parts of Pennsylvania caught the favorable attention of Alexander Baring as well, who saw that Maine might become an equally attractive destination for French *emigrés* fleeing the Revolution. In addition to refugees from France, Azilum's settlers included *emigrés* from St. Domingue, some with their servants (house slaves). It is likely therefore that Talon used his Dutch and Belgian financial connections to continue trading activities in the West Indies, although the records of Azilum show that he engaged actively in land speculation, mainly as an agent for the Azilum enterprise. He purchased land in central Pennsylvania from William Bingham in 1796, paying partly in bills of exchange on Europe, and partly in local notes.[24] Talon quickly sold that land again, however, and became financially embarrassed when his intended payments to Robert Morris through Morris' son in Paris, proved impossible due to the revolutionary government having seized his assets in Paris. For whatever reason, Talon was in Hamburg in 1798, possibly on one of his several clandestine returns to Paris under false passports while Coesvelt was in the West Indies. Talon

[24] Child, p. 89.

informed the British consul in Hamburg in March 1799 that the Dutch governor of Surinam, M. De Frédérici, was willing to surrender Surinam to the British. Talon's credentials were solid, both for the British, who had employed him as one of Pitt's agents during the early days of the French Revolution, and for the West Indies trade given his experience as founder of Azilum.[25]

Pierre Cesar, as the super-cargo in charge of the two merchant ships hired to carry back the tropical produce of Surinam, no doubt, was also compensated handsomely from the results of the Surinam venture, one that turned out much better than the earlier attempt made by Daniel Parker with the American ship, *Rosanna*, as discussed below. In late 1801, after the preliminary agreement for the truce of Amiens had been signed between Britain and France, Labouchere returned to Amsterdam, intending to complete the re-establishment of Hope and Company. Instead, he was directed to go immediately to Lisbon, to negotiate on behalf of Baring and Hope the terms of a loan to the government of Portugal that would enable Portugal to pay the tribute demanded of them by Napoleon (Buist, Ch. 14, "The Portuguese Diamond Loan"; Baring Archive, NP1.A19.7-8; Ingram, Damas, Albuquerque).

Earlier, when the First Coalition against the French Revolutionary armies had collapsed in 1797, Spain had switched sides to ally itself with France while Portugal had sought safety in neutrality. That led to an attempt by the Portuguese crown to elicit a loan on the London Stock Exchange in February 1797. They sought, if possible, a loan comparable to the loan to the Austrian Empire in 1795 that had been successfully engineered by the firm of Boyd and Benfield. According to the overture made to Sir Francis by the English firm of William and John James Stephens, members of the English Factory in Lisbon, if the Portuguese government could get a loan of £1,200,000 listed on the London Stock Exchange, they could offer as collateral uncut diamonds from Brazil for a greater value, or if these were not acceptable, they offered "to pledge or sell the Islands of Timor, Solor, & Bolea all which are subordinate to Goa."[26] Further, if these specific forms of collateral were not acceptable, proceeds from the lucrative tobacco tax could be pledged as well.

[25] Talon accompanied the British forces sent to take temporary possession of Surinam and was handsomely compensate by the British for his services (Griffith 2017).

[26] Baring Archive, NP1.A19.7.

It was clear that Portugal was desperate, and feared land invasion by either French or Spanish forces, given the recent victories of French armies in Italy and Belgium. Sir Francis took this very seriously, most likely on the advice of Henry Hope, who had desired a share in the Brazilian diamond trade for some years, and worked up a detailed proposal. When Sir Francis discussed the Portuguese loan with William Pitt, however, he found that Pitt was reluctant to take up any of the Portuguese territories in the East, occupied as he was with naval operations in the Caribbean. Further, February 1797 was not a propitious time for any new loans to be offered in London, given the drain on Bank of England specie reserves that month, which had forced suspension of payments in coin by the Bank, a suspension that was to last for the next 20 years. The combination of the "paper pound" with the increasing difficulties of servicing the Austrian Loan meant that no further issues of sovereign bonds would occur on the London market until much later.[27]

Instead, as the military situation of Portugal became more worrisome, Pitt allowed a subsidy of £500,000 for support of a contingent of British troops and further military supplies, which continued until 1801. Portugal's experience therefore set the stage for the subsequent British policy of subsidizing allies in the various coalitions that were to confront Napoleon in the future, rather than floating their loans directly on the London Stock Exchange (Sherwig, 136–142). In Portugal, the new Minister of the Marine and Colonies, D. Rodrigo de Souza Coutinho, undertook a domestic loan that required fresh taxes and forced circulation of paper money for the first time with the royal decree of October 24, 1796 (Silveira, p. 520).

Nevertheless, as Portugal's value to the British Navy in the subsequent successes against the remains of Napoleon's army in Egypt in 1798 and then the destruction of the Danish-Norwegian fleet in April 1801 became clear, further subsidies were paid out by Britain. From then on, however, all the British payments required that Portuguese land forces be under the command of a British general. Indeed, as early as 1801, when Pitt was replaced as prime minister by Henry Addington, the new Minister of War, Lord Hawkesbury, recommended that the Portuguese royal family depart to Brazil and continue control of the Portuguese empire from there,

[27] After the financial crisis of 1810, the London Stock Exchange responded by listing a large number of securities available to investors by their Members, including the Louisiana bonds and the remaining U.S. Federal bonds.

presaging their eventual departure at the end of 1807. In the meantime, desiring to maintain their own military against the ever-present threat of Spanish or French invasion, the Portuguese crown renewed their appeal to Sir Francis for a loan in 1801. This time, however, the loan would be strictly a commercial contract based on the collateral of a monopoly on the export of Brazilian diamonds, supplemented in case of shortfalls in diamond sales, by revenue from the tobacco monopoly in Portugal. No longer was there any mention of ceding overseas islands or ports, most of which by now were under British oversight in any event.

The detailed proposal that Sir Francis had made to the Lisbon promoters in March 1797 proved to be the basis for his agreement to the Portuguese diamond loan in 1801. As executed eventually by Pierre Cesar in February 1802, it also provided the template for financing the Louisiana Purchase in 1803. Denied a guarantee of a loan to Portugal by the British government, Sir Francis stated that a loan arranged by private individuals would have to have diamonds "amounting in value to more than sufficient to cover every contingent liquidation, shall be deposited in the Bank of England or some place of safety, in the name of 2 or 3 trustees, persons in whom the money lenders can place confidence, for the purpose of securing regular payment of the interest, and in due time, the liquidation of the principal."Further, "the calamities which have attended this very intensive, unprecedented war, render it necessary that a proportion of the net revenue arising from the Snuff contract shall be hypothecated, & remitted regularly, to pay the Interest on the Loan, & to provide a sum for a sinking fund."[28]

Many of these aspects of the Portuguese bonds that would be taken by Baring and Hope as the lead underwriters, if the Portuguese government agreed, were to be features as well of the Louisiana bonds that financed the Louisiana Purchase a few years later. In the meantime, with the Bank of England suspending convertibility of its notes in February 1797 and the Austrian court failing to make due remittances of the payments promised on both the bonds and the annuities they had issued in 1794, there was no hope for any private loan to Portugal. In lieu, Pitt authorized a contingent of mercenaries to be sent to Portugal's aid, at Britain's expense (Sherwig, pp. 136–141; Costa 2008).

[28] Baring Archive, NP1.A19.7.4.

By 1802, however, the Austrian loan had been taken over by the British government, even as the original lead underwriter for that loan, the firm of Boyd & Benfield, had declared bankruptcy.[29] Boyd's original scheme had been to entice foreign merchants involved in supplying Austrian armies to purchase the bonds, but the ultimate bondholders only desired regular interest payments, and these were not forthcoming until the British government itself undertook to make them. The same rumors of peace between France and Britain with the opening of negotiations for the Truce of Amiens in October 1801 that had encouraged Henry Hope to send Pierre Cesar and associates to Amsterdam to re-open the firm also stimulated Henry Hope to seize this opportunity to renew the diamond business in Amsterdam. The Brazilian diamonds offered as collateral for the Portuguese bonds allowed Sir Francis to see this loan as a strictly commercial transaction. The British government, now under the leadership of Henry Addington, and desiring peace as well as fiscal relief while temporarily ending Pitt's income tax, was even more determined than Pitt had been to avoid underwriting yet another government's bond issue. Addington, however, was very supportive of helping Portugal maintain its neutrality, even if meant helping French finances with the tribute that Portugal would be paying. Perhaps Addington and Hawkesbury hoped then that the Truce of Amiens would last longer than it did.

Labouchere undertook the negotiation willingly, and took the opportunity to visit Nantes, where his uncle still had contacts, thinking he could find a merchant ship that would take him and George Baring, the youngest son of Sir Francis who had been appointed to accompany Pierre Cesar, on to Lisbon. Failing to find a charter in Nantes, La Rochelle, or Bordeaux, however, the two finally hired a packer at Bayonne to travel overland to Lisbon via Madrid despite the winter hazards. Arriving finally in Lisbon at the end of January 1802, Labouchere found numerous letters of instruction awaiting him from both Henry Hope and Sir Francis.

The letters advised him to pay a great deal of attention to the credibility of the merchants in Lisbon who would be responsible for carrying out the terms of the Portuguese government's payments of interest and eventual reimbursement of the bonds to be issued. Shipment of the diamonds to

[29] Sir Francis was appointed chair of the bankruptcy commission formed to settle the affairs of the creditors, which enabled him to learn even more about the perils of relying on remittances from foreign governments to satisfy domestic investors (Baring Archive, NP1.A19.4.

London had to be carefully supervised and the commitment of the officials in charge of the tobacco monopoly to make up any delays in proceeds from the sale of diamonds was a point of special emphasis.

In the meantime, Henry Hope had received detailed information on the situation in Amsterdam from a trusted agent, David Berck, who reassured him that the moneyed men in the city would welcome the reappearance of Hope & Company, especially if it brought with them a renewal of the diamond trade. If Labouchere could succeed in finalizing the terms of the loan to Portugal, his chances of re-establishing the Hope & Co. operation in Amsterdam would be much greater. Labouchere was advised as well that some *tours de baton* (unrecorded side payments) would be needed to get approval by the authorities, although the Portuguese court was not as corrupt as that of Spain, according to Sir Francis.

With all these incentives and authority granted him by Hope and Baring, Labouchere managed to complete the necessary arrangements with the Portuguese court, the finance minister, D. Roderigo de Sousa Coutinho, and, most important, with the lead contractors in Lisbon for the Brazilian diamond monopoly, Joaquin Pedro Quintella, and the head of the tobacco monopoly, Pedro Rodriquez Bandeira, by the end of February 1802. After reassuring himself of Sir Francis' appraisal of the two leading merchants (while Quintella was richer, he owed much of his wealth to inheritance, while Bandeira was more a self-made entrepreneur), Labouchere provided each with drafts drawn on Hope & Co. & Baring & Co. that they could endorse in turn to the Minister of Finance. In this way, he assured their continued efforts on behalf of Baring & Hope for making the interest payments and eventual reimbursements of the bonds that were drawn up and printed for Labouchere to take with him to Amsterdam and London for eventual distribution. In the process, he also gave John Stanley, one of the initiators of the project with Sir Francis, a payment of £10,000 to keep him from interfering with the remainder of the project.

From Lisbon, Labouchere departed by a Dutch corvette to Gibraltar and then to Madrid and on to Paris. Arriving on April 17, 1802, his main task was to make the required Portuguese payment to Talleyrand. While unable to get Talleyrand to reduce the size of the payments, as he had promised the Portuguese Court he would attempt, he did persuade Talleyrand to extend the period of payment over a longer period. No doubt part of the reason for Talleyrand's acquiescence was that the payments were in bills of exchange, which Talleyrand would be in a position to pledge as collateral for his own recompense if occasion arose. Also, the formal Treaty of Amiens had just been signed in Amiens and Talleyrand knew that with peace, the Portuguese payments would be more secure. No mention is made of any side payments to Talleyrand to hasten his approval, but later correspondence in the Baring Archive dealing with the payments intended for Talleyrand over the Louisiana Purchase deal suggests that may have been necessary.

Flushed with success, Labouchere then returned to Amsterdam, where, according to the account in Buist, he then ran into difficulty with the Dutch authorities for the re-establishment of Hope & Company in Holland. The idea that the Dutch government should approve the issue of a Portuguese loan for purchase by Dutch investors in order to keep French troops out of Portugal while French troops were still in Holland, despite promises that they would leave, understandably struck the Dutch officials as offensive. Labouchere made matters worse, it appears, by insisting that it was stupid for the Dutch government to block the loan, given the obvious value of the diamond trade that it would create for Holland. Even the Portuguese Minister of Finance, D. Rodrigo de Souza Coutinho, who was responsible for initiating the loan proposal in the first place, expressed his concern over Labouchere's misstep in The Hague after all he had accomplished in first Lisbon and then Paris. D. Rodrigo was surprised by the ignorance of the Dutch that Labouchere had shown, but it showed him again that even the most adroit individuals are capable of unbelievable negligence at times.[30]

It took a breathing spell of several months to get the Dutch authorities to accede to the Portuguese loan being issued in Amsterdam after the bulk was issued in London (shared initially by Sir Francis Baring and Henry Hope, although Hope would later take over most of the loan). During this interval, Labouchere returned to London to gather up his family for the return to Amsterdam, which he accomplished in October 1802, about the time Alexander and his family, including William Bingham, were visiting Paris. In the meantime, the Portuguese loan was eventually approved for issue in Amsterdam, the argument that it would restore much of the diamond cutting and merchandising business that had been interrupted for several years finally taking precedence over the

[30] Silva, p. 531.

humiliation of the Dutch that they would be helping French troops to continue occupying parts of the Netherlands in lieu of parts of Portugal. In the interval, Coutinho had also reassured himself (and the Portuguese Court) that the Brazilian diamonds were fetching even higher prices in Amsterdam than he had initially anticipated.

Vincent Nolte, who became Labouchere's agent in New Orleans in 1807, recounts in his memoirs that Labouchere "was a man of most excellent and generous feeling. He had, assuredly without intention, fallen into the singular habit of speaking his mother-tongue—the French—with an almost English intonation, and English with a strong French accent. But he was most of all remarkable for the chivalric idea of honor in mercantile transactions, which he constantly evinced and which I never, during my whole life, met with elsewhere, in the same degree, however numerous may have been the high-minded and honorable merchants with whom I have been thrown in contact."[31] Nolte's praise is all the more noteworthy as he later recounts, with admiration, his impressions as well of Alexander Baring, Sir Francis Baring, and Henry Hope—the other leading figures in the financing of the Louisiana Purchase. Nevertheless, to Nolte at least, Labouchere remained the most admirable figure of the four financiers.

It is easy to understand, then, why Alexander's first recourse, once he learned of the intent of the United States to purchase New Orleans from France during the course of his Christmas holiday in Paris with his wife and father-in-law, was to ask Labouchere's advice whether, and how, to proceed. More puzzling is why Labouchere should list Daniel Parker among the four individuals who had to be bribed to ensure that Baring & Hope alone would finance the Louisiana Purchase. Livingston was clearly at the head of the American side of the negotiation, Talleyrand had earlier been at the head of the French side of negotiations, especially with the arrangement for paying France the proceeds of the Portuguese loan that Labouchere had arranged on behalf of Baring & Hope in 1802. The mysterious third person, unnamed for reasons no doubt given by Alexander in his letter, was most likely Pierre Samuel Du Pont de Nemours, who was on good personal terms with both Jefferson and Talleyrand.

But, why Daniel Parker, whose name has never come up in any previous account of the Louisiana Purchase? The Baring Archive reveals,

[31] Buist, p. 52.

however, that Parker had established a long-standing relationship with both Sir Francis Baring and with Talleyrand as well as with the leading American businessmen and diplomats in France, starting with Jefferson's tour of duty as U.S. Minister to France in 1785. Eventually, Parker would be the one American representing the interests of the United States to successive French administrations, starting with the Louis XVI in 1789 and enduring through the Terror, Napoleon, and Louis XVIII. While he was, perhaps, instrumental in arranging the finance of the Louisiana Purchase by Baring & Hope, his main interest was to recover losses that he had, along with other American merchants, suffered during the Quasi-War between France and the United States that preceded the Treaty of Mortefontaine in 1800.

References

Adams, Henry, ed. 1879. *The Writings of Albert Gallatin*, 3 vols. Philadelphia: J. B. Lippincott & Co.

Barbé-Marbois, François. 1796. *Réflexions sur la colonie de Saint-Domingue: ou Examen approfondi des causes de sa ruine, et des measures adoptées pour la rétablit* . . . Paris: Chez Garnery.

Costa, Fernando Dores. 2008. "Army Size, Military Recruitment and Financing in Portugal during the Period of the Peninsular War—1808–1811." *e-Journal of Portuguese History* 6 (2): 1–27.

Duffy, Michael. 1987. *Soldiers, Sugar, and Seapower: The British Expeditions to the West Indies and the War against Revolutionary France*. Oxford: Clarendon Press.

Dungan, Nicholas. 2010. *Gallatin: America's Swiss Founding Father*. New York: New York University Press.

Ferguson, E. James, ed. 1971. *Selected Writings of Albert Gallatin*. Indianapolis, IN: Bobbs-Merrill.

Griffith, Rob. 2017. "The Commerce of Treachery: The Selling of Suriname, 1799." Guest Post on https://adventuresinhistoryland.com/2017/11/10/the-commerce-of-treachery-the-selling-of-suriname-1799-by-rob-griffith/. Accessed December 21, 2020.

Jacoud, Gilles. 1996. *Le billet de banque en France (1796–1803), de la diversité au monopole*. Paris: Éditions L'Harmattan.

Knodell, Jane Ellen. 2017. *The Second Bank of the United States: "Central" Banker in an Era of Nation-Building, 1816–1836*. London and New York: Routledge.

Liss, Peggy K. 1983. *Atlantic empires: The network of trade and revolution, 113–1826*. Baltimore: The Johns Hopkins University Press.

May, Gregory. 2018. *Jefferson's Treasure; How Albert Gallatin Saved the New Nation from Debt.* Washington, DC: Regnery History.

McCraw, Thomas K. 2012. *The Founders and Finance: How Hamilton, Gallatin, and Other Immigrants Forged a New Economy.* Cambridge, MA: Belknap Press of Harvard University Press.

Sylla, Richard. 2011. "Financial Foundations: Public Credit, the National Bank, and Securities Markets." In *Founding Choices: American Economic Policy in the 1790s*, edited by Douglas A. Irwin and Richard Sylla. Chicago: University of Chicago Press.

United States, Department of the Treasury, *Annual Reports, 1801–1823.* Accessed at https://fraser.stlouisfed.org/

Walters, Raymond, Jr. 1957. *Albert Gallatin: Jeffersonian Financier and Diplomat.* New York: The Macmillan Company.

Wright, Robert E., and David J. Cowen. 2006. *Financial Founding Fathers: The Men Who Made America Rich.* Chicago: University of Chicago Press.

CHAPTER 6

Daniel Parker, Expatriate Extraordinaire

Daniel Parker clearly had the respect of Pierre Cesar Labouchere in January 1803 when he replied to Alexander Baring's letter, the letter that led Baring & Hope to finance the Louisiana Purchase. Labouchere put "Livingston & Parker"[1] as the first recipients of the various *pots-de-vin* he felt were necessary to "grease the wheels" for getting the Baring-Hope finance proposal accepted by the ultimate decision-makers for the United States and France. Further, even James Monroe clearly acknowledged the authority of Parker as speaking for the Baring investment bank when Parker told Monroe of the financing available from Baring and Hope ($10 million) immediately upon Monroe's arrival in Paris in April 1803.[2] To date, however, Parker's role in the financing of the Louisiana Purchase has been overlooked, as well as his early influence upon Sir Francis Baring for financing the U.S. Federal government's operations in

[1] Parker was clearly Daniel Parker; Livingston could have been either Robert R. Livingston, the American minister to France at the time, or Robert L. Livingston, the son-in-law of the minister, who was engaged in later deals with Parker.

[2] Deviosse, p. 344, fails to name Parker as the "*ami providentiel*" who informs Monroe of the $10 million loan that Baring & Hope are prepared to make.

L. Neal, *The Forgotten Financiers of the Louisiana Purchase*, Palgrave Studies in the History of Finance,
https://doi.org/10.1007/978-3-031-56277-8_6

Europe.[3] Several files in the Baring Archive, however, demonstrate how deep and wide-ranging were Parker's affiliations with Sir Francis Baring.[4]

In fact, Sir Francis Baring, in the course of refuting Hope & Company's claim that their contribution of "Capital and Labour" to the financing project entitled them to 2/3 of the profit, states that he had first heard of the proposed offer by the United States to purchase New Orleans from Daniel Parker, in September 1802, well before Labouchere's letter of January 30, 1803.

> I observe by your letter that Labouchere has discovered the Louisiana business to have originated with himself: I wish he would be content with the merit which is his due, but the first syllable I ever heard was from Parker in September 1802 when it was coupled with a French proposal to which Labouchere listened or rather entered into, but discovered no predilection for the other. I think that on that occasion, I stated to him, the operation treated for, should be a joint concern, a common cause, between the two houses. I say, that I think, because I have no memorandum to refresh my memory, & therefore I do not insist on the point of time, although it cannot have been long afterwards. The real negotiation only began however on the arrival of Alexander, in consequence of which, communications were had, & letters exchanged, by which means, the business had made such progress, that about the beginning of the year Labouchere made a proposal to divide:
>
> ½...Hope
> ¼...ourselves
> ¼... Alex. & Bingham
>
> This was in early stage of the business, & I think the first proposal for division from you, which distinctly marks the share you wished to hold.
> [The Baring Archive, NP1.A4.55(4)]

So concluded Sir Francis, in his much revised and rewritten draft of a letter to Henry Hope, which succeeded in its goal to divide the

[3] The classic history of Baring's role in financing the early national U. S., Ralph Hidy (1949) has no entry for Parker, nor do more recent works by Tearle (2017) and Ziegler (1988). Buist (1974) mentions him in a footnote referring to the work by Fugier (1930), which refers to a deal Parker and Livingston proposed to Talleyrand after the Louisiana Purchase.

[4] Without the aid of Clara Harrow, head archivist, I could not have uncovered the materials for this chapter.

profits equally between the two firms. But Sir Francis' letter also brings Daniel Parker into the very start of the financial narrative of the Louisiana Purchase. Sir Francis' memory probably was correct. He was one of the many English visitors to France during the brief Truce of Amiens, spending much of the month of September 1802 in Paris where he had every reason to contact Parker at the time. Further, he visited Parker's estate at Crécy on his return to England. Not only was Crécy on the way to Le Havre, but, presumably, there was his mutual concern with Parker over the fate of the *Rosanna*.[5] Parker could very well have been made aware of the proposal to purchase New Orleans, which Du Pont de Nemours had already delivered to Livingston. At the time, however, Sir Francis was probably more concerned with Labouchere's handling of the Portuguese loan proceeds to France, and Livingston was still concerned with persuading France to compensate American merchants for their losses to French privateers during the Quasi-war of 1798–1800. Recall that Labouchere's initial letter recommended "greasing the wheels" by equal amounts paid to Talleyrand, Livingston & Parker, and the third party who set the project afloat. It appears, however, that Daniel Parker should be honored at some point for his critical role in initiating the financing of the Louisiana Purchase.

Parker had dealt with various bills of exchange on France while contracting to provision French army and naval forces in New England at the end of the American war. Indeed, his break with his partners in military contracting, William Duer and John Holker, came when he informed them in 1783 that he was going to speculate on the French bills of exchange. That may have upset those partners at the time, but it did not stop George Washington from appointing Parker as one of the three U.S. commissioners to oversee the evacuation of British forces from New York that year. Nor did it stop Robert Morris, William Duer, and John Holker from using the services of Daniel Parker & Co. to build, outfit, and stow cargo on the first American commercial endeavor to trade directly with China—the *Empress of China*.[6] Moreover, Parker was active in outfitting and chartering six other, smaller ships—the *Columbia*, the *Comte*

[5] In NP1/A9/8, "Paris: Account by Sir Francis Baring of his visit to Paris during the Truce of Amiens."

[6] Ver Steeg (1954) refers briefly, but gives more detail in Ver Steeg (1953), highlighting the essential role of Parker. Smith (1984) focuses on the $2300 taken by Parker from the ship before sailing.

d'Artois, the *Bourbon,* and three whaling vessels. The *Columbia* sailed for Charleston, picked up cargo for Europe, and returned successfully to New York in September 1784. The *Comte d'Artois* and the *Bourbon* both went with cargo to France where they were sold. When the *Empress* returned from China, entering the New York harbor on May 10, 1785, its cargo of tea and porcelain from China cleared profits of $37,727, a return of over 30% on the original investment.[7]

Nevertheless, Parker's reputation with the other backers of the enterprise was to be blackened forever, due to a combination of two events:

1. Parker sailed from the United States to Europe himself in August 1784, leaving his accounts still unsettled with William Duer, John Holker, and Robert Morris;
2. Samuel Shaw, one of the super-cargoes on the *China Empress* responsible for the sale of the out-cargo and purchase of the return-cargo was surprised in Canton when the crates containing the Spanish dollars were unpacked to find $2,300 of the intended $20,000 missing. They had never been replaced as promised to Shaw by Parker when he put the dollars on board. Parker, reluctantly, signed a document years later that exculpated Shaw, who as super-cargo had been legally responsible for delivering the cargo in Canton as attested in the bills of lading. Shaw returned to China with the next voyage of the *China Empress*, served as American consul in Canton, and eventually escaped having to replace the funds that Parker had taken.

William Duer, who had originally been designated as the super-cargo on the *China Empress*, had excused himself from the actual voyage while busying himself to become Hamilton's secretary in the U.S. Treasury. He misused his access to Hamilton's operations to refinance the U.S. Revolutionary War debt and establish a national bank to speculate on his own in the ill-fated Scioto Company. Duer then speculated against the stock of the first Bank of the United States, causing the first financial panic in New York (Sylla et al. 2013) which led to his downfall in 1792, and imprisonment for debt. It appears that Duer never settled accounts with any of his partners, save perhaps Henry Knox, who was actually saved

[7] Ver Steeg (1953, pp. 6–7, 12).

by the loans of William Bingham, who became a joint partner with Knox in the Maine lands described earlier. Duer, however, obviously bore no ill will against Parker, as he recommended Joel Barlow, the agent he sent to France to sell shares in the Scioto Company to gullible Frenchmen, to begin by joining forces with Parker, which Barlow did when he arrived in Paris. Even Robert Morris recommended Gouverneur Morris to meet with Parker at the beginning of his stay in Europe, virtually at the same time Barlow arrived. Gouverneur Morris was sent as the partner of Robert Morris to France with the aim to refinance American debt to France and to market American tobacco through his prospective firm.

By that time (1789), Parker's advice and contacts in Europe were seen as useful for both projects. All the more remarkable is that the last "Morris note" of $20,000 sent to Parker in 1783 as military contracting was ending was never repaid by Parker. After Robert Morris died in 1806, Albert Gallatin, Secretary of the U.S. Treasury, found that the Treasury was still owed repayment of advances of $38,829.41 (including the $20,000 Morris note) made to Daniel Parker & Co. in 1784. Joseph Nourse, the registrar, calculated the accumulated interest since 1783 at 6% annually to present a claim against Parker of $96,430.81 on July 26, 1809.[8]

Earlier, in 1794, when Parker's finances were shaping up in Europe thanks to his deals with both Dutch and English bankers to speculate on the success of Hamilton's refinancing of American debt, he apparently made an offer to repay some of the advances. Congress considered his petition to the House of Representatives on January 1, 1794, which pleaded that he be "relieved against the losses he sustained, under a contract entered into in the year one thousand seven hundred and eighty-three, for the supply of the Continental army with provisions, during the whole of the said year; which contract was terminated in a few months after it was entered into, by the unexpected event of the treaty of peace, and the consequent disbanding of the army."[9] The committee appointed to examine the merits of Parker's offer, however, decided to reject it. Apparently, they took seriously the conjecture from Alexander Hamilton that they might get more repayment from Parker in the future

[8] Daniel Parker Letter Book, p. 178.

[9] *American State Papers*, Journal of the House of Representatives of the United States, January 1, 1794.

by compounding the interest due, especially if Parker's fortunes continued to improve in Europe.[10]

Thereafter, Parker remained in Europe to the end of his life, while maintaining cordial relations with most of the American expatriates and diplomats. He even entertained Gallatin at his Draveil estate when Gallatin became the U.S. Ambassador to France (1816–1823). On the other hand, John Holker, an expatriate Frenchman who came to the United States with the French forces in 1778 as the agent of Pierre-Augustin Caron de Beaumarchais and then remained to become French Consul-General in Philadelphia as well as one of the military contractors for Washington's army, pursued his claims against Parker to the end of his days, as will be described below.

Back in New York in 1783 and 1784, while the *China Empress* was being constructed, equipped, and laden along with six other vessels under the supervision of Parker, the remaining British forces (along with Loyalists and escaped slaves) in New York were being evacuated under the supervision of the three commissioners appointed by General Washington. The other two commissioners with Parker were William Stephens Smith, Washington's aide-de-camp at the end of the war, and Egbert Benson, one of the signers of the Declaration of Independence. Later, William Smith accompanied John Adams as secretary of the American legation in London. In 1786, he married the daughter of John Adams ("Nabby" Abigail Adams), with the grudging acceptance by Adam's wife, Abigail, who reported that Daniel Parker was one of the two witnesses chosen by Captain Smith to the wedding ceremony in London.[11]

While London was clearly Parker's base in Europe in the 1780s, he followed up the possibilities of dealing in French commercial and financial affairs as well. Thomas Jefferson gave official passports to Daniel Parker in 1787 (November 30 for 2 months), 1788 (May 6, again for 2 months, but this time for Mrs. Daniel Parker and servants as well), with renewals

[10] "Report on the Petition of Daniel Parker, [13 January 1794]," *Founders Online*, National Archives, https://founders.archives.gov/documents/Hamilton/01-15-02-0459. [Original source: *The Papers of Alexander Hamilton*, vol. 15, *June 1793 – January 1794*, ed. Harold C. Syrett. New York: Columbia University Press, 1969, pp. 635–637.] Hamilton noted that all the contractors had become insolvent temporarily, which he knew very well as he had been legal advisor to John B. Church, one of Parker's creditors (and Hamilton's brother-in-law).

[11] "Abigail Adams to Mary Smith Cranch, 4 July 1786," *Founders Online*, National Archives, https://founders.archives.gov/documents/Adams/o4-07--2=0088.

later in July and October 1788, each time for 2 months as well and then in February and July of 1789 for 2 months stretches. The first passport was issued when Parker carried letters of introduction to Jefferson from John Adams and William Smith in London. Both vouched for Parker as "presenting to you a fund of Commercial and political knowledge, which you may draw freely upon during his stay at Paris, without being in the least apprehensive of failure or protest" (Smith) and "an intelligent American, and well informed as any Man you will see from hence" (Adams).[12]

In 1789, as the French Revolution was developing and Jefferson was packing up to return to America, Parker was conferring with Gouverneur Morris (passports issued in March and July 1789) to convince Jacques Necker, the French minister of finance, to refinance the American debt to France. That Morris-Parker proposal (at the initiative of Robert Morris back in Philadelphia) was for France to replace their existing bonds with new bonds backed by land available for sale in the new Northwest Territory, as established by the U.S. Confederate Congress' Northwest Ordinance of 1787. Gouverneur Morris' journal refers frequently to his collaborations with Parker in Paris in the Spring of 1789. Both had meetings with Jacques Necker, the Swiss banker called back by Louis XVI to help reorganize French finances, as well as with the Comte de Montmorin, who continued to serve the French king as minister of foreign affairs.

Together, Morris and Parker seemed persuaded that Necker was amenable to their proposal to pay off the American debt to France in the manner they proposed. Necker, however, insisted that a large sum of ready cash (40 million *livres*) be posted as collateral before he would agree to their proposal. It became Parker's duty to find reputable bankers, whether in Paris, Amsterdam, or London, who could be persuaded to back their proposal by advancing the sum desired by Necker.

It appears, however, that Parker had exhausted his good-will with the Dutch bankers with his earlier arrangement to take over their claims on the bankrupt firm of H. Fijnje & Puller in 1785. A letter written to Parker in London from the Dutch firm of Daniel Crommelin & Sons

[12] "To Thomas Jefferson from William Stephens Smith, 26 October 1787," *Founders Online*, National Archives, https://founders.archives.gov/documents/Jefferson/01-12-02-0282, and "From John Adams to Thomas Jefferson, 28 October 1787," *Founders Online*, National Archives, https://founders.archives.gov/documents/Adams/99-02-02-0259.

in January 1790 expressed doubts about the latest proposal Parker had made to assume ownership of the claims they had on the Fijnje & Puller assets in the United States. In return for allowing them the sum of f2300, which they had already claimed, Parker could be reimbursed by whatever additional sums he (and his agent in the United States) could obtain from Congress.[13]

Parker had earlier proposed, through Jefferson, to establish a regular mail packet service between Boston and Le Havre, no doubt putting to profitable use the various ships that he had commissioned in earlier years. Parker even bruited a competitive scheme for providing tobacco shipments from the United States for the tobacco monopoly held in France by the *Fermiers-Générales*, one of several schemes for expanding trade between France and the United States that Parker ran by Thomas Jefferson during the period before the French Revolution.[14] These included a preference for American whaling enterprises, which eventually culminated in the establishment of the Quaker enclave of Nantucket Island in Dunkirk in 1785.[15]

Jefferson had also issued passports to Joel Barlow in 1789, who would join forces with Parker in the 1790s to their mutual benefit, but at the time Barlow was focused on getting French investments in the Scioto Company that William Duer had formed in 1787. James Swan, another military contractor from the American Revolution also showed up in France in 1788. His later career as the primary manager of the American debt owed to France served as a counterpoint to Parker's career.

[13] "Letters to Daniel Parker in London, January & March 1790," by H. Fijnje for Daniel Crommelin & Sons. [Stadsarchief Amsterdam: 654—Inventaris van het Archief van de Firma Daniel Crommelin & Soonen]. Winter (1977), gives more details of Parker's various arrangements with Crommelin in Chs. 4 and 7, but describes Parker, Duer, and Holker as "all of them adventurous merchants without much financial or moral backbone, in constant straits for money and always ready with another plan." P. 147. Parker's reputation is further blackened in a recent article by Cutterham (2018).

[14] Price, p. 834, mentions Daniel Parker as one of the associates of James Swan who tried to organize a group to pay the American debt to France in exchange for American produce needed by the revolutionary government in 1791.

[15] Bizardel, pp. 72–77, describes the arrival of 150 Quakers and 30 ships from Nantucket in 1785 and the subsequent acceptance of their privileges, which included pacifism and religious tolerance in addition to exemption from French import duties on their whale oil.

Both Parker and Swan ended their lives in Paris in ill-repute, but lived very well in the meantime (Rice 1937).

Joel Barlow's mission in 1787, however, was to convince a number of French settlers to voyage to the United States to take up land that William Duer had persuaded the Confederate Congress to cede to his Scioto Company. Duer obtained his reputed land grant by agreeing to absorb the 3.5 million acres of the Ohio Territory that the legitimate and seriously funded Ohio Company had declined to bid for, instead contracting for only 1.5 million acres in the eastern part of the future state of Ohio, closest to Pittsburgh. Both companies contracted to pay 2/3 dollar per acre in installments, the Ohio Company in two equal annual payments and the Scioto Company in 6 equal annual installments. Both could pay in specie, loan office certificates, or "certificates of the liquidated debt of the United States" (Jones, p. 120). The Ohio Company fulfilled its contract and settlers moved in promptly (McCullough, 2019).

Unfortunately for Barlow's well-intentioned efforts to recruit French settlers (and their finances) for the Scioto Company 's claims farther west, Congress had not received any of the required payments and so no legal title was available for the "first 500" settlers led by Count Jean-Joseph de Barth when they arrived in Ohio in 1790. Duer's continued speculations, based on taking advantage of Hamilton's funding program, culminated in his spectacular failure in the summer of 1792, and subsequent imprisonment for debt.

Joel Barlow, however, avoided repercussions in France, convincing his friends, mainly Brissot de Warville who had become, briefly, the most powerful figure in the French Revolution before the Terror, that he had acted in good faith. Indeed, as the French Revolution unfolded and Robespierre came to power, the *commission des subsistances* was set up in October 1793. The Convention came to rely on people like Barlow (and Parker and Swan) to organize the provisioning of the French armies through their American compatriots and their commercial contacts on both sides of the Channel, contacts they had established while organizing the overseas provisioning of American revolutionary forces.[16] The operations that Gouverneur Morris had initiated in 1789 with Jacques Necker to import wheat from the United States were carried on after Gouverneur left France by his one-time colleagues Daniel Parker and Joel Barlow.

[16] See for example, Tearle, *Merchants of War*, and Alberts, *The Golden Voyage*.

While Rice (1937) found that James Swan was the chief purveyor of goods for the French Convention, later authors focus on examples of other Americans involved in the surreptitious trade.

> Why else would Mark Leavenworth, Daniel Parker, and Benjamin Hitchborne have gone into partnership to charter the *Cumberland*? Its papers in order, the schooner left its British port with a cargo of rice and flour destined for Bilbao in Spain. As it reached the mouth of the Gironde under full sail, it suddenly tacked toward Bordeaux, where everything was in order to receive its cargo.
> (Bizardel, p. 219; Buel, p. 183)

The question left open and the answer taken for granted is just how these merchant voyages were organized and financed. It seems too easy to assume that American shippers could just sail hither and yon, taking advantage of the neutrality proclaimed by its fledging government. Indeed, one document from The National Archive in Kew suggests that Parker had some setbacks in this otherwise profitable trade. In early February 1795, the Duke of Portland, then Home Secretary of Great Britain, received a request from the marine insurance company of Turnbull & Forbes, who had insured "a cargo of flour & rice from Baltimore in America on the Swedish ship *Argo* John Schale Master bound for Gibraltar," which had been captured by a French frigate and taken to Toulon, that a passport be issued to Mr. Daniel Parker, Esq. "a citizen of the United States of America now residing in England, to whom the said cargo belongs, as you can certify, to proceed to France for the purpose of claiming the said Property, without incurring any of the penalties expressed in the traitorous correspondence & French Property Bills to which he otherwise would be liable."[17]

A note on the cover of the letter indicates that the request would be forwarded. It is not clear if Parker went to France, and then, whether he reclaimed the cargo to forward it on to the British Navy base at Gibraltar. It appears more likely that he did go to France, sold the cargo to the French authorities, and then used part of the proceeds to purchase a prime residence in Paris, the Hotel de Montmorin, in June 1795 as discussed below. The perils and potential profits of these ventures in

[17] *TNA*, HO 42/34, f. 147.

general, however, are spelled out in detail for one example in the Baring Archive.

An extensive file deals with the sad tale of the American ship chartered by Daniel Parker in 1796, the *Rosanna* (*Baring Archive*, HCOS_ 22). In London on March 10, 1796, Daniel Parker handed Captain Nathaniel Sargent of Boston a letter appointing him Super Cargo of the ship *Rosanna*, which Sargent had chartered with Captain Pollard for a voyage to Surinam and back to Europe. Enclosed in the letter were an order for ten thousand Spanish dollars and a letter of credit from Messrs. Hope & Co. of Amsterdam to M. Frederici, the Governor of Surinam for ninety thousand current guilders of Holland. The dollars were to be taken on board the *Rosanna* while the letter of credit was to be delivered to the Governor of Surinam, who would advise Sargent on what cargo to take on board for the return voyage. High-quality rum was the first choice, but Sargent was given leeway to fill up the ship with other tropical goods available, starting with molasses but possibly including coffee, cotton, or sugar. Once fully laden, the *Rosanna* should be cleared for Boston and Hamburg.[18] In Hamburg, Sargent would find other orders awaiting his arrival with the local firm Bell. They would have orders either from Parker or from "my Friends and Correspondents here Messrs. John & Francis Baring & Co. of London," which Sargent would "attend to and obey." Sargent would receive as payment for his services 5% on the amount of cargo he purchased. Sargent dutifully signed the copy left with Parker, acknowledging he had received the ten thousand dollars and the letter of credit and he promised to obey the instructions given by Parker "in all its parts." (*Baring Archive*, HCOS_022, ff. 1–2).

Nearly two weeks later, on March 23, 1796, Parker sent another letter to Sargent, informing him that Parker had requested "my friends Messrs. John & Francis Baring & Co. Merchants of this city" to dispose of the cargo of the ship *Rosanna* "at such market as may be most advantageous at the time of her arrival." (Apparently, Parker was now aware that Barlow had left Hamburg to take up his mission to Algiers, where he succeeded in ransoming American sailors with funds channeled from Barings.) Now the Baring brothers had the direction of the project. Presumably, they had also supplied the Spanish coins and arranged for the letter of credit

[18] For 14 months, Spring 1794 to Fall 1795, Joel and Ruth Barlow had supervised supplies to the French Directory from Hamburg, during which time Barlow established his fortune. (Buel, ch. 10, "Commercial Interlude.")

from Hope & Co. to present to the Governor of Surinam on arrival. The letter of credit by Hope & Co. would have been drawn earlier, probably by one of the clerks left behind after Alexander Baring and Pierre Cesar left Amsterdam in January 1795, most likely Robert Voûte. The potential profitability of the *Rosanna's* cargo, however, must have been the motivation for the later joint venture of Baring with Henry Hope, when they used Willem Coesvelt as their agent on-site in Surinam and Pierre Cesar Labouchere as super-cargo for the two ships, *Eurydice* and *Queen Charlotte*. (*Baring Archive*, NP1.A7.6).

Unfortunately for the first venture of the Baring brothers into the trade with the Dutch West Indies, Parker had to alert them in late November 1796 that he had received a letter from Captain Pollard in the French port of La Rochelle that explained why the *Rosanna* and its cargo were not in Hamburg or Guernsey as expected. Instead, while sailing toward Guernsey, the *Rosanna* had been taken by a British privateer, the *Diana*, out of Liverpool, on October 23, 1796. Captain Pollard and several of the crew, along with all the ship's papers, were taken to Liverpool by the *Diana* while Sargent remained on board the *Rosanna*, which was ordered to be taken as a prize to Falmouth. On the way there, however, it was retaken on the 5th of November, this time by a French privateer out of Nantes, *l'Actif*, which took them to the French port of La Rochelle to be appraised at the prize court there.

Parker used his friendship with the American consul at La Rochelle to appeal that the *Rosanna*, with cargo and crew, were all American and under the treaty of 1778 between France and the United States were therefore not eligible to be taken by French privateers. The court at La Rochelle agreed, but the owner of the French privateer, *l'Actif*, appealed its decision to the next higher court in Saintes, Lower Charentes. There, on a technicality so dear to French bureaucracy even then, that court ruled that the *Rosanna* did not have the appropriate legal form, a *Rôle d'équipage*, that had recently been declared necessary by the Directory in France. It turned out that Sargent could produce a similar *Rôle d'équipage* among the ship's papers that had been taken to Liverpool with Captain Pollard, which Parker and Labouchere used as the basis to appeal the court's decision at Saintes to the *Cour de Cassation* in Paris. Unfortunately, that court ruled, finally and definitively, in favor of the French privateer, *l'Actif*, saying the form of the French *Rôle d'équipage* produced by the Americans was out of date and no longer valid given the recent changes decreed by the Directory.

All was lost, except for the possibility of getting the insurance claim paid on the cargo, which it turned out that Sir Francis had insured, at Sargent's request from Surinam, but for only half the value of the cargo, presumably his half of the enterprise. The rest of the archive is taken up with the documentation produced by the French authorities, Daniel Parker, and Captain Sargent along with the discussion of Barings' lawyers about the validity of the British insurance claim on the loss of the cargo. It's not clear whether Barings recovered at least the insurance, or if they shared that with Parker. What is clear is that Parker certainly had an interest in seeing his share of the *Rosanna* restored as part of the American claims that were agreed to be settled by the American government's part of the Louisiana Purchase price, the $3.75 million designated in the Third Convention of the treaty.

On that score, Greg Williams (2009), in his comprehensive record of American merchant marine losses to French privateers, shows that the cargo of the *Rosanna* was sold in France for 369,782 francs, equal to $66,560. (Parker had estimated the value of the cargo at 500,000 francs in his correspondence to Baring Brothers.). Further, "On July 2, 1827, Daniel Parker assigned his claim to Thomas Barlow, of Pittsburgh, for the benefit of Frances and Harriet Preble." (Williams, p. 307). Williams goes on in detail to record subsequent amendments to the claim filed for $74,980.99 on the *Rosanna*, which eventually included numerous grandchildren of Nathaniel Sargent, the original super-cargo. But, like so many other claims initiated by U.S. merchants and their descendants, these were likely never paid off (Williams, p. 42).

Why would Parker assign his claim to Thomas Barlow, the nephew of Joel Barlow, a full thirty years after the cargo had been sold in France and a quarter-century after the claim had been submitted to the American commissioners who arrived in France in 1804 to begin settling the claims of American merchants? This was likely from Parker's last will (one source claims he died in 1829 and he was 60 years old in 1814, when he bore witness to the death of another American ex-patriot, Benjamin Rumford). True, there had been a close connection between Joel Barlow and Daniel Parker, obviously earlier during the Directory when Barlow was organizing shipments by American vessels for France from Hamburg and Parker was chartering ships from his American fleet, but again much later when Barlow was the American ambassador to France.

For example, it was Daniel Parker who took on the task of writing to Ruth Barlow in the United States the circumstances of her husband's death in January 1813, the task being too painful for Barlow's nephew and aide, Thomas Barlow, to undertake (Egan, 1983, p. 186). Earlier, moreover, Egan states that "Draveil, Parker's magnificent estate, provided a beautiful setting for the wedding of Thomas Barlow (nephew to Joel Barlow) and Francis Anica Preble (whose mother was rumored to have been Parker's mistress) on July 28, 1817." (Egan, p. 190)

Despite the loss of the valuable cargo of the *Rosanna*, Parker's other commercial ventures, such as the *Cumberland* in 1793, as well as the *Bourbon*, *Columbia*, and *Comte d'Artois* in earlier years, must have paid off handsomely. Further opportunities for entrepreneurial expatriate Americans in revolutionary France became available with the financial problems of the Directory, forced to finance its war with the monarchical powers of Europe by issuing paper *assignats* on the imputed value of estates expropriated from émigré nobles and clerics. The idea of issuing paper certificates to enable the purchase of land newly available was one that Parker (and Barlow and Morris and Swan) had helped promote earlier with U.S. land certificates. While the Scioto Company proved bogus, however, American merchants could use the *assignats* they received for shipments from America or the West Indies to buy available properties, which could then be resold for hard cash.

Daniel Parker, according to Bizardel, was the most stunning American businessman to have ever appeared on the banks of the Seine during the French Revolution. He involved himself in shipping, sale of tobacco, purchase of paintings, sale of rice, and commission for provisions against the sale of champagne, at 8 livres a bottle. Moreover, in addition to his profitable operations, he won a prize in the national lottery of 1795—the Paris mansion of the *emigré* Lalle-mant de Nantouillet located on the corner of la rue d'Antin and rue Neuve-des-Petits-Champs. (Bizardel, 1972, pp. 141–142).

On June 3, 1795 (15 Prairial an III), Daniel Parker purchased the Hôtel de Montmorin, the palatial quarters of the former Minister of Foreign Affairs under Louis XVI, Comte de Montmorin. Montmorin was the French official most favorable to the scheme proposed by Morris and Parker in 1789 but had the misfortune to be assassinated in prison in 1793. Parker "flipped" the Hôtel de Montmorin three years later (March 9, 1798) for 400,000 livres in specie, not assignats, along with the adjacent dwelling that Parker had won in the national lottery (Saulnier, p. 89). The banker who bought the mansions had to sell at a loss at the end of October 1805, no doubt one of the victims of the banking failures that occurred in Paris that month (Chapter 8 below). It is likely that Parker took his profits from shipping in the form of the rapidly depreciating assignats and, as an American citizen, used them to purchase property abandoned by an aristocrat exiled or executed under the Terror, as was the case with Montmorin (and his wife and son).

Indeed, on July 9, 1796, Parker was in Chartres at the office of a notary public to sign the various forms that gave Thomas Auzoux his power of attorney to take possession of all the properties that comprised the estates of Crécy and Comteville in the surrounding countryside. They were among the multiple assets of another *emigré*, the prince of Montmorency, that had been seized as "national goods" by the Convention, and auctioned off to speculators. Both estates were extensive, with illustrious histories. Crécy had been the favorite retreat of Louis XV and Madame Pompadour and Comteville had been the residence of Saint-Simon. This estate consisted of "*616 hectares of château, jardin, parc, bâtiments, moulins et terres laborables, estimés en 1812 plus de 800,00 F.*"[19] Two of the farms were sold by Parker to Jean Auguste Sevène in An VII (1798).[20] Nevertheless, Parker's charge to his agent was clear: he only wanted to sell off the various parcels for their market price, and he resold Crécy in a few years to M. Mariarty, who finished demolishing the once magnificent chateaux while breaking up the property into smaller parcels (Jusselin, p. 152).

Thomas Auzoux was one of the minor officials in France who affirmed their credentials as revolutionaries in the early years of the French Revolution and then turned their expertise toward business affairs arising from the sale of properties abandoned by *emigré* nobility. Parker, after signing the required forms in Chartres returned to Paris at his new residence on rue Neuve des Mathurins, no. 678 (where he wrote to Baring about the fate of the *Rosanna*), while Auzoux left his office in Chartres to oversee the acquisitions of Parker around Crécy and La Ferté-les-Bois, another estate of a noble *emigré*.

A similar transaction took place the next year on June 26, 1797 (8 Messidor, an V), when Daniel Parker acquired the great building of the *emigré* Montmorency-Laval, situated at the corner of rue de Rennes, 157, and Boulevard de Montparnasse, 73, 75, and 77, although Parker

[19] Bergeron, p. 86.

[20] ibid., p. 159.

had to agree to make all the alignments and retrenchments that might be required by the public works.[21] All of these activities must have made Parker a wealthy man, at least as wealthy as Joel Barlow, who had become wealthy just on the basis of his commissions from authorizing the commodity shipments that took place with Parker's ships.

But it was not until the summer of 1804 when it was clear that the Louisiana Purchase was a complete success for the combined merchant-banking houses of Baring and Hope, that Parker acquired his "magnificent estate of Draveil." Unlike the earlier estates of nobles that Parker had bought with *assignats* and then resold, either in whole or in parts, in specie, Draveil was closer to Paris, with its buildings in good shape. Located 12 miles upstream with a view of the Seine, it was where Parker could receive honored guests in high style, beginning with Lafayette in 1804 and continuing with distinguished American visitors and French officials until he sold it in 1821.[22] During the Napoleonic period and the first restoration of the Bourbon, Parker was the most visible representative of American interests, with a luxurious town house in Paris and the country estate of Draveil, which he maintained in style, actually employing a British spy, John Short, in 1810 as one of the groundskeepers. When Louis XVIII reentered Paris for the second time, he visited the convent reserved for Protestant women, where he was greeted by the young ladies singing, "God save the King," in English, led by Mrs. Daniel Parker6.1.

Parker's success could not be kept secret, of course, from his former associates in the United States. As noted above, his creditors Robert Morris and William Duer ended their lives in disgrace and bankrupt and Samuel Shaw died at sea, so their various claims on Parker were extinguished as were their debts to their creditors. John Holker, however, did not succumb to the perils of speculation either on American paper assets or real estate. Further, as a French citizen, albeit expatriate in the United States, Holker could travel to Paris on occasion to press his claims against Parker, even if he had cleared a nice profit from the results of the *Empress of China*.

[21] *Bulletin municipal official de la Ville de Paris*, 13 juin 1899, p. 1911.

[22] Draveil is still listed as a historical monument in France, with the park maintained by the commune of Draveil, but the ground floor of the chateau is now occupied by a nursing home and the stables converted to a movie theater. The magnificent salon, however, is now an exhibit in the Philadelphia Museum of Art, purchased in 1928.

Fig. 6.1 Chateau de Draveil (*Source* Chateau de Draveil, front view, http://www.chateau-fort-manoir-chateau.eu/chateaux-essonne-chateau-a-draveil-chateau-de-paris.html)

In 1797, Holker pressed a claim against Parker over unsettled affairs left from their dealings with Duer and Morris as contracts for supplying the American army were being wound up. The court in Boston named three individuals to determine what should be settled among the various claimants.[23] By October 1799, one of their decisions was to condemn Parker to pay Holker the sum of $5000 (25,000 French francs), which was duly assigned to Holker three days later on Parker's assets. But Parker and his assets, which were considerable by now, were in Paris all this time, and when Holker showed up in Paris in 1800 with his court order from Boston, Parker asked for time to determine how he could settle or contest Holker's claim.

Holker and Parker signed an agreement on 2 *brumaire an* 9 (October 24, 1800) naming two arbiters to determine how to proceed to the liquidation of their former partnership. In 1801, however, Parker finally learned formally of the sentence pronounced against him in Boston, but he pleaded to the *tribunal de commerce* in Paris that the agreement made

[23] Issue of *Journal du Palais*, 1819.

earlier in Paris should take precedence over the ruling in Boston. Parker's plea was rejected, however, and the Paris tribunal ordered on November 19, 1802, that the compromise agreed on in Paris should be executed. Parker appealed this decision to the *Cour d'appel de Paris*, which on May 25, 1803, overruled the judgment of the lower court of commerce, and declared Holker was ineligible even to demand fulfillment of the compromise agreed to in 1800, unless he could provide the documents from Boston on which his judgment there had been based. Holker returned to Boston, and it was no doubt at this time that Parker used his *pot de vin* from Alexander Baring to purchase the magnificent estate of Draveil.[24]

Parker feted the various American diplomats that followed Monroe and Livingston in Paris at his estate and all went well until Holker reappeared in Paris, this time in 1813. During the previous decade, Holker had gone through his accounts from dealing with Duer, Morris, and Parker in 1783 in quite some detail. During the War of 1812, in fact, Holker was able to get approval to receive reimbursement for loan certificates that must have been destroyed in the fire that burned down his office in Philadelphia in 1780, certificates with a face value of $426,800. Given the market depreciation of the notes, most issued from the loan office of Pennsylvania, Holker had likely received them in payment for goods and services worth no more than $43,000. Nevertheless, after 25 years and no record of the certificates having been redeemed as promised in Hamilton's plan of 1790, the acting Secretary of the Treasury, A. J. Dallas , recommended that Holker be paid the face value of the certificates.[25] Holker's success in that case might have been inspired by his success with an earlier judgment he received from a circuit court in Boston.

On May 14, 1814, that court annulled the 1799 judgment and then condemned Parker to pay Holker the sum of $203,000 principal plus another $336,920 in accumulated interest, for a total of $539,940. It was that Boston judgment that motivated Holker to return to France in 1815. This time, he got the president of the *tribunal civil de la Seine* to declare attachments on the funds of Parker's debtors as well as to put liens on all his buildings, including Draveil. On August 18, 1815, the *tribunal de première instance de la Seine* declared the judgment of the Massachusetts

[24] Two separate issues of the *Journal du Palais*, 1819 and again in 1823.

[25] HeinOnline, "Memorial of John Holker for renewal of lost loan office certificates (14-1), 36 *American State Papers*: Claims 470 (1815).

court valid in France against Parker but restrained Holker to just take mortgages on the buildings, while suspending all liens for a period of 4 months to allow Parker time to justify why the Massachusetts judgment of May 4, 1814, should not be enforced in France. That decision was appealed, of course, first by Parker and then by Holker, and then again by Parker to force the case to the highest court of the land, the *Cour de cassation* in Paris. This time, unlike the case of the *Rosanna* previously, Parker prevailed. The high court ruled, in elaborate detail, that laws of sovereign states could only be enforced in other sovereign states if the respective sovereign rulers had formally agreed to do so by formal treaty beforehand. As that was not yet the case between France and the United States in 1814, Holker's case was dismissed.

Nevertheless, Parker sold Draveil in 1821, well before his death in Versailles on April 1, 1829 (Daniel, p. 146). No doubt he was clinging still to the possibility that his claims on the cargo of the *Rosanna* might end up being redeemed eventually and help mollify the descendants of one of his disappointed agents, Nathaniel Sargent. His various creditors, starting with Robert Morris and John Holker, did not do so badly. True, Morris spent time in debtor's prison, before he was allowed freedom at the end of his life at the expense of his junior partner, Gouverneur Morris.

Gouverneur Morris' dealings with Parker while he was in France and England and Hamburg enabled him to commission an entire ship to carry back the rich furnishings he had acquired from the expropriated estates of the royal family and emigres, to adorn his mansion at Morrisania. John Holker, it appears, was frustrated in his attempts to share in some of Parker's accumulated wealth in France, but nevertheless, he died a wealthy American landowner in Virginia. The original creditor of Parker, of course, was the Treasury of the United States, which never recovered the original $20,000 in Morris notes, or the accumulated interest at 6%—unless, of course, we put part of the Louisiana Purchase to Parker's credit.

References

Bizardel, Yvon. 1972. *Les américains à Paris pendant le revolution*. Paris: Calmann-Lévy.

Buist, Marten G. 1974. *At Spes Non Fracta: Hope & Co. 1779–1815*. Amsterdam: Bank Mees & Hope NV.

Cutterham, Tom. 2018. "'A Very Promising Appearance': Credit, Honor, and Deception in the Emerging Market for American Debt, 1784–92." *William and Mary Quarterly* 75 (4): 623–650.

Fugier, Andre, 1930. Napoleon et l'Espagne, 1799–1808, 2 vols., Paris: Librairie Felix Alcan.

Egan, Clifford. 1983. *Neither Peace nor War: Franco-American Relations 1803–1812.* Baton Rouge, LA: Louisiana State University Press.

Hidy, Ralph W. 1949. *The House of Baring in American Trade and Finance: English Merchant Bankers at Work, 1763–1861.* Cambridge, MA: Harvard University Press.

McCullough, David. 2019. *The Pioneers: The Heroic Story of the Settlers Who Brought the American Ideal West.* New York: Simon & Schuster.

Rice, Howard C. 1937. "James Swan: Agent of the French Republic, 1794–1796." *The New England Quarterly* 10 (3): 464–486.

Smith, Philip Chadwick Foster. 1984. *The Empress of China.* Philadelphia: Philadelphia Maritime Museum.

Sylla, Richard, Robert E. Wright, and David J. Cowen, 2009. "Alexander Hamilton, Central Banker: Crisis Management during the U. S. Financial Panic of 1792." *The Business History Review* 83 (1): 61–86.

Tearle, David. 2017. *Merchants of War: Barings Bank and William Bingham, Revolutionary Bankers from the War of Independence to the Louisiana Purchase.* Modbury, Devon, UK: The Incorporated History Press.

Ver Steeg, Clarence L. 1953. "Financing and Outfitting the First United States Ship to China." *Pacific Historical Review* XXII (1): 1–12.

Ver Steeg, Clarence. 1954. *Robert Morris: Revolutionary Financier: With an Analysis of His Earlier Career.* Philadelphia: University of Pennsylvania Press.

Williams, Greg H., 2009. *The French Assault on American Shipping, 1793–1813: a history and comprehensive record of merchant marine losses.* Jefferson : McFarland & Co.

Winter, Pieter J. van. 1977. *American Finance and Dutch Investment, 1790–1815: With an Epilogue to 1840.* English Adaptation of the Rev. Version of the Dutch Original ed. Prepared for Publication with the Author's Assistance by James C. Riley, 2 vols. New York: Arno Press.

Ziegler, Philip, 1988. *The Sixth Great Power: A history of one of the greatest of all banking families, the House of Barings, 1762–1929.* New York: Alfred A. Knopf.

CHAPTER 7

The Deal Is Done, But Problems Arise Everywhere: America, London, Paris, and Amsterdam

Problems in America

In the Baring archive, the next recognition that the treaty has been signed in Paris to the mutual satisfaction of the French and American negotiators comes with a series of letters and enclosures addressed to Robert Gilmor, a merchant banker in Baltimore. Gilmor, a trusted associate of both Baring and Bingham, was given the power of attorney to act in place of Alexander Baring in case misfortune should prevent his arrival safely in Washington. A full accounting of the number of certificates, their denominations, and their division between F. Baring & Co. in London and Hope & Co. in Amsterdam was included (Appendix A, Panel A). The instructions were that "The certificates should be to bearer, the only way to secure an easy transfer and to encourage many people who look for a solid and advantageous investment, but trust to nobody as themselves are not to be trusted. Nor is it always convenient for them that their name should appear" (*NP1.A4.16*).

These instructions, however, were not those carried out by Albert Gallatin and Alexander Baring in Washington while they awaited word from New Orleans that the "cession of Louisiana" from Spain to France and then to the United States had been achieved. Gallatin apparently insisted that his system of recording each government bond—when issued, to whom, and where, when, and how much interest was to

L. Neal, *The Forgotten Financiers of the Louisiana Purchase*, Palgrave Studies in the History of Finance,
https://doi.org/10.1007/978-3-031-56277-8_7

be paid—should be maintained for these new bonds as well. Consequently, Alexander, rather than dividing the certificates simply between Amsterdam and London, depending on where interest would be paid, instead had six separate packets of certificates printed up (Appendix A, Panel B.). The number of certificates remained the same as requested by Sir Francis and Henry Hope, 5071, as did their total face value, $11,250,000, but now they were divided into six separate packets, four destined for Amsterdam and two for London. Within each packet, A through F, the certificates were numbered sequentially for each denomination, even though each packet contained a variety (13) of denominations for the individual certificates (Fig. 7.1).

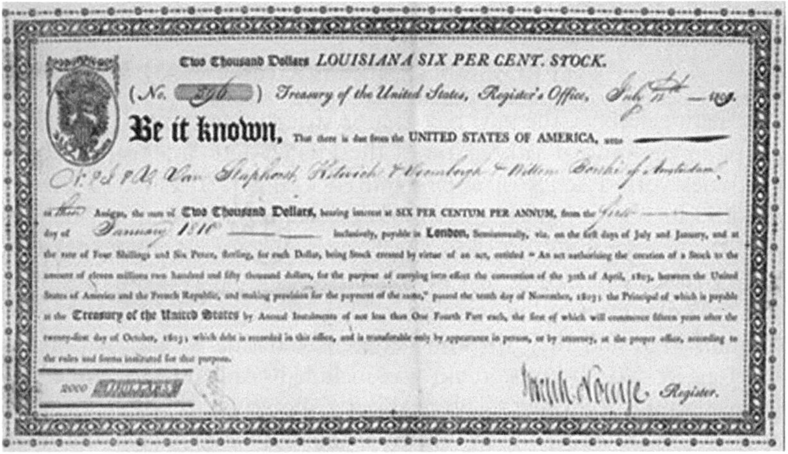
Two Thousand Dollars LOUISIANA SIX PER CENT. STOCK.

(No.) Treasury of the United States, Register's Office,

Be it known, That there is due from the UNITED STATES OF AMERICA, unto

or their Assigns, the sum of Two Thousand Dollars, bearing interest at SIX PER CENTUM PER ANNUM, from the day of inclusively, payable in London, Semiannually, viz. on the first days of July and January, and at the rate of Four Shillings and Six Pence, sterling, for each Dollar, being Stock created by virtue of an act, entitled "An act authorising the creation of a Stock to the amount of eleven millions two hundred and fifty thousand dollars, for the purpose of carrying into effect the convention of the 30th of April, 1803, between the United States of America and the French Republic, and making provision for the payment of the same," passed the tenth day of November, 1803; the Principal of which is payable at the Treasury of the United States by Annual Instalments of not less than One Fourth Part each, the first of which will commence fifteen years after the twenty-first day of October, 1803; which debt is recorded in this office, and is transferable only by appearance in person, or by attorney, at the proper office, according to the rules and forms instituted for that purpose.

2000

Register.

Fig. 7.1 Sample certificate for Louisiana Purchase bonds (*Source* https://lewis-clark.org/media/loupur_stock-certif.jpg, accessed March 6, 2023. This rare specimen appears to be a certificate transferred to a group of Amsterdam investors in place of one (or more) of the original certificates issued in Amsterdam. After Napoleon's Continental Blockade made it difficult to collect interest payments in Amsterdam, the Dutch proprietors could shift payments to London. While interest was payable in London, the bond "is transferable only by appearance in person, or by attorney, at the proper office, according to the rules and forms indicated for that purpose." The exchange rate of the dollar to the pound is still fixed at the original rate agreed in 1803. One of the owners, Willem Borski, died in February 1814, which may be why this replacement certificate still exists in the U.S. archives.)

This elaborate production surely undercut the intent of Sir Francis Baring and Henry Hope in London to maintain the easy marketability of the bonds. It did, apparently, satisfy Gallatin that he could keep abreast of his progress toward his cherished goal of eliminating all of Hamilton's debt that he had inherited in 1801.[1]

In any event, Alexander arrived safely in Washington and reported back regularly on the progress that Jefferson and Madison were making in getting the approval of Congress. He was getting Albert Gallatin to print up the 5071 certificates once Congress had approved the treaty. Alexander refused to accept them, however, until word came that the physical transfer of Louisiana from Spain to France (for less than a month) and then to the United States had been completed at the end of December 1803. (The letters and instructions for Gilmor never appeared, however, apparently lost at sea.)

Before Alexander arrived in America to take charge of the Baring & Hope loan to the United States, he had alerted Albert Gallatin to the impending transaction by direct correspondence. This private channel of communication enabled Gallatin to reassure Jefferson that the terms of the deal could be met easily by the Federal government. True, Gallatin felt that Baring & Hope had cut themselves a very handsome commission for the task they were taking on. The contract sent as an enclosure with Alexander's letter to Gallatin, said nothing about the form or number of the stock certificates to be printed up in Washington. It began with the French government giving Alexander an act "authorizing the American government to transfer to the said houses or their representatives the 11,250,000 dollars American stock."[2] Gallatin assumed that Alexander would want the certificates in denominations small enough to be readily marketable, say $1000 each. That would mean printing up 11,250 separate certificates, each to be engraved to foil efforts at counterfeiting, and then each signed individually. Gallatin noted all these details to let Jefferson know that the completion of the transaction would take several

[1] Hassler, pp. 78–79, by contrast, shows a certificate, No. 956, for $1000 of "Louisiana Domestic Six Cent. Stock," but issued in 1815 to the executors of the estate of William Bingham, with interest payable quarterly at the Bank of Pennsylvania. The originals would have had interest paid quarterly as well, according to De Knight, p. 48. The confusion over the exact form of the certificates arose during the hectic years of the War of 1812, when the United States. Treasury initiated new forms of financing without the services of the Bank of the United States. See Chapter 11.

[2] *Writings of Albert Gallatin*, v. 1., Gallatin to Jefferson, August 31, 1803.

weeks at least after legislation had been passed and signed by Jefferson. In the meantime, however, Gallatin set the wheels in motion to prepare paper, ink, and clerks for providing the physical forms of the "American stock." The final form of each certificate, according to Gallatin, "must express the nature of the stock, the law by virtue of which issued, and, what cannot be done without Baring's consent, the mode of transferring the stock, the place where the interest is payable, the mode of paying it, and the rate of exchange, all of which is left indeterminate in the convention, the rate of exchange with Paris only excepted." Consequently, the gears of the American government could not be engaged until the arrival of the personal agent of the houses of Hope & Baring and it would take another three weeks to print up, sign, and verify all of the certificates. It was simply not feasible to speed up the ratification process on the American end, despite the pleas for immediate action coming from Livingston and Monroe (in response, it must be said, to pressures by Napoleon on Barbé-Marbois.)

Gallatin's close reading of both the official conventions between the United States and France and the further convention between France and Baring, however, persuaded him that "it is impossible that Bonaparte should not consider his bargain as so much obtained for nothing; for, however valuable to us, it must be evident to him that pending the war he could not occupy Louisiana, and that the war would place it very soon in other hands." Consequently, Gallatin assured Jefferson that the anxiety communicated in the letters of Monroe and Livingston to hasten the completion of the American side of the bargain arose, not from Bonaparte, but from Baring and Livingston. Baring was anxious "that a convention by which he and his associates will gain near three millions of dollars should not fail in its execution," while Livingston was concerned that "no modifications should be made by Congress in the mode of settling and paying the American claims, as well as a natural desire to persuade us that he has made a most excellent bargain."[3] Gallatin did not impute any side-business being done between the Barings and Monroe, but he did suspect that Napoleon would be upset to see Barings receiving the first installment of interest on the American debt before they were committed to begin paying the French Treasury to sums agreed in weekly installments.

[3] Ibid.

That was indeed the case, as reported in Barbé-Marbois's account of the sale of Louisiana. It was also due to Sir Francis agreeing that an advance payment should be made to Napoleon, given his experience with the previous loans arranged to cover tributary payments to Napoleon. That possibility had even been raised in Madison's instructions carried by Monroe to Paris. It was really the combination of Monroe in London with the $2 million already authorized by Congress to cover foreign obligations, and deposited with Barings, that enabled Sir Francis to make the advance payment to Napoleon, albeit through the intermediation of Hope & Co. in Amsterdam.

Gallatin, however, added the 8 million francs commission that Barings had arranged with France to the 3.6 million francs they would get from the United States in interest paid during the two years before they completed payment to France. His calculation led him to infer that Barings were implicitly pricing the American stock at 78½ percent. He went to some pains to assure Jefferson that all the outstanding American securities were being traded in Philadelphia and New York at close to par, and, further, that the American 3% redeemable bond was trading in London at a slightly higher price than the vaunted English Three Per Cent Consol! (He conveniently omitted that the interest on the Consols was subject to the just renewed income tax imposed by Addington, while the American securities were not.) Nevertheless, as a recent historian of Gallatin remarks, "Whatever his misgivings about the payment terms, Gallatin worked amicably with Alexander Baring—the young banker who came to Washington to complete his firm's bond purchase—and he began to adjust his overall plan for repaying the public debt to take account of the new obligations."[4] That assessment is certainly correct, but the historian omits the prior relationship that Alexander had established with Gallatin. In early 1802, Alexander purchased the remaining shares held by the Federal government in the Bank of the United States at a premium of 45%. This was a major operation in itself as it was a huge step toward Gallatin's goal of paying off the Federal debt, but it was also accompanied by Alexander undertaking to pay off the remaining debt owed by the Federal government to the Dutch creditors.[5] Gallatin made sure, at the conclusion of his report, to include details of a competing offer made

[4] May, p. 132.

[5] All this was happily reported by Gallatin in his annual report of December 1802, p. 254.

by the Manhattan Company in New York and the refusal of the Bank of the United States to undertake the remittances to the Dutch, finally mentioning Alexander by name.[6]

In the months Alexander was in the United States, from September 1803 to January 1804, when he set sail for his return to Europe, he made other arrangements to lay off the bonds to interested investors but declined Gallatin's offer to take the entire commitment from Baring and Hope, arguing that his principals and partners in Europe had made earlier commitments that he had to honor. Given the high opinion that Gallatin had of the quality of American government debt at that date, Alexander wrote his father that he was sure that it was his prior relationship with Gallatin that enabled the deal to go through just as agreed in the two contracts for which he was the responsible agent. The first contract was between Alexander and the three government ministers who had signed the conventions for the Louisiana Purchase in Paris. The second was the contract in London to divide the 5071 certificates among the London and Amsterdam merchant bankers as determined by his father, Sir Francis. Again, Gallatin was enthusiastic about the basic structure of the financial arrangement but only wanted to get an even better deal for his government, if Alexander would be flexible. Alexander, no doubt buoyed by the confidence in him shown by his father and his father-in-law as well as by his brother-in-law, stuck to his terms, and refused even to accept the already printed-up bonds prepared by Gallatin until official word was received in Washington that the final cession of New Orleans to the United States had taken place on December 20, 1803. Interest on the bonds, consequently, would begin December 21, 1803!

"Of the five thousand shares in the stock of the Bank of the United States, originally subscribed by the United States, 2780 shares had been sold in 1796, by virtue of the act entitled "An act making provision for the payment of certain debts of the United States," and for the purpose of discharging a part of the debt due to the bank. The remaining 2220 shares were now, under the same authority, sold at 45 per cent. advance. The 1,287,600 dollars which they produced, were, in conformity to the provisions of the same act, applied towards discharging an equal amount of that part of the debt which had become due to the bank before or during the year 1796; and the purchaser of the stock sold, at the same time, to the Treasury, an equal sum in bills on Holland, at 41 cents per guilder; the securing of which large amount, at that rate, was the inducement, on the part of Government, to dispose of the bank stock on those terms."

[6] Ibid., p. 261.

Problems in London

While the tedious business of creating physical certificates was going on in Washington under the careful eye of Alexander Baring, the war between Britain and France resumed. The new Prime Minister, Henry Addington, and his Secretary of State and War, Lord Hawkesbury, had been informed of the upcoming transaction earlier and had approved, thinking that New Orleans was better in the hands of the Americans than in Napoleon's. With the expenses of renewed war, however, Addington realized that Napoleon's finances were being augmented each time France cashed the bills of exchange already accepted by F. Baring.

Sir Francis explained in detail the commitment he had made, and the importance for his firm (and its ability to continue in the major financing of the British war effort) to honor these commercial contracts. In his letter to Addington of November 12, 1803, he laid out in detail ("which I have endeavored to make as concise as possible") first, the operation in France, in English and French money, with the periods or installments when the money becomes payable. Second, he gave the particulars of the debt due from America in Holland, including the Dutch plan so as to discharge £600,000 in 1803 and £500,000 in 1804.[7] This plan, initiated by Labouchere in Amsterdam, included three of the richest houses in Europe (Hope & Co., R. & G. de Smeth, Wm. & G. Willink). They had set up a joint venture, by which they would receive nearly the whole of the American debt to be paid off and repackage the obligations as shares in a 15-year investment fund paying 5% interest in guilders to any investor wanting to receive payment in Amsterdam.

Sir Francis noted that his firm had sent to Holland bills on various places for the American account over the past 9–10 months totaling about £770,000. Of that "£450,000 was money received from W. King & from the Am. Government towards the discharge of the loan due in 1803." The remaining £320,000 was in part for the Louisiana Purchase, and of that, about £90,000 belonged to Americans "concerned with us in the business." (Presumably, these were William Bingham and Robert Gilmor,

[7] *Baring Archive*, NP1.A4.22. "Sir Francis Baring to Henry Addington 12/11/1803. Copy of letter written following a meeting between Baring, Mr Addington and Lord Hawkesbury; explains options for repayment of the loan; importance of doing nothing to upset the negotiations; damage caused by a letter from Lord Hawkesbury to Mr King; the three houses involved in the loan, Francis Baring & Co, Hope & Co, and De Smeth & Co."

as Bingham was credited with $300,000 of the Louisiana loan by the executors of his estate in 1805.) To placate the fears of Addington and Hawkesbury, Sir Francis elaborated:

> In the agreement we have an option to make the debt payable in England or Holland, or France. But as the liquidation must be beneficial to the country where it is made, & being desirous not to introduce a currency & circulation between countries where it doth not exist at present France has been omitted. When our agent (my son) went to America we were not so sanguine about our success in Holland, his directions, therefore, are, to divide the debt.
>
> 5 millions for Holland
> 6 ¼ mill. For England
>
> Our views were, that as America was in the practice of redeeming a considerable portion of her foreign debt annually, that we might dispose of a large proportion of that sum to the American government. At any rate we should find a little difficulty in converting the English into Dutch debt & vice versa. Thus is disposed of

5,000,000 in Holland
1,500,000 in England
4,750,000 unappropriated making 11,250,000 dollars

Here, Baring minimized the role he was playing in financing Napoleon by claiming it was essentially American and Dutch money that was and would be going to France. He raised the possibility that the Dutch would be doing the bulk of the financing with the resources they had available. Later, as we shall see, he argued to Henry Hope, on the contrary, that he could have taken the entire sale of American bonds.

> We do not know whether the Houses in Holland, who are accustomed to hold a large sum, have made a provision for themselves out of the 5 millions but they write very distinctly that they can make further progress at any time & with care. With regard to the funds to enable them to discharge their acceptances they are more ample than I thought, on further investigation, & which I can explain very distinctly whenever you may think proper in conversation, as I humbly conceive it is necessary to be known to Lord Hawkesbury & to yourself.

Sir Francis concluded his appeal to the British government by reminding them of the strategic importance of New Orleans, in particular, to the United States. The United States would have been willing to pay much more, but for the intervention of his company's agent, Alexander Baring, to divert part of the American purchase price to recompensating their own merchants, not Napoleon's forces.

> The acquisition of Louisiana is of the last importance to America, & for which she could not pay too dear; it is admitted moreover that the measure must be beneficial, & of course desirable to this country. The demand of France was originally 100 million of livres; & I believe that Mr. Livingston & Mr. Monroe will allow, that merit was due to my son for reducing the price & facilitating the arrangement, which owed its termination however to the political circumstances which existed at that period. It is the more desirable that the slightest pretence should not be suffered to disturb the cession, for in consequence of the quiet but judicious letter from Lord Hawkesbury to W. King on the subject of the treaty, the political merit which France sought to obtain with America is vanished, & it is viewed by Americans in general as a mere bargain of purchase & etc.
>
> What I have submitted to the consideration of Lord Hawkesbury & yourself, I can prove by documents, or a reference to Mr. Monroe who was actively employed on the occasion: I therefore flatter myself you will not listen to any insinuations to my prejudice which may come from abroad without hearing what I may have to say, & for which request I have particular reasons. (*Baring Archive, NP1.A4.22*)

In his extensive presentation to the British Prime Minister, Sir Francis minimized his role in financing the Louisiana Purchase and suggested that the Dutch firms might take the bulk of the American bonds, contrary to his earlier correspondence with Labouchere. Further, the total owed to France was reduced substantially by Alexander's efforts in the Paris negotiations. (No mention is ever made of Alexander's role in that decision in the later accounts by Livingston, Monroe, or Barbé-Marbois for that matter.) The political advantage of the transfer of Louisiana from France to the United States was very much in Britain's favor, and the Americans considered it as a commercial, not politically strategic, transaction, according to Sir Francis. (This, however, was quite the opposite of the opinion expressed by Jefferson in his open letter carried by Pierre-Samuel Dupont de Nemours to Livingston in 1802!) Finally, Sir Francis emphasized for Addington's benefit the importance for the future of his firm's role in international finance that required him to continue to fulfill faithfully his commitments to other financiers (as well as to the British government for which he had become the lead subscriber to their successively larger war loans).

For all the forthright explanation by Sir Francis of the way funds were being funneled into England and Holland, Addington ultimately responded by ordering, very diplomatically, Sir Francis to put a stop to the further remittance of funds to either France or Holland (as Dutch funds would be sent on to France) in his letter of December 16, 1803 (Appendix D; *TBA* NP1.A4.28). The formal letter, apparently, was sent to provide Sir Francis written evidence that he was reneging on his remaining acceptances only under duress of His Majesty's Government. For Sir Francis had already complied with the command, having sent a letter to Labouchere on November 22, 1803, that requested him to retain in his hands or to make remittances to Sir Francis "for the whole of what may be due to you for your account F, deducting only the value of 500,000 dollars or about £90,000—which belongs to Mr. Bingham & another American friend."[8] Labouchere's response on December 6, 1803, was prompt and obliging, assuring Sir Francis "that it will suit our convenience in every respect, as we are most amply provided with funds to enable us to discharge the engagements we have entered into on behalf of ourselves & our friends Messrs de Smeth & Willink."[9]

Problems in Paris

Unmentioned in Pierre Cesar's letter were the engagements that Labouchere had made with Barbé-Marbois to speed up the payments of the accepted bills, so that the previously accepted bills were no longer at issue. He explained, instead, the arrangement he had made for payments in place of the accepted bills of exchange, as well as making an advance payment to the French Treasury. This had been done by making a payment of 10 million francs to the French Treasury before word of formal acceptance of the treaty by the Americans was received in Paris. The arrangement, made with the knowledge of Livingston and Monroe, counted as a payment of 2 million dollars from the money deposited with

[8] NP1.A4.25, Sir Francis Baring to Hope & Co. 22 Nov. 1803.

[9] NP1.A4.31.

F. Baring by the United States while Monroe was on his voyage to France, with an assurance that this was paid in the United States. The remaining 8 million francs were itemized by Labouchere at the foot of the formal agreement by various French securities, bank notes, and assorted bills of exchange accepted by Hope & Co. in Amsterdam or drawn on Leghorn. In return, the accepted bills numbered 2–4–6–7–9–11–12–14–15–16–18–19–21–22–24–25, were returned to Sir Francis, taking him off the hook for the coming year. Further, Livingston sent Sir Francis a note to assure him that if, worst outcome, the United States rejected the treaty, the French government would then repay Barings the 10 million francs being advanced.[10]

Problems in Amsterdam

Fortunately for all concerned, Alexander returned to London in April 1804 with the packet of 1/3 of the U.S. certificates safely for distribution in Britain, and a U.S. Navy ensign arrived in Paris with the other 2/3 of U.S. certificates. Livingston turned them over to Labouchere, who presumably transferred them to his partners in Amsterdam. By December 1804, the *Amsterdamsche Courant* could advertise that the "*Origineele Louisiana Schuld*" with annual interest of 6% payable each six months starting from January 1804 was available at the offices in Amsterdam of Willem & Jan Willink, Nicolaas Jacob en Roelof Van Staphorst at a guaranteed exchange rate of 50 stuivers to the dollar. These were the original partners in the funding of earlier American obligations, obligations that were now being paid off by them, as advertised as well in the paragraphs above the Louisiana notice. The new Louisiana bonds were a desirable replacement for the previous American bonds that had proved so profitable to the original Dutch investors but were now being paid off. The exchange rate was the same as indicated in the Dutch proposal that Sir Francis has presented to Henry Addington the previous year (Appendix E). Only later do we see advertisements for that partnership: the Willinks with Hope & Co. and the De Smeth brothers. The appearance of two Dutch firms advertising sales of Louisiana bonds was the result of Labouchere's efforts to spread even further the risk of his participation in the deal arranged by Alexander in Paris.

[10] BA NP1.A4.34.

Fig. 7.2 Amsterdam Advertisements for various American securities, December 25, 1804 (Source *Amsterdamsche Courant*, December 25, 1804)

In Amsterdam, while sales of certificates held in London continued to take place at a brisk pace, advertisements began to appear in Dutch newspapers announcing that European investors could acquire their shares of the Louisiana "*schuld*," again with attractive yields and fixed exchange rate, but directly from the joint partnership of Hope, Willink, and Staphorst. At the same time, the Dutch bankers for the American government, the partnership of the Van Willinks and the Van Staphorsts, were redeeming in full the notes for the "liquidated United States of America debts" that they had marketed 15 years earlier. Their intent, obviously, was that investors could "roll over" their lucrative and passive investment in American sovereign debt and thereby maintain a comfortable rate of return. Everyone involved in Amsterdam and London could well congratulate themselves for having pulled off a magnificent concern (Fig. 7.2).

Complications in London

In London, Sir Francis produced a printed flyer, dated April 3, 1804, that advertised the availability of "American Louisiana Stock" to the London market. The flyer emphasized that the stock was irredeemable for fifteen years and then would become reimbursable in the four following years by four equal payments. The stock bore interest of 6% per annum, from the first day of January 1804, and would be paid in London half-yearly as it became due. "The first Dividend of Three per Cent. will be paid in July next, by Sir Francis Baring and Company of London." Moreover, the flyer noted that "The Interest is payable at the par of exchange of four shillings and sixpence Sterling per dollar, free of Commission and Charges, the risk of Bills being for account of the United States." Further, it was noted that the Proprietor of the Stock could exchange the certificate for one bearing interest quarterly, payable in America. In this way, bondholders might avoid paying the British income tax, if the Exchequer agents became aware of this source of their income (Fig. 7.3).

> A List of the Proprietors will be sent from Washington every half-year; and those Persons, in whose names the Stock stands on the first of January, are entitled to receive the six months' dividend, due the first of July following; and in like manner those Persons, in whose names the Stock stands on the first of July, are entitled to receive the six months' Dividend due the first of January following.[11]

This assertion in the printed prospectus obviously belies the original intent of Sir Francis to make each bond certificate payable to the bearer, and therefore easily sold from one person to another. The flyer asserts that the United States Treasury maintained a registry of all persons or firms who would be entitled to receive the semi-annual interest payments, for each of the numbered certificates held abroad. While the total number of certificates came to 5071, as instructed to Alexander, they were divided among four different firms and set into 13 different denominations, so that no single set of certificates numbered more than 250. (See Appendix A, Panel C for a complete listing of the original certificates printed up at the direction of Albert Gallatin and Alexander Baring). Gallatin's insistence on keeping a nominal list of all recipients of the interest payments by the United States over the 15-year life-span of each bond would make the marketability of individual bonds much more cumbersome for the London firm, unlike the marketing scheme previously set up by the Amsterdam group.

Originally, the names in which the certificates stood were the two firms that held certificates for payment of interest in London and the two firms with certificates for payment of interest in Amsterdam. Later, Baring Bros. began to ship some numbered certificates back to the United States to be replaced by other names, but most of those certificates were sent back

[11] The Baring Archive, NP1.A4.45.

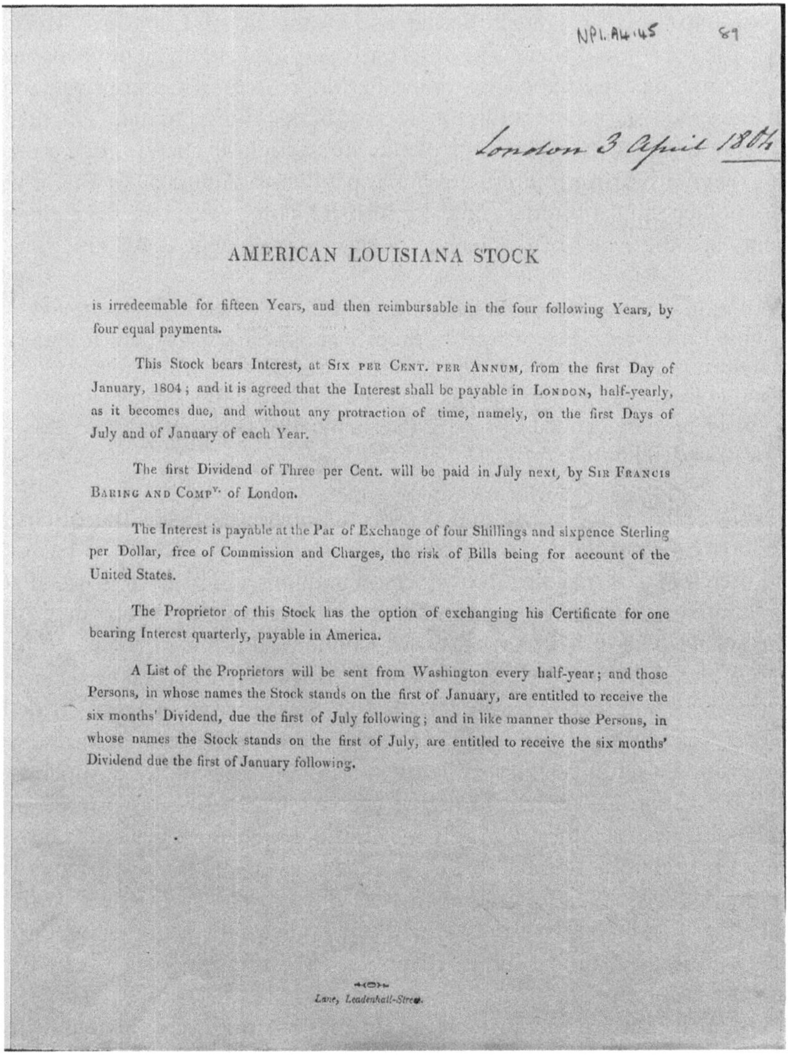
NP1.A4.45 89

London 3 April 1804

AMERICAN LOUISIANA STOCK

is irredeemable for fifteen Years, and then reimbursable in the four following Years, by four equal payments.

This Stock bears Interest, at SIX PER CENT. PER ANNUM, from the first Day of January, 1804; and it is agreed that the Interest shall be payable in LONDON, half-yearly, as it becomes due, and without any protraction of time, namely, on the first Days of July and of January of each Year.

The first Dividend of Three per Cent. will be paid in July next, by SIR FRANCIS BARING AND COMPY. of London.

The Interest is payable at the Par of Exchange of four Shillings and sixpence Sterling per Dollar, free of Commission and Charges, the risk of Bills being for account of the United States.

The Proprietor of this Stock has the option of exchanging his Certificate for one bearing Interest quarterly, payable in America.

A List of the Proprietors will be sent from Washington every half-year; and those Persons, in whose names the Stock stands on the first of January, are entitled to receive the six months' Dividend, due the first of July following; and in like manner those Persons, in whose names the Stock stands on the first of July, are entitled to receive the six months' Dividend due the first of January following.

Lane, Leadenhall-Street.

Fig. 7.3 The baring prospectus for the Louisiana bonds in London (*Source* Baring Archive, NP1.4.45, "1804, Apr: Prospectus for Louisiana 6% Loan.")

to Barings and, presumably, turned over to the new titleholders. (See Appendix B for details.) These individuals then had to make their own arrangements for receiving their semi-annual interest payments, perhaps including using the services of Baring Bros. to avoid receiving the interest payments in England and paying the British income tax. The Louisiana bond transferred from the name of Baring Bros. to another creditor wishing to receive the interest payment in the United States, however, paid the interest quarterly, in common with the other U.S. bonds, rather than semi-annually in London or Amsterdam.

The combination of a high rate of interest and a fixed exchange rate with the dollar locked in for at least 15 years and possibly longer proved irresistible. Sales were boisterous, beyond the fondest expectations of either principal and very close to face value, putting to rest the original doubts of Sir Francis Baring and Henry Hope in London and Pierre Cesar Labouchere in Amsterdam. Further, the United States proved capable of remitting the semi-annual interest payments to the respective bankers ahead of the dates announced for distribution to the ultimate holders, which gave the bankers advance money as well as reassurance. While Baring and Hope had made a substantial payment to the French Treasury in advance of ratification of the treaty in the United States, the firms had received by mid-July 1804 the interest on the total of $11,250,000 for six months plus the 11 days at the end of 1803 after formal possession of the Louisiana Territory by the United States took place on December 20, 1803.

On the 25th of July, 1804, Alexander Baring wrote to Albert Gallatin to confirm that he had received sufficient money from the United States to cover accumulated interest on the $5,000,000 of Louisiana 6% bonds held in Amsterdam, $2,000,000 in the names of Hope & Co, and Francis Baring & Co. and $3,000,000 in the joint names of W. & J. Willink, R. & T. De Smeth, and Hope & Co. Interest was paid for the 11 days from the 20th to 31st December, and then the six months through June 30, 1804. Total interest was in current florins, amounting to cf399,657.10.8, calculated at 40 cents per current florin. For the bundles of stock held in London, divided into $2,500,000 in the name of Sir Francis Baring & Co., and $3,750,000 in the name of Hope & Co. and Sir Francis Baring & Co., the total interest due amounted to £44,961.9.2 sterling. Twenty-five days after interest was promised to be paid, however, Alexander had received bills of exchange that amounted to only £30,000. Consequently, he credited the United States for the £30,000 and debited it for the £44,961.9.2, but, graciously, charged no commission, or further interest for the amount being covered out of pocket by Sir Francis Baring & Co., at least for the time being.[12] Of the total of $11,250,000.00 bonds issued by the United States to Alexander Baring in December 1803, $500,000.00 were committed to close associates of Sir Francis

[12] Library of Congress, Baring mss. bound volume "MMC 2475" "Copies of letters addressed to the Treasury department of the United States of America by Sir Francis Baring & Co.", ff. 50-51.

Letter to Gallatin, London 25 July 1804.

"In consequence of the articles of agreement I had the honor of signing with you at Washington the 16th of January last I have now to wait upon you with the following receipts for interest on the Louisiana six pCent Stock payable both in this place and at Amsterdam to the 30th of last month."

On Amsterdam stock

Cf 9863.	for interest from 20th to 31st December 1803 on Drs. 2,000,000 in the names of Hope & Co & Francis Baring & Co.
Cf 14,794.10.8.	for the same on $3,000,000 in the names of Hope & Co., R&J de Smeth,& H & J. Willink.
Cf 225,000.	for 6 months interest to the 30th Ult. on the stock last mentioned [$3,000,000].
Cf 150,000.	for the same on $2,000,000 in the names of Hope & Co, & Francis Baring & Co., amounting together to Cf399,657.10.8 for which I have received payment from you at 40 cents the current florin.

On London Stock

£1109.11.8.	for interest from the 20th to 31st Dec. 1803 on Drs. 2,500,000 in the name of Francis Baring & Co.
£1664.7.6.	for the same on Drs. 3,750,000 in the names of Hope & Co. & Francis Baring.
£25,312.10.	for 6 months interest on the stock last mentioned to 30th Ult.
£16,875.	for the same on Drs. 2,500,000 in the names of Francis Baring & Co.

Making altogether £44961.9.2 sterling. For the amount of the two sums first mentioned for interest due 31 December last I received from you payment in full. On account of the two following sums amounting to £42,187.10 being the exact amount of interest due here the 30th Ult. I received the value of £30,000. It appears to me however more regular to make out the receipts for the full sum, and Messrs. Barings in the accounts they will this day furnish, will carry the total amount of Six months dividend £42,187.10 to the debit and the £30,000 received by me to the credit of the United States, and on no part of this operation will any commission be charged."

[signed] Alexander Baring

Baring (and friends and in-laws of Alexander), but it appears that the actual certificates came to London with Alexander. It also appears that he took from Amsterdam some of the certificates made out to his father, and, possibly, some in the name originally of Henry Hope.

Alexander's letter of July 25, 1804, however, clearly put the London house of Sir Francis Baring & Co. (then in the course of becoming reorganized as Baring Bros. & Co.), in control of the future servicing of the entire new debt issued by the Federal government of the United States, wherever the certificates might be held physically. Whether American sovereign debt was held by investors in Amsterdam or London, their interest payments came from London, whether in current florins, pounds sterling, or American dollars. This further cemented the commitment of the London firm to supporting the credit of the United States government, much as Sir Francis had promised in his original letter of February 11, 1803, when he accepted, gladly, the sole responsibility for handling the European finances of the American government. Later, matters would become increasingly complicated, especially during the War of 1812!

Problems Between the Houses of Hope and Baring

At the moment in mid-1804, however, an internal issue arose—how should the proceeds of the sales be shared between the two firms, one in London and the other in Amsterdam? A letter to Sir Francis by Alexander from Amsterdam dated June 4, 1804, alerted Sir Francis that Labouchere and John Williams Hope in Amsterdam felt that their efforts to accelerate payments to Napoleon, sooner and more rapidly than had originally been agreed, entitled them to 2/3 of the profits from the sales of the 5071 certificates.[13] Recall that 2/3 of the certificates had been sent to Paris, while Alexander departed Washington with only the remaining 1/3. Alexander apparently had been sent over to Amsterdam to make final arrangements for completing the division of the certificates and to settle accounts among the partners. When he returned to London to review the accounts with the United States, however, it appears that either he had reclaimed some of the bonds sent to Paris, or that those bonds had smaller denominations than the bonds Alexander had carried back to London. Whatever, the total face value of the Amsterdam bonds was $5 million

[13] The Baring Archive, NP1.A4.50.

while the London bonds made up the remaining $6.25 million. While 2/3 of the bonds had been sent originally to Paris, over one-half of their face value had come to London.

Labouchere's success in bringing the two other Dutch firms, the Willink brothers and the De Smeth brothers, into the marketing of Louisiana bonds in Amsterdam meant that the house of Hope & Co. in Amsterdam would have a smaller share of the final proceeds. Jointly, the two active partners in Hope & Company in Amsterdam, Pierre Cesar Labouchere and John Williams Hope, convinced themselves that they, along with Henry Hope in London, should get credit for 2/3 of the profits from marketing the Louisiana bonds, leaving Baring and Co. with 1/3. They felt, no doubt sincerely, that the labor they had gone through to convince the original bankers for the American government in Amsterdam to let the rejuvenated firm of Hope & Co. in Amsterdam take the lead in arranging the Louisiana loan entitled the two firms, Hope & Co. in Amsterdam and Henry Hope & Co. in London, to 2/3 of the profits. This, although Alexander had taken over half of the total bonds to London, some in the joint names of Francis Baring and Henry Hope, and over half of the interest owed semi-annually by the American government would be administered by Baring Bros. for the duration of the loan. The suggested split of 2/3 for Hope and 1/3 for Baring merely meant a manageable reduction in the share of profits for both Baring and Hope according to the arguments made by Labouchere and John Williams Hope in Amsterdam. The bulk of the Louisiana file in the Baring Archive recapitulates the arguments made on both sides and reveals in the process the pressures both Alexander and Pierre Cesar endured to bring the deal to a successful conclusion.

The news brought back to London by Alexander in June 1804 came at an emotionally fraught time for the London house. Alexander's father-in-law, William Bingham, had returned from Paris in poor health at the end of 1803. Sent to Bath with his daughter in the hope of recovering, he died there on February 7, 1804. In addition, Sir Francis' wife was suffering what would prove to be her final illness, which required treatment at Bath, where she died on December 3, 1804. Meanwhile, Alexander was at sea sailing back from New York with 1/3 of the Louisiana bonds. In the midst of these travails, and with the safe return of Alexander, it is understandable that Sir Francis would decide to retire from active duty in the firm, but he now devoted himself to sustaining his family by insisting they claim a full half-share in the profits from the boisterous sales of the Louisiana bonds.

In Sir Francis' presentation to Prime Minister Addington in November 1803, he had minimized the further commitment of the house of Baring for disposal of the bonds to be issued by the United States. Then, he stated it was for only $1.5 million of the bonds on his account, $5 million for the Amsterdam account, with the remaining $4.75 million still unallocated. Labouchere's letter to Sir Francis from Amsterdam on December 26, 1803, apparently took this division as then agreed, stating that while the contents of Sir Francis' letters (three during the past month) had surprised him,

> We have no objection to the discontinuance of your remittances, as we shall not want them. But we cannot comply with the rest of your request as for reasons which appear to us unanswerable. In the first place, we must acquaint our associates, who would impute the reasons to motives very injurious to the character & credit of your bonds, whatever we may urge to the contrary. In the second place it is but natural for us to suppose that one restriction may follow another after the very injudicious conduct of your government during the last war. [Referring to the difficulty imposed against listing the Portuguese bonds in London that Labouchere had arranged in 1802.] Your remittances are for the general concern, and for which you may reimburse yourselves easily, at the same time we must insist that you sell no more of the stock in your place without our consent, as there is a demand here which will enable us to sell more than we want to dispose of, & we have the pleasure to tell you that with the cordial & powerful aid of our colleagues we shall be enabled to execute the whole of the business without any inconvenience, We do not mean however to prevent the delivery of what has been actually contracted for with you, which we know must be complied with, the amount however is comparatively trifling.
>
> [*Baring Archive, NP1.A4.40*)

Nevertheless, Alexander returned with nearly 1/3 of the bonds to be sold in London, not Amsterdam. Further notes in the Baring Archive show that Sir Francis (or one of the chief clerks) calculated that the net profit from acquiring $11.25 million bonds (converted to pound sterling at 4s.6d per dollar) and dispensing 52 million francs (converted to pound sterling at 24.10 francs per pound sterling) created a surplus of £409,000.

Deducting commission charges of 2% left a balance of £358,350, essentially double the profit that Labouchere had calculated as possible in his letter of January 30, 1803.[14] Further notes in the Baring Archive show how the various Louisiana bonds were being divided up after Alexander's return to London (Table 7.1).

Clearly, Alexander had disposed of a half-million dollars of the bonds while in the United States, which would be to the account of Baring & Co., but the bonds allotted to Holland (the partnership of Hope, Willinks, and De Smeth), France (probably Baguenault), Henry Hope in London, and Hope & Co. in Amsterdam totaled $7,160,000 or nearly 2/3 of the $11,250,000 issued by the United States.

The claim that profits then should be shared in proportion: 2/3 Hope, 1/3 Baring, therefore seemed plausible. No mention is made of what would be the division between Henry Hope in London and Hope & Co.

Table 7.1 General estimate

Dollars			Florins
$5,000,000	Holland	circa	*cf* 12,000,000
$105,000	America	remitted	250,000
$210,000	Gilmor	to be remitted	500,000
$225,000	Willing & Francis	ditto	540,000
$160,000	France	do	430,000
$1,500,000	in London	F. B. co	3,500,000
$7,200,000			*cf* 17,220,000
1,000,000	H. H	[Henry Hope]	
1,000,000	H. & co	[Hope & Co.]	
1,000,000	F. B. & co	[Francis Baring & Co.]	7,180,000
10,200,000			24,400,000
1,050,000	surplus		2,800,000
11,250,000			*cf* 22,200,000
	To pay originally frs	52,000,000	
	paid in America	2,000,000	
		50,000,000	
	Discount circa	2,800,000	
		Frs	47,200,000
		or *cf*	22,200,000

Source *Baring Archive*, NP1.A4.48

[14] Baring Archive, NP1.A4.44.

in Amsterdam, but it is clear in the arguments made by the disputants—John Williams Hope and Pierre Cesar Labouchere in Amsterdam and Sir Francis in London—that the share in Amsterdam ($5,000,000) would have to be split with the Willink and De Smeth brothers.

The gist of Sir Francis' argument, which takes up many pages of emotional outpourings over the next two months, was that it was Pierre Cesar's own fault to have brought in the two Dutch firms in July 1803. Apparently, according to Sir Francis, Pierre Cesar was "panicked" (sic) when he learned that Alexander had committed to the 92 acceptances, payment of which would begin whenever the initial payment was made to France. Pierre Cesar had clearly stated earlier that any initial payment should be withheld until they were assured that the bonds were issued by the United States and delivered safely back to Europe. Nevertheless, Sir Francis had seen the advantage of making an initial payment to France in order to maintain Napoleon's commitment to the deal. Only when the Willinks made it clear that they would place the forthcoming Louisiana bonds with their clients as they redeemed the earlier American bonds that were then in the course of being paid off and offered to take up an equivalent amount did Pierre Cesar relax and acquiesce in Alexander's contract with Barbé-Marbois, Livingston, and Monroe.

Why Pierre Cesar then brought in the De Smeth brothers into the arrangement when he returned to Amsterdam was clearly his initiative and his responsibility, according to Sir Francis' decided opinion. Further, Sir Francis cast some aspersions on Pierre Cesar's judgment in general. Pierre Cesar had always been more optimistic about the Portuguese loan that he had arranged earlier, even though those bonds had not sold well, at least until Henry Hope had decided to take up a large part of them. By contrast, he was always fretting about the American bonds, which proved to have a very robust market, both in Amsterdam and London, and could have been sold in America as well.

In his final letter to Henry Hope on the subject, composed October 3, 1804, while in Bath attending his ailing wife, Sir Francis concluded,

> [W]hilst I fear that I may have expressed myself with too much energy on some occasions I have certainly forborne to use arguments of which I might have availed myself, but Lab: [Labouchere] in pursuit of his object will never admit the possibility of forbearance nor enter into any consideration that is not favorable to his own view of the subject.

The warmth of his imagination & the fluency or facility of his pen often carries him off his legs, of which you will please to accept the following proof from his letter of the 9 August last in speaking of the transaction with De Smeth brothers.

"I would have proposed to grant them my share for their assistance because without it, according to my notions of the spot here, & of the peculiar situations in which we were I certainly thought success impossible."

This quotation offers so many points of view, that it is really impossible to embrace them & I cannot perceive one which is favorable to his judgment. I do not think it very friendly to De Smeth to propose to him a concern the success of which was impossible without the magic of the De Smeth name for the funds he was to furnish were too insignificant. Nor can I comprehend what Magic that name can perform superior to those of Hope & Co. He totally forgets that there were resources (& those with a certainty of success) for the whole of the loan independent of Holland, even if not a single dollar had been sold in Holland. His aversion, his objection, to the operation has been uniform ^varying however perpetually in the form^ but I cannot understand the motive.

[*The Baring Archive,* NP1.A4.49]

Further, Sir Francis obviously felt pride in the achievement of his son Alexander, who had negotiated the printing of the 5071 bonds successfully in Washington, while also making sure that the transfer of Louisiana from France to the United States had been officially recognized in Washington before he took possession of his share. Alexander assured his father that while everything was concluding well, there had been details that only he could have dealt with on the spot.

The foolishly exalted opinion the Secretary [Gallatin] & people here generally have of the value of their funds made them unaccommodating from false notions of the value of our contract & I see clearly that no terms we could ever have made with their ministries would have been ratified here, indeed I have every day more reason to be pleased with the form of our proceeding & several circumstances which at first appeared objectionable. The Secretary offered par for the whole payable in 1. 2. 3. Years. In the uncertainty what had been done & indeed in the certainty that some part was engaged I refused but offered part which was rejected with the comment that his object was to clear the whole away. A good deal of old stock is coming out & keeps prices down. I therefore doubt whether I

shall sell here & as my last letters from Amsterdam of the 22 August are encouraging, ¼ of the whole sum being there engaged with fair prospects.
[*Baring Archive,* NP1.A4.19. "Alexander Baring to Sir Francis Baring—21 October 1803."]

Subsequent letters by John Williams Hope to Sir Francis acknowledge the quality of Alexander's efforts, both in Paris and in Washington, even while taking credit for having trained him so well when he was in Amsterdam in 1793. Much more effusive is the letter by Pierre Cesar to Alexander composed over several days before he posted it on August 10, 1804. For pages, he defends the claim first put forward by John William Hope for 2/3 Hope and 1/3 Baring, while also denying that he was "panicked" in the sense of losing his senses. Rather, he was fully aware of the dangers that lay in dealing with the French government as well as the need to bring on board the most powerful merchant bankers in Amsterdam so they would not undercut the attempt to restore the house of Hope & Company under the new government. Nevertheless, he hopes that Alexander will be able to mediate the dispute between Sir Francis and Henry Hope and that the two houses of Hope and Baring will continue as a powerful combination in the world of finance. He concludes,

I hope that in conversation with M. Hope & your father you will as mediator be able to unite all opinions, but I am satisfied that nothing that can further be wrote from here can have any but a most pernicious tendency.

You are, my dear Alexander, the only person to whom I could open my mind so fully and unreservedly—we have known each other long and in every different position that we have met with in life—to you I leave to determine whether my course has been marked by consistency, and what must be my feelings on this occasion. God bless you, my dear friend, and all yours & believe me always, most truly faithful, yours
P. C. Labouchere [*magnificent signature!*]
[*Baring Archive,* NP1.A4.57]

Ultimately, both John Williams Hope and Pierre Cesar agreed that the final division of profits would remain in the hands of Sir Francis and Henry Hope. The material in the archive has marginal notes by Sir Francis, all clearly intended to lay before a Court of Equity if the issue continued to be disputed by Henry Hope. No doubt, Sir Francis would have had the "home court" advantage in such a suit, although it would not have been politically astute for Sir Francis to have aired the dispute in public. (Already, William Cobbett in his *Political Register* was accusing Baring of aiding Napoleon's military ambitions by purchasing Louisiana for the United States, which may explain why Sir Francis had been at pains to minimize the role of Barings in his earlier presentation to Prime Minister Addington.) Nevertheless, he threatened it to Henry Hope and it is clear that the mass of preserved correspondence was recovered precisely to make the legal case clear to Henry Hope and to enable a continued, mutually profitable relationship between the two establishments.

In fact, the mutual efforts and combined resources of the two firms would resume shortly, perhaps due to Alexander responding positively to Pierre Cesar's plea. Labouchere had already passed on a proposal to Alexander to forward to his father in July 1804. This "Mexican silver" proposal would lead to one of the most celebrated adventures of the two firms. Eventually, it led to the Mexican mint delivering silver coins in bulk to American vessels and, on two occasions, to Royal Navy warships. Their ultimate shipment to Amsterdam and London and beyond (including Canton in one case) was overseen by agents of Baring Bros. & Co. and Hope & Co. located in Vera Cruz, New Orleans, and Philadelphia. This episode has fascinated historians ever since, but none with the benefit of insights from the Baring Archive. The background to this adventure, however, requires going back to Paris in 1804 and the adventures of Barbé-Marbois while he dealt with Napoleon's increasing financial demands to pay the rising price of his quest for glory.

CHAPTER 8

Meanwhile, More Trouble Back in Paris

The standard histories of the Louisiana Purchase agree that the sum paid to France helped Napoleon finance his renewal of war with Great Britain. The timing seems clear as war was declared on both sides the week after the formal signing in Paris of the three conventions for the Louisiana Purchase. True, troops had been massed beforehand on the west coast of France and in the occupied Netherlands while troop ships were being constructed for the intended invasion of Louisiana or, possibly, England. When Barbé-Marbois presented his accounts to Napoleon in mid-March 1803, shortly before he was called upon to arrange the sale of Louisiana, his accompanying letter noted that on the night of March 11 Napoleon had ordered him to prepare for extraordinary needs. Indeed, Barbé-Marbois had to conjure up some miracles in addition to the proceeds from Baring and Hope.[1] Not only would he have to cover the expense of invading England, which required building up the French navy, but later in the summer of 1805, when Austria declared war as well against Napoleon, he would have to cover the further expense of a continental war.

[1] Branda, Ch. 18, "La crise de 1805," and fn. 519.

L. Neal, *The Forgotten Financiers of the Louisiana Purchase*, Palgrave Studies in the History of Finance,
https://doi.org/10.1007/978-3-031-56277-8_8

It appears in retrospect that the funds obtained from the sale of Louisiana were used in part to cover the expenses of outfitting the invasion fleet being assembled at Boulogne, but in larger part to cover the costs of installing Napoleon as Emperor in 1804. The finances derived from the sale of Louisiana, while very satisfying to France given the loss of St. Domingue, paled in comparison to the other "extraordinary" receipts that Barbé-Marbois had to conjure up for Napoleon from a variety of sources, some of which would require him to call again upon the ingenuity of Baring and Hope, but especially Pierre Cesar Labouchere.

At the outset, the 50 million francs obtained from Baring & Hope spread over two years were overshadowed by the 75 million francs that Spain was forced to pay annually in lieu of providing military and naval support to its new ally (Treaty of Subsidies, December 1803). Another 64 million francs were claimed annually as well from the new Republic of Italy, created by Napoleon after his victory at Marengo (14 June 1800). Extraordinary revenues included 60 million francs in security bonds (*cautionnements*) posted by the new officials created to collect customs and excise duties. Further sales of national lands brought in another 49 million francs. The total of extraordinary revenues for the years leading up to the declaration of Napoleon as Emperor of France in May 1804, came to 304 million francs. The expenses of preparing for war, however, still left a deficit of 66 million francs.[2]

The shortfall would not be covered by a public loan, or by imposing a new tax upon the French citizens, even if they now included residents of surrounding territory that had previously been independent of the French kingdom. Napoleon had no thought of imperiling his stature as "the man on horseback" and First Consul for life by risking resistance to a new tax or a failed public loan, as had been the case with the Directory that he had replaced in 1799. Barbé-Marbois was finally persuaded, with the acquiescence of Napoleon, to rely on the promises of a group of military contractors, the *Négociants Réunis*. This partnership was led by Gabriel-Julien Ouvrard, the richest man in France (or, at least, the most flamboyantly wealthy individual in France), and the most important supplier to both army and navy in France.

Ouvrard's partners included Ignace-Joseph Vanlerberghe, the major dealer in grain since the Revolution and supplier to the Army of the

[2] Branda, Ch. XVII, "Du rêve américain au camp de Boulogne," "*Recapitulatif des finances publiques sous le Consulat*," Kindle loc. 6068.

North and then Napoleon's Army of Italy. Just as Daniel Parker's service to the American Revolutionary Army had brought Parker to the favorable attention of George Washington, Vanlerberghe's efficiency in supplying Napoleon's army in Italy had brought him the favorable attention of the emperor. Other partners who had successfully provisioned Napoleon's troops in Italy were the Michel brothers and Armand Seguin. Organizing themselves into a new *Compagnie des Négociants Réunis*, they relied on Ouvrard's contracts in Spain to take responsibility for the debt of Spain. So much so, that they paid into the French Treasury on their own account the total sum owed by Spain. Their offer was approved by Napoleon, who was apparently confident that, based on their previous performance in the Italian campaigns and now reorganized under Ouvrard's leadership, the new company could continue to supply his forces being assembled on the west coast of France.

Napoleon's forces, originally intended to reestablish French Louisiana, were now poised to invade England. With the connivance of Médard Desprez at the Banque de France, the obligations of the *Négociants Réunis* used to replace the debt payments from Spain were faithfully discounted at the Banque, but its reserves were drained. When England declared war against Spain in December 1804, the Spanish supplies of silver coins from Mexico were cut off and Spain's remittances, whether to the French Treasury or to Ouvrard, ceased as well. As Napoleon left Paris in mid-1805, rumors flew that he had taken even the last metal reserves from the Banque de France and bank runs began to accumulate, leading to a number of failures and bankruptcies. The ongoing financial difficulties posed by Napoleon's demands for funds while shaking up the financial structure of France found their focus in the office of the Treasurer, Barbé-Marbois. His correspondence with Napoleon over the course of the year 1805 took on increasingly desperate tones.[3]

While Barbé-Marbois had demanded that Ouvrard send him the royal orders on the Mexican mint for 10 million piastres, half of the total Ouvrard had received in December 1804, neither Ouvrard or Barbé-Marbois had any way to send the orders securely to Mexico and then to receive the specie in return. Briefly, Barbé-Marbois may have thought of Labouchere. In his letter to Napoleon of 22 September 1805, when Napoleon had just reversed course to march his army against Austria and

[3] Branda, Ch. XVIII—"La Crise de 1805."

Russia rather than invade England, Barbé-Marbois pleaded that he had scoured all of Europe for coins to pay the French soldiers. He had even thought for a moment to try drawing bills on London. But, he explained, he had refrained once he found how high the expense would be.[4] Later, it would turn out that Mollien, Barbé-Marbois's successor as Minister of the Treasury, would not be reluctant to use Labouchere's American connections to import the Mexican coins to France even as those connections were winding up in 1807.[5]

Nevertheless, after lambasting Barbé-Marbois for failing to supply him the specie needed to keep his soldiers from deserting, Napoleon diverted his forces from the coast of France to send them marching toward Vienna through various German states. Along the way, he was able to supply his troops as usual by pillaging much as he had in his earlier campaigns in Italy. Now considered one of Napoleon's most brilliant military successes, his victory over the Austrian army at Austerlitz on December 2, 1805, may have been initiated by Barbé-Marbois's failure to supply payments to the French troops billeted at Boulogne. Flushed with his historic victory at Austerlitz, Napoleon took his time to return to Paris from Vienna. When he arrived in late January 1806, he found his financial system in complete disarray.

Who was to blame? Historians ever since blame, of course, Napoleon, who had refused to raise new taxes or to float a new loan as he set off for Boulogne. True, it was a brilliant military feat to turn his entire army away from the coast and march toward Vienna by stages. But, part of the motive for this turnabout was the failure of the man he had put in charge of supplying funds to pay his troops, namely Barbé-Marbois. Barbé-Marbois's failure, in turn, was due to Spain's failure to make its promised payments to Paris. The *Négociants Réunis* had provided funds to Barbé-Marbois, however, while counting on payments from Spain, thanks to the interventions of their lead merchant, Gabriel-Julien Ouvrard, into Spain in late 1804. Ouvrard's mission had been precisely to arrange ways for Spain to make its agreed remittances monthly to France.

[4] Letter of Barbé-Marbois to Napoleon, 16 September 1805, AN, AFIV 1082, as cited in Branda, fns. 544–545.

[5] Nolte, Ch. VI, describes how he exchanged some of the bills given him by Parish in Philadelphia for a single drawn to his order in Havana—a bill for 945,000 dollars on the viceroy of Mexico.

On arrival, however, Ouvrard found the situation in Spain to be as bad as the Spanish authorities had claimed. Spain required immediate assistance to feed its own troops and urban populations, much less provide subsidies to French troops. Using his network of grain merchants in France to supply Spain's temporary needs, Ouvrard wrangled in exchange a monopoly of trade with Spain's American colonies. Dated December 26, 1804, the contract included requisitions on the Mexican mint for coins to an extent of the obligations now owed by Charles IV to Ouvrard, namely 20 million piastres. Converted to francs at the going rate in Paris, this amounted to 100 million francs, nearly double the amount gained by France in its deal with the United States from offloading the Louisiana Territory.

Clearly, this tribute by Spain, as arranged by Ouvrard with the help of Godoy's influence with Charles IV, was much more valuable to Barbé-Marbois than the arrangements he had already made with Labouchere for paying off the Louisiana Purchase in April 1804. The only problem, given the declaration of war between Spain and Britain, and British control of the Atlantic sea lanes, was how to get the Mexican silver to either Spain or France. Spain had agreed to pay monthly installments to Napoleon by a treaty signed in October 1803 but could not receive the Mexican silver even on its own account. Ouvrard, knowing how cleverly Labouchere had managed to use his credits on Russian bonds to provide payment on account of the Louisiana purchase, knew that the cutouts of American neutral shipping might provide the means to ship Mexican coins to European ports.

Accordingly, Ouvrard had approached Labouchere and John Williams Hope in Amsterdam to make a deal in May 1805. Ouvrard turned over his remaining obligations on the Mexican authorities to Hope & Co. in Amsterdam in exchange for their commitment, after they had cashed the obligations with the Mexican viceroy, to ship the silver or Mexican goods back to Europe using American neutral ships. By the account in Nolte, Labouchere and John Williams Hope were initially dubious, but when convinced that Ouvrard's obligations were valid on the Mexican mint, they signed a contract insisting on complete control of the subsequent arrangements for settlement of the contract.[6] Not mentioned by Nolte or Ouvrard, but surely relevant to the decision by Labouchere and John

[6] Nolte, Ch. IV, "The Mexican Business of Messrs. Hope & Co."

Williams Hope was their disappointment with having to share more of the gains from the sales of the Louisiana bonds with their Dutch partners than they had anticipated.

It would take time, of course, for suitable arrangements to be made, in cooperation with the American mercantile shipping interests as well as with the house of Baring. Indeed, the first sign of a plan by Barings is dated 7 October 1805.[7] Only then, after Napoleon had departed Paris to begin his reputed assault on England, and as Nelson was about to destroy the combined French and Spanish fleet at the battle of Trafalgar, did Sir Francis Baring begin to take Labouchere's plan seriously. The marginal notes at the head of the Baring Archive file read, "Communications to D. P., 7 October 1805; speculations at that time before we even applied to; papers prepared by ourselves when the business first began with Mr. Pitt."[8]

D. P., most likely, was "Daniel Parker."[9] A year earlier, in the winter of 1803, Parker had already proposed, in company with Robert L. Livingston (the son-in-law of the American minister to France, Robert R. Livingston), the same idea—use American neutral shipping to take on Mexican piastres in Vera Cruz with other cargo to send to Hamburg. Their profits then would have derived from selling the specie at a higher price in French francs than they would pay for them in Mexico.[10] It appears that the plan Labouchere sent to Sir Francis via Alexander was very similar, but no longer included either Parker or Livingston.

The problem now was that Spain had declared war on England (December 12, 1804), which meant that shipments of Mexican silver, even in ships flying neutral colors, could be confiscated. Further, the Royal Navy, especially after Nelson's victory at Trafalgar over the combined Spanish and French fleets, was in control of the sea lanes of the Caribbean. So, the Mexican silver plan of Hope & Baring now needed

[7] Baring Archive, NP1.B8.1.1.

[8] Baring Archive, NP1.B8.1.2.

[9] "D. P." could refer to David Parish, who directed the operation in the United States, but Labouchere had been aware of the possibility of acquiring Mexican silver from Parker before he hired Parish (Buist, p. 290).

[10] Fugier, vol. 1, pp. 265–267. Their proposal in the winter of 1803, while Ouvrard was in Spain making his arrangement, had been to ship 15 million piastres to Hamburg, Amsterdam, and Paris, for payment of 57 million francs in four equal installments. Talleyrand was enthusiastic, but Godoy preferred dealing with Ouvrard at the time.

legal protection of cargoes from confiscation by British warships or privateers. The task of Sir Francis Baring, therefore, was to persuade William Pitt to authorize letters of protection for the American ships entrusted with the Mexican silver. The many drafts of such documents take up several folios in the Baring archive and cover all sorts of possible forms in which the piastres could be transported. Possibilities included tropical goods for sale in Europe and letters of exchange on various destinations, all designed to give the agents on board the ship captured by a British frigate or privateer the greatest possible latitude to avoid seizure of their cargo, whether Mexican silver or goods.

Given that Pitt had returned to office only in May 1804 after war had been declared, first against France, and then against Spain as France's ally, and, further, that Pitt had to deal with the frustration of his plans to create a Third Coalition comprising Austria, Prussia, and Russia—the result of Napoleon's stunning defeat of the Prussian and Russian forces at Austerlitz in December 1805—it has puzzled historians ever since just why Pitt eventually assented to Sir Francis's request for the licenses. It is possible that Pitt was unaware of the agreed division of the Mexican silver between London and Amsterdam, a division that Sir Francis made clear at the outset in his letter to Labouchere would be 50/50 between the two houses of Baring and Hope. Sir Francis was taking no chances that a similar conflict over the division of spoils that had occurred after the finance of the Louisiana purchase would take place at the end of this new adventure. It may also be that Pitt was persuaded that Baring's share of the silver could be put to good use in part for Wellington's expedition to Portugal as well as in part for the East India Company's need for silver for its trade with China. Probably, Pitt would be assured that other steps could be taken to avoid any remaining Mexican silver from finding its way to Napoleon's troops in France or Iberia. The British frigates sent to anchor offshore from Vera Cruz clearly established control over the formally authorized shipments of Mexican silver and monopolized the trade while they were present.

A final term of the arrangement between Baring and Hope (at this stage, really between Alexander and Pierre Cesar as the two active principals), was to supply 1½ million piastres in four American ships of 300 to 400 tons each, to be carried from Louisiana to Canton. They would have licenses to protect them from British cruisers. "The same anticipation of 20% to be paid down on producing the licenses on your side, & the remainder to be paid by drafts on the E. I. Company at six months, &

half at twelve months at sight."[11] Further notes deal with the arrangement to take Mexican silver on board British frigates of the Royal Navy. In that case, receipts for the silver were to be signed in quadruplicate by the captains in the presence of a known representative of Hope & Baring (who turned out to be Charles Baring, youngest brother of Alexander).

While these details were being worked out between Sir Francis and Pitt the Younger, and between Alexander and Pierre Cesar, Labouchere had already dispatched three agents to the shores of North America to carry out Ouvrard's scheme. Already in Spring 1804, he had summoned Vincent Nolte from his cousin's firm in Nantes to Amsterdam in order to serve as Hope & Co.'s agent in New Orleans. He then sent him off to America in early July 1805, after signing the contract with Ouvrard. In the meantime, Labouchere persuaded David Parish to leave behind his firm in Antwerp to oversee operations in Philadelphia. Nolte states that Barings had thought of Samuel Labouchere, Pierre Cesar's younger brother, to be the Philadelphia resident, but Pierre Cesar knew that Parish had the great advantage of a personal relationship with Talleyrand. They had met during Talleyrand's sojourn in Hamburg back in 1796, but the relationship was reinforced during Talleyrand's visit to Antwerp with Napoleon in early 1803.

Finally, Armand Pierre Lestapis, the clerk in the House of Hope in Amsterdam responsible for its Spanish business, was picked to be the agent in Vera Cruz.[12] Lestapis had previously been in the service of a Spanish merchant in Santander, where he had come into possession of the birth certificate of another employee of that house, José Gabriel de Villanueva, whose identity he could assume in Vera Cruz. These three agents were sent off to their respective ports in the first half of 1806, bearing not only the Spanish *libranzas* (orders of payment) to acquire silver from the Mexican mint but also the British licenses designed to protect the cargoes of American ships from seizure by British cruisers.

Meanwhile, Napoleon had returned from his triumph in Austerlitz to Paris in late January 1806. There, he found his Treasury, overseen by Barbé-Marbois, at the end of its resources thanks to the *Négociants-Réunis*, led by Ouvrard, unable to pay the Treasury at least 70 million francs. Naturally, Napoleon focused blame on Barbé-Marbois and the

[11] Baring Archive, NP1.B8.2.2.

[12] Nolte, Ch. IV, "The Mexican Business of Messrs. Hope & Co."

Négociants-Réunis for letting this happen while he had been fully occupied with defeating the combined armies of Prussia and Austria. The loss of the combined fleets of France and Spain at Trafalgar (October 21, 1805), of course, had eliminated the flow of Mexican silver and the possibility of Spain paying its debts to either France or Dutch investors.

Nevertheless, immediately upon his return to Paris the night of January 26, 1806, Napoleon called a meeting of his Council of State the next morning. The purpose was to humiliate Barbé-Marbois in front of his chief ministers and to proclaim that he would imprison the chief partners of the *Négociants Réunis* and seize their assets until they had paid the full 70 million francs to the Treasury, and, if need be, invade Spain to seize the Mexican silver by force. Barbé-Marbois began the meeting by calmly reviewing the events that had created the financial crisis in Paris during Napoleon's campaign in 1805. When he came to the part where he explained why he had loaned Desprez 50 million francs to enable him to continue supplying the armed forces, Napoleon exploded. He was outraged that instead of receiving a subsidy from Spain, his Treasurer, in an act of sheer stupidity, had instead subsidized Spain! Barbé-Marbois protested meekly, that, surely, Napoleon did not think he was a robber? Napoleon replied, as reported in the memoirs of Mollien, "No, but I would have preferred that one hundred times, as cupidity has its limits but stupidity none!"[13] Whereupon, Napoleon publicly dismissed Barbé-Marbois from office, banishing him to his recently purchased estate in Normandy.

Ten days later, Napoleon finally called the members of the *Négociants Réunis* on the carpet to carry out his earlier threats. He raised their debt to 141.5 million francs in 1807,[14] while beginning his preparations to employ military force on Spain and Portugal in 1808 and calling on Nicolas-François Mollien to be his new minister of the Treasury in place of the disgraced Barbé-Marbois. Mollien's efforts to reorganize Napoleon's public finances succeeded sufficiently well to be maintained for the remainder of Napoleon's rule, including even the 100 days of the return from exile in Elba. Mollien had proven his value to Napoleon previously as director of the *Caisse d'amortissement*, the equivalent of the

[13] Branda, Kindle loc. 6518, Napoleon's "cinglante réplique," "Je le préférerais cent fois, la friponnerie a des bornes, la bêtise n'en a point."

[14] Branda, "Récapitulatif des valeurs employeés pour couvrir les dettes des Négociants réunis," Kindle loc. 6564.

sinking fund that had been proven so useful to William Pitt's financial regime in England (and which was being used successfully as well in the United States by Secretary of the Treasury Albert Gallatin).

In his new position, Mollien instituted reforms that, no doubt, Barbé-Marbois would have acceded to and welcomed, but did not have the mature experience with French and British finance, as well as industrial finance, that Mollien brought to the table. Mollien began by maintaining even closer oversight of the deliberations and actions of the Banque de France than Barbé-Marbois had tried but failed to achieve. (In the case of the *Négociants réunis*, for example, he had been misled about the Banque's lending by his clerk, Roger.[15]) Most importantly, however, Mollien imposed military-like controls over the regional tax collectors scattered throughout France, and now the French Empire, as well as tightening his oversight of both the Banque de France and the *Caisse d'Amortissement*. In addition, Mollien replaced the previously fragmented system of tax collection by establishing two new financial agencies directly under his supervision: the *Caisse de Service* and the *Cour de Comptes*.

The *Caisse de Service* replaced the previous system of departmental tax collectors, *receveurs générales,* who were responsible for the annual amount of taxes collected locally to be remitted to Paris. They co-existed with departmental offices, *payeurs générales,* who were responsible for covering the local government expenses. In the typical case, especially when Napoleon was mobilizing his troops somewhere in the Empire, the Treasury in Paris needed funds immediately, which it had to borrow from the various collectors against the anticipated tax revenues to be delivered at the end of the year (or next year, or the next). The collectors, for their service, charged remunerative rates of interest to the central Treasury. Barbé-Marbois had complained constantly to Napoleon about the high rates of interest he felt forced to pay the local *receveurs générales* and counted it a triumph whenever he could negotiate a lower rate to pay against the eventual receipts.

Mollien's *Caisse de Service*, instead, instituted a system of double-entry accounting for each *receveur* and each *payeur*, each of whom now had to operate within the new institution. In addition to consolidating central control over each tax collector, Mollien's system allowed easy movement of funds from one locality in France with a surplus of funds on hand to

[15] Deviosse, p. 397, "Roger a touché un million pour témoigner de la solvabilité et de la bonne foi du codirecteur des Négociants réunis."

another with a temporary deficit. This innovation eliminated the costly transfer of funds to Paris and back to wherever the troops needed to be paid. In addition, it eventually allowed the *Caisse de Service* to become effectively a branch banking system within the ever-expanding French empire.[16] Thanks to the introduction of double-entry accounting in each departmental office of the *Caisse de Service*, individual tax collectors could lend locally or beyond on their own accounts, but monitored by Mollien's officers and by the restored *Cour de Comptes,* which was charged with auditing the accounts submitted regularly by each local authority.

On the recommendation of Barbé-Marbois's long-time friend and mentor, the one-time Third Consul with Napoleon, Charles-François LeBrun, who had risen to be Arch-Treasurer of Napoleon's Empire in 1804, Napoleon appointed Barbé-Marbois to be the initial governor of the *Cour de Comptes,* starting on September 28, 1807. Mollien also expressed his strong approval of this appointment to head a crucial agency for implementing Mollien's reforms effectively. Barbé-Marbois's continued demonstrations of his devotion and loyalty to Napoleon also helped restore him to favor. But it was his probity and diligence in carrying out the duties of auditing rigorously thereafter that maintained him in office for the next several decades. Only during the 100 days of Napoleon's attempted return to power in 1815 was he removed from office, largely due to his new commitment to bring order to the finances of the restored Bourbon king, Louis XVIII while making Louis a constitutional monarch, at long last. Essentially, Barbé-Marbois became the chief auditor of the public finances of Napoleon's empire, while Mollien reorganized them to ensure that the crisis of 1805 could not reoccur.[17]

It is amazing, in retrospect, that Mollien's introduction of double-entry accounting was an innovation for French public finances, the advantages of which had long been experienced in the public finances of various city-states in Europe as well as the kingdom of Naples, not to mention the newly formed United States of America, but such was the laggardly pace of effective financial innovations in France under Napoleon's dictatorial rule. Nevertheless, Mollien's three innovations

[16] Branda, Ch. XIX, "Un nouveau depart," extols Mollien's reforms, many of which have persisted to the present day in France.

[17] Branda, Ch. XIX, "Un nouveau depart."

combined to allow continued finance of Napoleon's increasingly expensive wars. Pierre Branda estimates, for example, that the use of the regional offices of the *Caisse de services* to facilitate payments among private merchants created a floating debt, which the state could use for its own purposes and which rose to 80 million francs annually under the Empire.[18]

Mollien also made the Banque de France more effective as a source of support for Napoleon's finances, by extending its charter for another 25 years, doubling its capital stock, and replacing its governing board, previously elected by the shareholders, with a governor and two sub-governors all appointed by Napoleon. Now very much under the control of the imperial government, the Banque gradually recovered from the crisis of 1805 to help finance Napoleon's continued wars, especially in 1812. Branda makes the point, however, that even then the Banque kept prudent control over the issue of bank notes, an effort that Mollien also supported by his efforts to recoin the mass of outstanding coinage from prerevolutionary times into the new Napoleonic *franc germinal*, and its various denominations.[19]

More and more, however, Napoleonic finance came at the expense of the satellite kingdoms, especially those put under the rule of one of Napoleon's family members. The exception, however, proved to be Spain. As Ouvrard had cautioned Napoleon in 1806, it proved impossible to extract Mexican silver from Spain by military force. Even the 118,000 troops he employed to invade the country in 1808 to install his brother, Joseph Bonaparte, as king could not manage to make Spain pay the debt still on the books of the French Treasury under Mollien. It was left to Mollien to retrieve the silver coins from the Mexican mint by trying to cash in the royal orders that Ouvrard had sent to Barbé-Marbois early in 1805. This meant using Labouchere and his network of agents now scattered across the North Atlantic.

Vincent Nolte, the agent that Labouchere had sent to New Orleans, had ended his tour of duty there when David Parish had found it more

[18] Branda, Ibid., Kindle loc. 6736. This exceeded annually the total received from the sale of Louisiana over the course of two years, as described above.

[19] Branda, Ibid., Kindle loc. 6859. The contrast with the Bank of England's increasing note issue and the rise of country bank notes during the height of the following war years are highlighted by Bordo and White (1991).

advantageous to work with the Oliver brothers and their fleet of fast-sailing ships from Baltimore or Philadelphia.[20] But Parish had another task for Nolte. He had received from Labouchere a packet of 105 separate drafts drawn by the Spanish Minister of Finance on the Consolidation Fund in Havana for a total of 700,000 piastres. These were among the documents that Napoleon had seized from Ouvrard and handed over to Mollien to see if he could cash them. Earlier, Mollien had sent them to the Spanish Ambassador in Philadelphia, who found no American merchants willing to take the risk of carrying them to Havana. Mollien then fell back on the services of Hope & Co. in Amsterdam, perhaps because some of the previous drafts that Ouvrard had put at the disposal of Hope & Co. had been cashed in with some returns to the French Treasury. These additional drafts, however, were as authentic as the original documents Ouvrard had confided to Hope & Co., but were drawn on the funds in Havana, not in Mexico. Nolte describes in vivid detail his success in getting the drafts exchanged in Havana for a single draft on the Mexican mint for the silver, netting, he claimed, a profit of nearly one million francs for Hope & Co. (net of the various bribes he paid to the Spanish officials in Havana).[21]

Nolte's adventure, however, was only a small part of the total enterprise undertaken by Hope & Co., according to his account. After his eventual return to Philadelphia, Jefferson's Embargo, imposed at the end of 1807, put an apparent end to the American role in the Mexican scheme. Nolte then spent nearly two years in Philadelphia before returning to Europe. His time was employed mainly in transcribing the various accounts of Parish for settling his partnership with Barings and Hope & Co. This was also when Parish became more interested in his land speculations in northern New York state, which became the focus of his entrepreneurial energies.[22] Upon his return to Europe, Nolte presented Parish's accounts

[20] Cf. Bruchey, Ch. VI, "Spanish Specie and South American Markets," describes how the Olivers developed their brief, but profitable, relationship with David Parish.

[21] Nolte, p. 124.

[22] The town of Parishville, New York remains as testimony to his commitment to American settlement. Located on land Parish bought from Gouverneur Morris in 1808, who had claimed the territory previously occupied by the Iroquois nations, but ceded to the United States after 1783. Negotiations for the Treaty of Fort Stanwix (1784) were actually witnessed by Barbé-Marbois at the end of his tour of duty in America (Deviosse, pp. 112–115).

to both Alexander Baring and Pierre Cesar, and in his autobiography asserts that the enterprise must have cleared at least 33 million Spanish piastres (over double the $15 millions of American bonds issued to pay for the Louisiana Purchase).

The drain of Mexican silver abroad, however, did not cease with the end of the Hope & Baring operation. A competing firm, Gordon & Murphy, also with headquarters in London, but also with family-affiliated merchants present in Philadelphia, Vera Cruz, and Cadiz also had documents drawn upon the Viceroy of Mexico by royal Spanish officials. Gordon & Murphy's documents, however, were drawn by Spanish officials who had opposed the contracts made between Carlos IV and Ouvrard in 1804. For a brief period in 1807 Gordon & Murphy's ships competed with the Olivers' ships for the Mexican business. When the Spanish revolt against Joseph Bonaparte broke out in 1808, however, Gordon & Murphy enjoyed the continued permission of the British government to extract increasing amounts of silver from Mexico. Gordon & Murphy's documents rested now on the authority of the Regency officials resisting Napoleon. Moreover, with the Gordon & Murphy operations, the silver made its way almost entirely to the benefit of the British, not the French, although some may have ended in the United States as well.

As Mexican authorities became more responsive to demands made by the Spanish officials remaining loyal to the Bourbon monarch, now Ferdinand VII, the silver exported by the ships of Gordon & Murphy, or by the frigates of the British or Spanish navy, came to London or Cadiz and thence to Wellington's troops in the Iberian peninsula or to Spanish rebel forces in Andalusia.[23] In the critical period of 1808–1811, when Spanish patriots were supported by the British navy in Cadiz and Andalusia, Marichal estimates that official remittances to Spain from Mexico amounted to 24 million silver pesos, carried mainly by British or Spanish warships.[24] These shipments nearly equaled the almost 28.5 million pesos of promissory notes that the *Caja de Consolidación* in Madrid had given Hope & Co. to be cashed at Vera Cruz (Marichal, p. 288). Marichal's point is that the continued extraction of resources from the Spanish Empire, especially from Mexico, eventually led to

[23] Jimenez Codinach, Ch. VI, "La Casa de Gordon y Murphy: Un Estudio de Caso."

[24] Marichal, p. 234 and Table 4.

bankruptcy of both Spain and Mexico. In the process, however, trade was lubricated for both British and American merchants, with the backing of Mexican silver.

Moreover, Baring & Hope clearly made a good deal of money from their role in the extraction of Mexican silver by order of Spanish authorities. Nolte, who had made up the accounts of David Parish for the final reckoning with Alexander Baring in London and Pierre Cesar Labouchere in Amsterdam, estimated that "the amount of profit remaining in this business was not less than the heavy sum of £778,750 sterling."[25] In addition, a further sum of £83,500 was set aside in case an ongoing lawsuit being waged against David Parish in Philadelphia by a purported Spanish agent of Charles IV, "a certain Sarmiento," should succeed. On the advice of Henry Hope, however, this sum was added to the total profits to be divided, making a grand total of £862,500. Note that the Mexican silver affair, which followed the conclusion of the financing of the Louisiana Purchase, far exceeded the total profits calculated for the Louisiana Purchase—£ 358,350 (see Appendix F). True, this amount comes from Nolte's account, written many years later, but Nolte got the figures from Parish, and he had spent months earlier transcribing Parish's accounts for delivery to Baring and Hope. Moreover, Nolte goes on in his account to state:

> In connection with this business there existed, in the hands of Messrs. Hope, a separate book account, which the uninitiated of the office had never been permitted to see. In computing this profit, no reference is made to the gain which flowed to the Messrs. Baring and Hope alone, without the participation of Parish upon the millions of Spanish dollars which were shipped at Vera Cruz, in the English frigates, and brought by them direct to London. Nor must we leave out of sight the great advantages secured by commissions on the sale of the numerous cargoes sent on American account to Amsterdam, Rotterdam, Antwerp, and Hamburgh (later Toenningen). According to the instructions given to Parish, the cargoes destined for Hamburgh were to have been sent to the Messrs. Matthieson & Sillem, Hope's own correspondent, but he [Parish] dispatched them to the house of his brother.
>
> [Nolte, p. 173]

[25] Nolte, p. 172.

The sums gained remain uncertain but were certainly far beyond those gained by the operation of the Louisiana Purchase. Some evidence of their value shows up in the account by Buist of the ease with which Hope & Co., on behalf of Russia, paid off a loan made by the Genoese firm of Regny & Co. in February 1809. "[I]n the end, Hope & Co. were obliged to send rixdollars [the Dutch silver trade coin], Mexican piastres, and bars of silver to cover the deficit."[26] The Russian loans managed by Hope & Co. on behalf of their clients in Amsterdam were to preoccupy Labouchere over the next two years. Indeed, the full impact of Napoleon's intensified Continental Blockade in 1810, which reinforced the trade embargoes imposed by Jefferson at the end of 1807 and continued by Madison right through the War of 1812, changed everything.

Reference

Bordo, Michael and Eugene N. White. 1991. "A Tale of Two Currencies: British and French Finance during the Napoleonic Wars. *The Journal of Economic History* 51 (2): 303–316.

[26] Buist, p. 215.

CHAPTER 9

The Financial & Personal Crises of 1810–1811

The financial crises that occurred in the Atlantic economies during the years 1810–1811 took their toll on the financial and personal affairs of Alexander Baring and Pierre Cesar Labouchere. The long-time leaders of their respective firms died within six months of each other: Sir Francis Baring on September 11, 1810, and Henry Hope on February 25, 1811. Thereafter, both younger men had to deal with re-organizing their respective firms in London and Amsterdam as well as coping with the fallout of the general economic crisis for their respective clients. Both men had to re-think as well what their own roles would be in each firm as well as with each other. All this while they had to deal with the unsettled political circumstances in each country and the rise of illicit commerce to evade the disruptions created by Napoleon's Continental Blockade and the British Orders in Council. In the years 1810–1815 that witnessed the culmination of the Napoleonic Wars and the War of 1812 between the United States and the United Kingdom, both men were to play decisive roles in the ongoing transformations of war finance that had historic consequences for the future of sovereign debt internationally.

L. Neal, *The Forgotten Financiers of the Louisiana Purchase*, Palgrave Studies in the History of Finance,
https://doi.org/10.1007/978-3-031-56277-8_9

Alexander Baring

In 1804, when Sir Francis had carried out his threat to retire from business, he had stepped down as partner and handed over the leadership to his son-in-law Charles Wall and his three oldest sons: Thomas, Alexander, and Henry. In 1807, their role was formally recognized as the name of the firm was changed from Sir Francis Baring & Co. to Baring Brothers & Co. Sir Francis left much of his capital on loan to the firm, however, and was instrumental in setting up the Mexican silver business as described above (Chapter 8). As the oldest, Thomas Baring and Charles Wall maintained a larger share of the firm's capital than either Alexander or Henry. It was only after Sir Francis died in 1810 that Alexander's role became dominant. With a growing family and a wide circle of similarly minded friends within the Whig party, his talents were increasingly put to test in the political arena when the War of 1812 with the United States occurred (June 1812–December 1814).

For Alexander in London, the political arena opened for him as a wealthy supporter of the Whig party. He became a Member of Parliament in 1806 for Taunton (a classic "rotten borough" in East Devon) and he would continue to serve in the House of Commons as an ambivalent Whig until 1835, when his long-cherished dream of a peerage elevated him to the House of Lords. Even though he was in the minority in Parliament much of the time, as a member of the Board of Directors of the Bank of England from 1805 to 1817 he was central to policy-making for Great Britain during this tumultuous time. He was one of the minority votes on the eventual report of the Bullion Committee in 1810, where he supported the Governor of the Bank who had argued that it was the Continental Blockade's disruption of commercial credit rather than an excess issue of bank notes under the paper pound regime that had caused rising inflation and a falling exchange rate of the pound sterling. Further, Alexander argued that the British Orders in Council, which would eventually provoke the Madison administration to declare war on Britain in June 1812, had only made the problems created by Napoleon's Continental Blockade worse for Great Britain.

His 196-page "pamphlet," *An Inquiry into the Causes and Consequences of the Orders in Council; and an Examination of the Conduct of Great Britain toward the Neutral Commerce of America*, was not published in London until 1808. But its genesis began earlier when the British government retaliated against Napoleon's Continental Blockade of November 1806 by first imposing their own version of a blockade against French controlled parts of Europe. Alexander meant to demolish the economic arguments that James Stephens had made in his very influential book, *War in Disguise: or, the Frauds of Neutral Flags,* in 1805. Publication of his response was delayed for reasons of personal health until 1808, but it must have been an outlet for Alexander's increasing frustration with his government's policy.

The fresh Orders in Council, specifically directed against American shipping between European ports controlled by France and overseas French and Spanish possessions, mainly in the West Indies, were promulgated by the new Granville "Ministry of All Talents," that included Charles Fox, leader of the Whig party, as Foreign Secretary. The so-called Fox Blockade, issued on 16 May 1806, was merely a paper blockade, as declaring all the European ports from Brest to the Elbe to be blockaded was clearly not enforceable. In response, however, Napoleon issued his Berlin Decree of 21 November 1806, which forbade any French trade with Great Britain, its allies, or neutrals—in effect also only a paper blockade. In further response, however, Britain issued new Orders in Council in 1807, first on 6 January and then on 11 November 1807. These orders did strike effectively at neutral, especially American, shipping to France. These were the British Orders in Council that Baring attacked in his 1808 pamphlet and they were the Orders in Council that would lead America to declare war on Great Britain in June 1812.

In his 196-page "pamphlet," Alexander reiterated the now classic economic arguments in favor of free trade. But he reinforced them with empirical evidence of the benefits for Britain of resumed trade with the now-independent American states. The American imports of British goods, mainly manufactures as well as cheap cotton for clothing the plantation slaves of the South, provided a profitable outlet for British manufactures, which Americans paid for with specie they earned with their highly profitable trade with the West Indies. To continue providing Britain payments in specie to cover their trade deficit with the previous mother country, Americans had to earn a surplus in their trade with the European continent. They re-exported the bulk of the goods they imported from the West Indies, especially sugar and coffee, to the European countries that could no longer rely on their country's shipping as a result of British domination of the sea lanes across the Atlantic. British Orders in Council to cut off American exports of West Indies goods to the European continent also reduced the ability of the Americans to import

British goods, and thereby hurt the British ability to finance their war against Napoleon.

Alexander used data from Gallatin's report to Congress on foreign trade in February 1806 to document his argument with the facts. These showed that the average exports of America to the West Indies over the three years of 1802, 1803, and 1804 amounted to $15,700,000 in domestic products of America (mainly grain and lumber), and $6,550,000 in re-exports of manufactured products from other countries (mainly cotton goods made in Britain), while average imports from the West Indies as a whole amounted to $20,000,000—an export surplus of $2.25 million that was paid in specie, specie that circulated within America and paid for goods from Asia.[1]

Later reports by Gallatin showed just how damaging were the combined effects of Napoleon's Continental Blockade and the British Orders in Council on what had been a very profitable trade for the new United States of America. His "Report on the Finances" June 1809, detailed a sharp drop in imports of sugar and coffee from 1807 to 1808. Sugar imports fell from $214,172,966 in 1807 to only $86,597,447 in 1808; coffee fell from $55,593,476 to $31,448,055 in 1808. Alexander used these data to strengthen his overall argument, but as a partner in the re-organized firm of Baring Bros. with its continued role as the financial agent for the American Federal government in Europe, he knew first-hand how his British government was hurting his overseas clients. Fortunately, his brother-in-law in Amsterdam had set up a very nice alternative way for Mexican silver to end up in the hands of American shippers (as described above in Chapter 8). This also provided the means to finance the British war effort against Napoleon. American grain and Mexican silver would now support Wellington's 1808–1814 campaigns in the Iberian Peninsula against the French armies.

By this time, it might be one of Alexander's nephews, William or George, who would oversee the shipment of silver on British frigates from Vera Cruz to London or Lisbon or Oporto or Cadiz as the situation warranted. In the meantime, Alexander made sure that the semi-annual interest payments on the Louisiana bonds in the hands of the Baring firm continued, as well as the dividends on the shares of the Bank of the United States. Although sometimes payments were made to a client's

[1] Baring (1808), pp. 64–65.

account in the U.S. in order to avoid paying the renewed income tax that Addington had restored in 1804.[2]

Further, the London Stock Exchange, as part of its effort to consolidate its monopoly position in marketing the continued outpouring of new issues of British sovereign debt to finance the war effort on the Continent, responded to the financial woes of 1810 by expanding greatly its listing of possible securities that could be purchased through its facilities. Wetenhall's *The Course of the Exchange,* issued by the authority of the Stock Exchange Committee, changed dramatically with the first issue of 1811. Although it continued to appear on Tuesday and Friday of each week, as it had since 1698, the list of possible securities more than doubled in number. In addition to the quotations of British government funds, 20 in number, there were now added shares of numerous canals, docks, insurance companies, and waterworks. In the January 11, 1811 issue, an extra space was inserted below the list of "Government stocks" and above the list of "Canals" to present "American stocks." These were consistently five in number: the 3% annuity, the "Old 6%," the "New 6%," the "Louisiana 6%," and "Bank Shares."[3] In October 1811, an adjacent cell was added which gave the latest quotes for all five American stocks in New York, usually four to six weeks earlier. Presumably, the New York price quotes were useful for investors deciding whether to pay the British income tax on their dividends held in Britain or, instead, pay the exchange rate commission on dividends paid to their account in the United States.

Surprisingly, the quotes persisted for both London and New York through the War of 1812. More surprisingly, even though notice was posted in the issues of February 8 & 12, 1812 that nothing was done in Bank shares, "advices having been received that no Charter will be granted," prices for shares of the first Bank of the United States continued to appear from time to time through 1815. Presumably these were sale offers by shareholders still waiting for their redemption by the Bank of the United States. Redemption delays, as well as delays of dividend payments

[2] Baring Archive, NP1.A4.45, "American Louisiana Stock" is a printed flyer informing "The Proprietor of the Stock has the option of exchanging his Certificate for one bearing Interest quarterly, payable in America.".

[3] Unlike the British government stocks or the canals, which have columns for three days ending either Friday or Tuesday (skipping Sunday) the American stocks have only one column, presumably for Friday or Tuesday, although the heading for the column is for 3 days earlier, Wednesday or Saturday.

on the government bonds, were due to the disruption of bullion shipments, which had earlier been carried to London and Amsterdam by U. S. naval frigates, which were exempt from seizure of stopping by either British or French privateers or naval vessels, unlike the private merchant American ships that were seized in large numbers by both British and French naval forces. The puzzle is how could the reputation of American sovereign debt in the Amsterdam and London stock exchanges be sustained during the active hostilities of the War of 1812?

The answer must lie in the way the Mexican silver had financed the American trade with Europe before 1808 and then expanded to provision Wellington's forces in Portugal and the revolutionary Spanish forces based in Cadiz. When the War of 1812 was declared by the American Congress in June 1812, the commander of British naval forces based in Halifax issued explicit orders to all British vessels to continue to allow American or other vessels flying neutral flags to be unmolested if they were destined for the Iberian peninsula with provisions for British or allied forces.[4] While acting beyond the limits of his authority at the time, the Board of Trade in London confirmed Admiral Sawyer's policy at least until 1814. Until a general blockade of the American east coast was declared that year, which culminated with the sack of the nation's capital in August 1814, American exports of wheat to Spain and Portugal reached all-time highs (Table 9.1).

[4] Hitsman, pp. 49–50. "Vice-Admiral Herbert Sawyer issued... the following:

> Whereas, Mr. Andrew Allen, his Majesty's consul at Boston, has recommended to me Mr. Robert Elwell, a merchant of that place AND WELL INCLINED TOWARDS THE BRITISH INTEREST, who is desirous of sending provisions to Spain and Portugal, for the use of the allied armies in the Peninsula; and whereas I think it fit and necessary that encouragement and protection should be afforded him in so doing.

These are, therefore to require and direct all captains and commanders of his Majesty's ships and vessels of war, which may fall in with any American, or other vessel bearing a neutral flag, laded with flour, bread, corn and pease, or any other species of dried provisions, bound from America to Spain and Portugal, and having this protection on board, to suffer her to proceed without unnecessary obstruction or detention in her voyage: *Provided,* she shall appear to be steering a due course for those countries, and it being understood this is only to be in force for one voyage, and within six months from the date thereof.

Given under my hand and seal, on board his Majesty's ship Centurion, at Halifax, this fourth day of August, 1812.

Table 9.1 American flour exports to Spain and Portugal, 1808–1815

Year	*Spain*	*Portugal*
1808	30,449	41,761
1809	40,047	65,149
1810	144,436	88,696
1811	306,074	529,105
1812	381,726	557,218
1813	430,101	542,399
1814	221	4,141
1815	67,866	47,163

Source Gilpin, p. 25, table from Timothy Pitkin, *A Statistical View of the Commerce of the United States* (New Haven, 1835)

Clearly, the trans-Atlantic commercial trade, initially financed by the Mexican silver scheme described above, continued after its first stages initiated by the Barings to supply the forces opposing Napoleon's forces in Spain and Portugal. British payments for American flour and other provisions delivered in Spain or Portugal to British or allied forces were bills on London merchant houses. The interest payments on American debt held in London could continue, preserving the reputation of American sovereign debt on the London Stock Exchange. American commerce with Spain and Portugal, until cut off in 1814, also established the credibility of Alexander Baring with the future Duke of Wellington. Alexander's reputation with Wellington would become central to Baring & Hope underwriting France's occupation expenses after 1815.[5]

Pierre Cesar Labouchere

In Amsterdam, Pierre-Cesar's activities had made him the evident head of the firm, Hope & Co., even though his share of the firm's capital remained below that of John Williams Hope, the clerk of Henry Hope who had married Henry Hope's niece in England. His share of the profits from the Louisiana Purchase had been whittled down, thanks to his

[5] Even ex-President Jefferson, not known for his financial acuity, touted the usefulness of the American grain trade with the Iberian Peninsula in 1813. "Besides, if we could, by starving the English armies, oblige them to withdraw from the peninsular, it would be to send them here; and I think we had better feed them there for pay, than feed and fight them here for nothing." (Gilpin, p. 38, citing Jefferson's letter to James Ronaldson.).

previous agreement to bring on board the Dutch firms of the Willink Bros. and the De Smeth Bros. Moreover, to set up the Mexican silver scheme, he promised a share of the eventual profits from that scheme to David Parish, and it would take years, as we shall see, for that arrangement to be settled as well. While Alexander was fighting the political battles in England to put an end to the British Orders in Council that harassed American shipping as well as facilitating the seizure of their crews to be impressed into British warships, Pierre Cesar had to cope with Napoleon's increasing political control over the Dutch nation.

When Napoleon abolished the Batavian Republic and replaced it with the Kingdom of Holland on June 5, 1806, he installed his younger brother, Louis, as king. Given Pierre Cesar's troubled relations with the ruling gentry of the Batavian Republic, troubles that had induced him to bring in the Willinks and De Smeth merchant houses as part of the Louisiana Purchase arrangement back in 1803, he was able, perhaps because of his French origin, to become a reliable and trusted source of funding for King Louis Napolèon Bonaparte. In turn, Louis tried to become a beneficent ruler for the Dutch by reducing the harassment of Dutch shipping by French forces, and, with the aid of Hope & Co., by raising funds to buy off Napoleon from imposing further tributes in kind on the Dutch nation. Pierre Cesar's vaunted successes with the Portuguese Loan in 1802, a Dutch loan in 1803, and the American loan in 1804 made him a favored resource for the Napoleonic network. The chronicler of the fortunes of the Hope & Co. operation in Amsterdam in these troubled years details his efforts to salvage the fortunes of the metastasizing Napoleonic empire on the European continent all the while he maintained the firm's solvency and his personal sanity (Buist, Chs. 12–14).

For reasons that must have been partly driven by family concerns as well, Pierre Cesar announced his desire to retire from the firm in 1810. This decision came after his brief "diplomatic" mission as a personal envoy of King Louis Bonaparte, sent to London to determine if England desired peace enough to keep Holland from being absorbed into the French Empire. Despite gaining direct access to Lord Richard Wellesley, Wellington's older brother and Foreign Secretary at the time (6 December 1809–4 March 1812), Labouchere had to report back that Britain was determined to continue the war against Napoleon. Further, his father-in-law informed him that much of the British population were doing well from the war expenditures, even though his brother-in-law had recently published his cogent arguments against the British Orders in Council, which were disrupting American shipping. The failed mission had the unintended effect of outraging Napoleon, who responded by deposing his brother as king and absorbing Holland into the French empire.

Napoleon also called Labouchere to Paris to explain his travels in person. Fortunately for Pierre Cesar, he was able to prove that he had been misled by letters that appeared to him to give Napoleon's sanction to his effort.[6] Nevertheless, Pierre Cesar lost his favored position with the powers to be in Holland with the exile of Louis Bonaparte. It is also possible that Labouchere learned that he was not in line to assume the position of head of the firm in Amsterdam when he met with the two ailing heads of the houses of Baring and Hope, Sir Francis Baring and Henry Hope, during his trip to London. Sir Francis had always hoped that his son Alexander would take control of the firm in place of John Williams Hope whenever Henry Hope retired fully. In the meantime, according to Vincent Nolte, Henry Hope still held out hope that his nephew-in-law would continue to head the firm in Amsterdam, despite his disappointing performance, both as a husband to his niece and as a financier.[7] By contrast, the French authorities, and all the finance people in Amsterdam, Hamburg, Frankfort, Lisbon, Naples, and Paris naturally assumed that Labouchere was the head of the house of Hope & Co. and would approach him directly when any matter of finance arose. Otherwise, his resignation from the firm could have been a realization that once Amsterdam was part of the French Empire that the new rules of the game for international finance under the Continental Blockade would end badly for the firm (as well as for Holland).

The diplomatic venture came at a critical time in the evolution of Napoleon's empire-building on the European continent and enforcement of his Continental Blockade, both directed against the financial and naval power of Britain. Frustrated by Louis Bonaparte's failure, even as king

[6] See Labouchere (1914), who explains the denouement of his ancestor's diplomatic mission, concluding that Napoleon would have done better to have invaded Spain rather than Russia!

[7] Nolte, p. 157, recounts the distress of Henry Hope at the affair his niece in Amsterdam was carrying on with a Dutch officer of dragoons while her husband, John Williams Hope, was in London. Nolte disliked Williams Hope: "He had a repulsive exterior, and pure egotism was visible in every line and feature of his countenance." (p. 162).

of Holland, to seal off Dutch shipping in support of the Continental Blockade, Napoleon threatened to depose Louis and incorporate Holland fully into his growing empire. Only if Britain rescinded its Orders in Council that interdicted French maritime trade with its Atlantic partners could he continue to grant Holland its independence.[8] Louis, with the support of his foreign minister and his ambassador to Britain, seized on this straw to induce Pierre Cesar Labouchere to use his contacts in London to approach the British authorities. Labouchere's mission was to determine the possibility that Britain would see the continued independence of Holland as reason enough to rescind the Orders in Council, something that neither American ministers earlier (James Monroe and William Pinkney in 1806) nor Alexander as a Member of Parliament (in 1808) had been able to persuade the British government to do, even after the death of William Pitt.

It remains unclear just why Labouchere undertook such a dubious mission. He did receive a copy of a letter sent by the current French Minister of Foreign Affairs, Champagny, the Duke of Cador, to the Dutch Minister that apparently contained Napoleon's marginal notes. A copy was apparently sent by Fouché or Mollien later in April 1810 directly to Labouchere in order to assure him that he had the authority of the French government to sound out the British authorities on behalf of the Dutch cause.[9] In January 1810, Labouchere left Paris in the company of the two chief Dutch ministers, Van der Heim and Mollerus, with their vague instructions to persuade the British government that they should not let Holland fall under the growing French empire, and that they could assure the independence of Holland if they opened the door to peace negotiations by rescinding the Orders in Council that blockaded the Atlantic coast of Europe. He did, in fact, meet with Lord Wellesley in early February, who promised to raise the issue in the British Council of Ministers, but after his meeting on February 12 with Wellesley, Labouchere had to tell the Dutch officials that the British government felt compelled to maintain their blockade while Napoleon was continuing to expand his empire into Spain and Portugal.

[8] Labouchere (1913), pp. 426–427, quotes at length Napoleon's threat to his brother Louis in his letter of December 21, 1809.

[9] Labouchere (1913), pp. 428–429.

Labouchere's failed diplomatic foray also occurred as his agents sent overseas to manage the Mexican silver affair returned to Europe to settle accounts. First, Vincent Nolte arrived in Europe, visiting first the London establishments of Sir Francis Baring and then that of Henry Hope, before traveling circuitously into Amsterdam to deliver the accounts of David Parish to Labouchere. A few months later, David Parish showed up himself to confirm the settlement and to see if there were other opportunities for financing Napoleon's ventures with Spain. (By this time in 1810, Napoleon had installed his older brother, Joseph, as King of Spain, hoping he could finance the French troops stationed in Spain and Portugal, much as he had been able to do earlier in the kingdom of Naples.)

There were no such opportunities, despite various proposals made by Daniel Parker. One, with David Parish, was for Spain to raise a fresh loan from the United States by ceding to it the parts of Florida that had not been included in the Louisiana Purchase. Given the dubious legitimacy of the new Spanish government, however, this proposal found few takers among the Dutch investors. Not finding another project in Europe worthy of his talents, Parish returned to the United States, just in time to help finance the American effort in the War of 1812.[10]

In the meantime, Labouchere had sent his sons to England to be educated among the English elite as well. The logical inference is that with the deposal of King Louis of Holland in July 1810, he realized that his future, and that of his family, lay in England, not in Holland or France. Further, his share of the profits from the dealings with Ouvrard and then Mollien to extract Spanish tribute from the mints of Mexico could have enabled him to set up a country estate in England and live comfortably thereafter. Further, perhaps Alexander mollified him further by transferring $100,000 of the Louisiana bonds held by Baring Bros. in London to Pierre Cesar in October 1807 (see Appendix B). It would take a few more years for him to sort these matters out in the midst of the turmoil of European and American war finance caused by the Peninsular war and the outbreak of the War of 1812 between the United States and the United Kingdom, culminating with Napoleon's ill-fated invasion of Russia in 1812. Nevertheless, Labouchere maintained his high prestige among the financial elite of Europe. These included his partners in Holland, but

[10] The critical moment in the financing of the War of 1812 by the U.S. Treasury came in mid-1813 when a $16 million loan was jointly underwritten by David Parish, Stephen Girard, and John Jacob Astor (Perkins, *American Public Finance,* 333).

also Gabriel-Julien Ouvrard and Walter Boyd, two early innovators in the international finance of sovereign debt. He continued his American connections by sending Vincent Nolte back to New Orleans and David Parish back to Philadelphia just as the U. S. was stumbling under the Madison administration into the War of 1812 with Great Britain.

In the meantime, despite announcing that he would retire from the firm of Hope & Co. at the end of 1811, Labouchere undertook a perilous visit to St. Petersburg at the end of June, 1811. Earlier, Labouchere had sent an agent, Robert Mervil, to Russia in 1808 to secure payments on Russian bonds that had been underwritten by Hope & Company. Mervil's mission, basically, was to aid Russia's attempts to circumvent Napoleon's Continental Blockade by exporting commodities in demand by Britain or Holland. These would be shipped out in ships sailing under neutral country flags, usually American or Scandinavian. Receipts in rubles would be exchanged then for payments in Dutch guilders in Amsterdam, which could be used to meet the interest and redemption payments on Russian bonds held by Dutch investors. As Napoleon tightened control of Hamburg and British Orders in Council harassed American shipping, however, the prospects for the sale of the commodities, which included potash, iron, sailcloth, flax, hemp, and masts, diminished in 1810. The situation required Labouchere to visit St. Petersburg in person, June to December 1811.[11]

By the end of his stay in Russia in the months that followed, Labouchere had managed to dispose of the stocks of various Russian commodities that the firm had taken possession of under Mervil's agency, which enabled Hope & Co. to continue payments on the Russian bonds held in Amsterdam. We are left to infer that the continued presence of ships flying neutral flags from Sweden, Denmark, or the United States enabled him to succeed. The continued penetration of the Continental Blockade in the Baltic Sea also motivated Napoleon to organize his fatal campaign against Russia in 1812. Ironically enough, Labouchere's efforts this time helped finance a war effort against Napoleon, in contrast to his earlier successes to help tributary states finance Napoleon. Labouchere's consistent motive, however, was to maintain the prestige of Hope & Co. with Dutch investors in the variety of bonds the company had underwritten.

[11] Buist, Ch. 7, "'Les Traites du Nord", describes the efforts of Robert Mervil in 1808 and Labouchere in June to December 1811.

Labouchere's travels after his return from Russia in December 1811 became increasingly erratic. John Williams Hope remained in London while trying to wrap up the firm's affairs in Amsterdam by withdrawing funds to the full extent possible. Labouchere in Amsterdam tried to maintain the allegiance of his most trusted colleagues—Lestapis, Sillem, Coesvelt, and his brother Samuel Labouchere. His ailing wife required care at various mineral springs, sometimes in the south of France, once in Kassel, while he also had to pay attention to the financial demands of Mollien in Paris, Bethmann in Frankfurt, and the entrepreneurs in Amsterdam who were ultimately responsible for placing the various bonds that Hope & Co. had underwritten for Holland, the United States, Portugal, Spain, Russia, and Naples. All this in 1812 while Napoleon declared war on Russia and the United States declared war on Great Britain. The continued problems of Russian finances after Napoleon's defeat even led Labouchere to visit the Czar in Frankfurt in 1813, where Russian financing was also being arranged with the house of Bethmann & Co.[12] By this time, he was clearly a principal figure among the merchant bankers who would negotiate the confused finances of postwar Europe.

Labouchere's agents for the Mexican silver scheme, Parish, Nolte, and Lestapis, had all returned at various times to render accounts and observe his activities, while thinking how to make their own fortunes, following his leadership. Their future adventures took place while Napoleon invaded Russia, Wellington conquered the Iberian Peninsula and the United States declared war on Great Britain. Meanwhile, the Louisiana bonds continued to pay regular interest payments to the holders in London and Amsterdam.

References

Baring, Alexander. 1808. *An Inquiry into the Causes and Consequences of the Orders in Council; and an Examination of the Conduct of Great Britain towards the Neutral Commerce of America*. London: J. M. Richardson.

Labouchere, M. G. 1913. "Un financier diplomate au siècle dernier: Pierre-César Labouchère (1772–1839)." *Revue d'Histoire Diplomatique* 27 (3): 425–455.

———. 1914. Un financier diplomate au siècle dernier: Pierre-César Labouchère (1772–1839). *Revue d'Histoire Diplomatique* 28 (1): 74–97.

[12] Buist, pp. 257–258.

CHAPTER 10

The War of 1812 and the Financiers of the Louisiana Purchase

After settling their respective accounts with Baring and Hope in London and Amsterdam, both Vincent Nolte and David Parish visited their families in Europe in 1811. Each man considered possibilities for further adventures with war finance, given their success with the Mexican silver scheme. Labouchere, who had already decided to retire from the firm in Amsterdam and wrap up its affairs as neatly as possible, encouraged Nolte to join his younger brother's firm back in Nantes, the same firm where Nolte had begun his apprenticeship as a foreign merchant. Labouchere then tried to divert Parish into working with Daniel Parker in Paris on yet another scheme to help Joseph Bonaparte solve the ongoing financial problems of Spain. This one, which Parker had tried to involve his friend Joel Barlow in promoting while Barlow was serving as U.S. Minister to France (February 27, 1811–December 29, 1812), was to have Joseph Bonaparte sell Spain's lands in Florida to the United States. Labouchere thought Parker might persuade Parish to invest in Florida rather than continue to develop his land holdings in upstate New York, which he thought had been a major mistake by Parish.

Ultimately, however, Labouchere's well-intentioned and well-founded advice was shunned by both men. Nolte took up an offer by Alexander Baring to set up a cotton brokerage firm in New Orleans, now firmly under American rule as Louisiana became formally the 18th state of the

L. Neal, *The Forgotten Financiers of the Louisiana Purchase*, Palgrave Studies in the History of Finance,
https://doi.org/10.1007/978-3-031-56277-8_10

U.S. in April 1812. Parish, content with his share of the profits from the Mexican silver affair, much of which he had invested in the purchase of lands from Gouverneur Morris in northern New York state (much to the disapproval of both Baring and Labouchere), decided to return to America to continue developing his property that bordered the St. Lawrence River.

Despite their mutual dismay at the declaration of war in June 1812 by the American Congress shortly after each had arrived back in America, both Nolte and Parish would play critical roles in the outcome of the War of 1812. Over the course of the war, Nolte would help Andrew Jackson win the battle of New Orleans; Parish would frustrate the war plans of the Madison administration to conquer Canada before he helped underwrite a critical war loan engineered by Gallatin in 1813. Meanwhile, back in London, Alexander Baring would continue to oversee the regular payments of interest on American debt to investors in both England and Holland, despite the difficulties of receiving American credits on British merchants, much less shipments of silver by American frigates as earlier.

Vincent Nolte

Nolte's adventures in the United States highlight that New Orleans was certain to become an international port, even though Jefferson's Embargo Act of 1808, followed by Madison's Non-Importation Acts in 1809–1810, served to divert local energies into smuggling activities rather than riding the eventual boom in both cotton and slaves. Well-developed over the preceding decades of Spanish rule, coastal trading with various British, French, and American settlements scattered throughout the Caribbean basin continued under a variety of flags, including those of pirates based in the Barataria islands at the mouth of the Mississippi. The recent introduction of superior varieties of sugar cane from Haiti and Cuba and the adoption of Whitney's cotton gin had created a rapid growth in both sugar cane and cotton, which had displaced the previous reliance on indigo and tobacco as export commodities when Nolte returned to America.[1]

Illegal slave trading was especially active following the ban on foreign slave trade passed by Congress in 1808. Because payments for illegally

[1] Clark, Ch. 12.

imported slaves had to be made in specie, local commercial banks were often short of cash to redeem their bank notes, which led to repeated local banking panics. Nolte's ready access to advances from Baring & Hope enabled him to guarantee favorable prices to local growers and to stabilize the local banking community. He quickly set up a model cotton gin and packing plant to become the leading export merchant in New Orleans.

Nolte recounts with relish his various involvements with the resident grifters and land speculators who had descended on New Orleans after its purchase by the United States. To prove his worth among the leading American citizens, he had to survive two duels. As Nolte expands on the background of each duel, he assures the reader,

> so as to present a fair view of the social condition of things in New Orleans, at that period. It was not only a nest of pirates, but a place of resort for every description of schemers and scamps, against whom nearly every other community was closed.[2]

Adapting quickly to the local *mores*, Nolte engaged in his own smuggling operations, loading bales of cotton onto a fleet of small schooners. Then, by directing them to English merchant ships that would anchor at Pensacola, still nominally owned by Spain but in fact occupied by British warships, he managed to carry out a profitable exchange of his cotton bales for warm clothing that was in high demand in New Orleans as winter approached.[3] Nolte, although he embodied the mercantile ethics of Baring and Labouchere as well as enjoyed their financial support, managed to adapt readily to the sharp practices of the American merchant class in New Orleans. He also gained the respect of the resident Creole elite with his financial expertise.[4]

When General Andrew Jackson made his appearance in New Orleans in December 1814 to organize the defenses of the city against the British forces assembling in the Floridas, however, Nolte's cotton smuggling enterprise suffered a severe loss. Most severe was the destruction of

[2] Nolte, p. 198.

[3] Nolte, pp. 198–199.

[4] It's also possible that his smuggled exports of cotton to British merchant ships helped maintain U.S. Treasury payments of semi-annual interest on Louisiana bonds in this period. Until bills of exchange stopped arriving in 1814, U.S. payments were increasingly bills drawn on Liverpool merchants.

hundreds of bales of cotton destined for Nolte's next profitable venture and already loaded on the schooner *Pallas* and ready to sail. Its valuable cargo was summarily unloaded at Jackson's command so the bales could provide stable mountings for the 24 heavy cannons that Jackson had placed along the banks of the canal linking the Mississippi with Lake Borgne. This was valuable cotton, cleaned, ginned, and baled at Nolte's expense, but Jackson, on Edward Livingston's advice, refused to compensate Nolte for his loss. Further, Nolte later found that the woolen clothing he had stored for eventual sale locally had been commandeered by Jackson's Tennessee volunteers. Little wonder that his memoir is filled with acerbic remarks about the character of Andrew Jackson and his sycophants who followed Jackson afterward to the presidency (Fig. 10.1).

Nolte pays special attention to the activities of Edward Livingston, the younger brother of Robert R. Livingston, who is still memorialized in Louisiana as the key American responsible for the Louisiana Purchase (cf. Ch. 1). On Nolte's account, Edward Livingston made a nice living

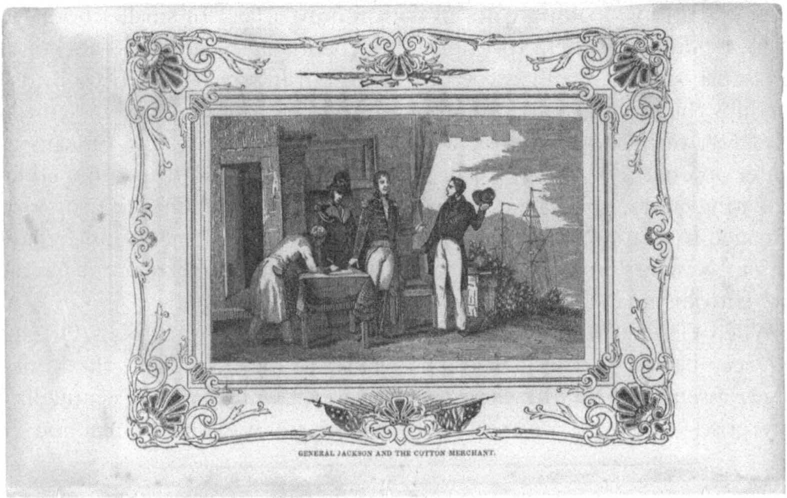

Fig. 10.1 Vincent Nolte confronts General Andrew Jackson, 1815 (*Source* Historical New Orleans Collection, http://hnoc.minisisinc.com/THNOC/SCRIPTS/MWIMAIN.DLL/128817035/5/1/217840?RECORD&UNION=Y, accessed July 8, 2022)

defending the shadier characters involved in illegal trading and even piracy based in the island chain of Barataria, often in company with his brother-in-law, Auguste Davezac. Edward Livingston had left New York in 1804 for New Orleans when a shortage of funds was discovered in the municipal accounts under his charge as Recorder for the Municipal Council. The discovery was made after he had recovered from the yellow fever epidemic in New York City and had returned to his office. Edward Livingston, to maintain his family's honor, accepted full responsibility for repaying the missing funds, $40,000. He eventually accomplished this feat, including with the accumulated interest, which proved the wisdom of his move to New Orleans. There, he capitalized on the opportunities awaiting capable American lawyers in the new territory that his older brother had worked so hard to acquire for the United States.

Shortly after arriving in New Orleans, Edward Livingston married Davezac's sister. The Davezac family had fled Haiti in 1803 after the final defeat of the French forces, going first to Jamaica, and then to New Orleans. There, they were quickly assimilated by the growing Creole population that had also been driven from Santo Domingo. Edward Livingston and Auguste Davezac thereafter laid the basis for their growing fortunes by taking their legal fees in the form of property claims. Their joint expertise in both American and French law made them especially prominent in the legal transformation of the Louisiana economy. While Nolte despised their lack of mercantile ethics, he did appreciate their usefulness to General Andrew Jackson as military advisors and for establishing Jackson's authority with the local population of newly arrived French speakers and American opportunists. Both Edward Livingston and Davezac worked well after 1815 to enable Jackson's eventual rise to the presidency of the United States in 1828 as the reputed "hero of New Orleans." Edward Livingston extolled Jackson's feats and virtues with his pen while Davezac lauded Jackson with his voice on the campaign circuits in the following election years.

More interesting for our understanding of how the United States could continue to service the Louisiana and other bonds held by Dutch and British investors during the hostilities of the War of 1812 are Nolte's descriptions of the activities of David Parish, Stephen Girard, and John Jacob Astor. These three wealthy immigrants proved to be the major underwriters of the American war debts issued throughout the War of 1812. Nolte describes how each of them managed to evade the strictures of the Embargo and Non-Importation Acts that preceded the open hostilities of June 1812 to February 1815 and thereby maintained their ability to finance the American war effort.

Parish, upon his return to Philadelphia, persuaded Gallatin that "non-importation" surely did not include the Mexican dollars that were already contracted to return in American ships from Vera Cruz. Girard and Astor subsequently convinced Gallatin that these Mexican dollars could also be part of the "ballast" that said ships could carry outbound to retrieve goods already contracted and paid for in foreign ports, China in Astor's case.[5]

All three "lords of finance" managed in various ways to keep their previous trade and finance activity in operation through the following years of trade restrictions and war. Stephen Girard, for example, lost only one ship over the period despite never taking out insurance on any of them, relying instead on the quality of his captains and crews. He also stepped into the breach left in public finances when the Bank of the United States had to close in 1811 after its charter was not renewed in 1810. By then, Girard had become the largest shareholder in the Bank, purchasing much of the shares held by Baring Bros. from the profits made on his shipments to Europe.[6]

John Jacob Astor managed to pass off a Chinese sailor as a merchant from Canton wanting to claim silver from Astor for what he was owed for previous shipments of tea to the United States. When the claim was allowed, Astor's silver financed another profitable voyage to China. Nolte comments, "A stroke of skill had been achieved, whose morality no one in the United States doubted for a moment." (p. 143).

Nolte's admiration of the smuggling ingenuity of Americans who had enjoyed the expanded trading opportunities given to neutral shipping in the years before Napoleon's Continental Blockade and the British Orders in Council was ruefully confirmed by Gallatin in his Report of the Treasury in December 1810. Gallatin alluded especially to the smuggling sieve provided by the Canadian border.

[5] Ibid., pp. 139–148.

[6] Adams (1972).

> Some additional provisions will be necessary to enforce the law on the northern frontier of the United States: amongst which may be reckoned the erection of some new collection points, particularly on the river St. Lawrence, and in the eastern part of the State of Vermont. . . . . And it must be added, that the peculiar situation of those districts will render condemnations extremely difficult, unless the obligation be imposed on persons claiming merchandise seized there to prove the same was legally imported.[7]

Gallatin must have been referring to David Parish's extensive land holdings in northern New York State, which bordered the St. Lawrence River. As the historian Alan Taylor notes, "The smuggling doubly damaged the American war effort, for while supplying the enemy, the diverted supplies increased the cost of feeding American troops, a grave concern given the financial distress of the national government."[8]

David Parish

The major town in Parish's holdings, Ogdensburg, had been established originally by the early French fur traders on the southern banks of the St. Lawrence River and lay directly across from the town of Prescott on the Canadian bank. Both towns provided waystations for shippers navigating the river between Lake Ontario and the rapids downstream above Montreal. Trade was active between both towns well before the War of 1812, and continued amicably until near the end of the war in late 1814. From the military perspective of the U.S. government under the leadership of the Virginia Dynasty (President James Madison, Secretary of State James Monroe, both keeping in close touch with former President Thomas Jefferson), Ogdensburg was precisely the strategic place from which to attack Canada. "American troops might have commanded the river by erecting batteries of cannon along their shore and by filling the river with gunboats. Better still, they could have crossed the river to seize and fortify the key Upper Canadian river town of Prescott."[9] Instead, the Madison cabinet dispersed their limited, under-paid, and under-equipped

[7] Report by Mr. Gallatin on the Finances, December 10, 1810, p. 425.

[8] Taylor (2010, p. 291).

[9] Alan Taylor (2012, p. 269). His Ch. 10, "Northern Lights," argues at length that David Parish was singly responsible for this misplaced military strategy.

forces, mostly state militia or short-term volunteers, over three widely separated sites along the 600 mile border between Upper Canada and the U.S. territory. A three-pronged attack at Detroit, Niagara, and Lake Champlain ended with disastrous results at all three sites in the first year of the war.[10]

Alan Taylor explains that "A savvy British officer, who had served at Prescott, hinted that the Madison administration kept troops away from the valley to appease 'the private interests of a very influential individual in the States.' Unnamed in the officer's account, that 'very influential individual' was David Parish."[11] Taylor adds, "By loaning millions of dollars to the Madison administration, Parish procured a tacit understanding that the government would keep its troops away from Ogdensburg. Neutrality in the St. Lawrence Valley best protected his property, but it compromised the war effort that his loan money kept barely afloat."[12]

That loan, jointly underwritten by David Parish, Stephen Girard, and John Jacob Astor on April 7, 1813 in Philadelphia at a meeting with Gallatin for that purpose, was for $16,000,000. On one account,

> whereby Parish and Girard jointly took $7,055,800 of the 6 per cent stock at 88, while Astor took $2,056,000 of it at the same figure. By the efforts of the German-born Parish and Astor, the French-born Girard, and the Swiss-born Gallatin, accordingly, the greatest financial transaction during the War of 1812 was concluded, and the United States was saved from insolvency.[13]

The enthusiasm of the historians who wrote that paean was not shared by the historian Alan Taylor, who focused on the efforts made by Parish to keep his settlements neutral—free from British invasion or American military presence.[14]

[10] All accounts agree on this, regardless of their overall perspective. Cf. Borneman, Hickey, Hitsman, Morales, as well as Taylor.

[11] Ibid., p. 269.

[12] Ibid., p. 270.

[13] Walters and Walters (1944, p. 161).

[14] McCraw (2012), pp. 301–302, makes much of the observation that all six men involved in the agreement with the private syndicate to underwrite the $16 million loans were foreigners who had immigrated to the United States: Astor, Girard, and Parish for the syndicate and Campbell, Dallas, and Gallatin who served as Secretaries of the Treasury during the War of 1812. He doesn't mention that the three private financiers

Similarly, Nolte discounted Parish's financial aid to the United States. He comments that Parish found it difficult to lay off his share of the loan, and despaired that the merchants he helped to enrich during the height of the Mexican silver scheme had closed their books to him. Only Girard, grudgingly, loaned him a portion of the funds borrowed. At one point, Parish even sent a batch of the bills he had underwritten to Alexander Baring, thinking they could find buyers in London. Naturally, Alexander sent them back, noting that the two countries were at war![15] A later proposal by Parish, concocted in partnership with Girard, was for Parish to return to Europe with bonds to sell in Antwerp or Amsterdam. That scheme did not come to fruition, but the turn of events that led to hopes for peace based on serious negotiations in Ghent between the British negotiators and the American team led by Gallatin in late 1814 did restore the market value of the American bonds still held by Parish. As Nolte recounted in his memoirs, when asked by Alexander Baring what he thought of Parish's abilities, Nolte replied that he thought "Mr. Parish shows more ability in getting out of scrapes than in avoiding them." Alexander nodded in agreement.[16]

Alexander Baring

During the course of the War of 1812, however, Alexander Baring helped Albert Gallatin and the Madison administration get out of the fiscal scrape they had got into with their ill-advised confrontations with the British. There were other ways he could assist than in helping Parish find buyers for his bonds among Baring's clients. For example, Alexander made sure that the semi-annual interest payments due on the Louisiana bonds were covered faithfully, probably in the majority of cases by switching funds from one account to another. As the official agent of the Federal government for all payments in Europe, Baring Bros., as they were named then, paid the interest owed on debts held in Britain as well as the expenses of the American commissioners when they arrived in Europe, first in

all had substantial accounts with Baring Bros. in London and Hope & Co. in Amsterdam as well.

[15] Nolte, pp. 186–187.

[16] Nolte, p. 160.

St. Petersburg at the end of 1813, and then in London and finally in Ghent.[17] In these ways, Baring Bros. kept faith with their private clients in Britain and occupied Europe, but also with their public client—the Federal government of the United States.

Thanks to the firm's concern to maintain continuity of their contracts with existing clients, the market value of American sovereign debt, Hamilton's legacy, was sustained throughout the War of 1812. Despite the sharp decline in U.S. tariff revenues as a result of the interruption to legal trade, interest on the Louisiana bonds and earlier debts of the Federal government continued to be met. Indeed, in his later report of December 1812, when hostilities were well underway, Gallatin commented:

> It may be proper also to state, that, notwithstanding the addition thus made in the public debt ($13,100,200), and although a considerable portion has been remitted from England and brought to market in America, the public stocks, which had at first experienced a mild depression, have been for the last three months, and continue to be, at par.[18]

It was likely during the "first mild depression" in the bond prices that Gallatin authorized the purchase of $118,500.00 of Louisiana stock, which cost 98.5% of par: $116,761.17. He also managed, while preparing U.S. finances for the war, to pay off the last claims of American merchants from the Louisiana Convention, the remaining $4992.86.[19] By mid-1814, however, U.S. finances were in disarray, Congress failing to enact Gallatin's recommendations on raising property taxes. Instead, Congress merely doubled the tariff duties on the sharply reduced amount of legal trade. One must conclude that it was probably more the care taken by Baring Bros. to sustain their reputation as the leading merchant bankers in Europe than the financial reputation of the American government at the time that explains why the prices of the American bonds on the London

[17] Hidy, p. 52, notes, "Barings continued to perform their normal functions for the Federal government, including the liquidation of outstanding converted 6 per cent. Bonds, the payment of interest to holders of American bonds, and the acceptance of authorized drafts for account of the American peace commissioners from 1813 to 1815." Hidy cites successive letters by Alexander to the current Secretary of the Treasury over those years.

[18] Report by Mr. Gallatin on the Finances, December 1, 1812, p. 469.

[19] Ibid., p. 483, Tables D & E.

Stock Exchange remained remarkably high and steady throughout the period of the War of 1812, as shown in Fig. 10.2.

Indeed, reading the successive letters by Baring Bros. to the various Secretaries of the U.S. Treasury during this period,[20] one is struck, first by the repeated advice given to the U.S. Treasury officials how to maintain the marketability of their various Federal debt issues in the London market; second, by the measures taken by Baring Bros. to maintain access by the Dutch bankers of the American government, Willinks and Van Staphorst, to the semi-annual American interest payments by drawing bills on Barings; and, third, by the increasing amount of advances made to the U.S. government by their London banker, a total that came to £120,000 by the end of July 1815.[21]

Fig. 10.2 American funds on the London Stock Exchange, 1811-mid-1817 (*Source* Edward Wetenhall, *The Course of the Exchange*. 1811–1817)

[20] The bound volume, Library of Congress, MMC 2475, "Copies of Letters addressed to the Treasury department of the United States of America by Sir Francis Baring & Co."

[21] Letter from Alexander Baring to A. J. Dallas, Secretary of the Treasury, London, 26 July 1815, pp. 293–298, Ms. MMC 2475, Baring Mss., Library of Congress.

Eventually, Baring Bros. felt themselves forced to charge both interest and occasionally, commissions, on the advances they made to various creditors of the United States in Britain and Europe rather lose their access to the sovereign debt of the U.S. government. After all, the American economy would be expanding rapidly into the economic space created for American agriculture by the Louisiana Purchase. Nevertheless, the fact remains that Baring Bros. sustained the regular payment of interest on the Louisiana bonds held both in London and Amsterdam during the War of 1812. This remarkable show of confidence in the good faith of the American government to "make good" on its accumulating debt reflected, ultimately, the strength of the personal connection that had been established between Alexander Baring and Albert Gallatin, back in 1802 and again in 1803 as described above. It also must reflect the continued bond between the two men while Gallatin was in Europe negotiating terms for ending the War of 1812.

Earlier, advice to Gallatin on marketing the existing debts of the U.S. government held by clients of Baring Bros. came from Sir Francis Baring in April 1804. In a carefully worded and rewritten draft to Gallatin, Sir Francis pointed to the difficulty of transferring ownership of a particular security in Europe if the seller and buyer had to appear in person before an American consul rather than sending their agents with powers of attorney to make the transfer, as had long been the custom in England and Europe. Sir Francis added for good measure, "I think I may say without presumption that no man has exerted himself or contributed more to facilitate & to impress the minds of the publick with confidence in the good faith which is due to the American government than myself."[22] After Alexander arrived with the bulk of the 5071 certificates created at his direction in Washington, however, the London certificates began to be sent back to Philadelphia to be transferred into the names of the initial purchasers of the bonds, rather than being transferred readily among clients available in Britain. This cumbersome procedure obviously added another layer of transaction cost. Once the transfer was recorded in Washington, moreover, the new certificates came back to London for distribution to their new owners. The U.S. Treasury then billed Barings for the cost of transfer,

[22] BA, NP1.A17.8.1, "Sir Francis Baring to Albert Galatin (sic), Concerning the above act of Congress." 20 April 1804. No copy of this letter is found in the U.S. archive, however, so it either was not sent or went to Gallatin personally, rather than officially.

and Barings typically had their correspondents in Philadelphia, the firm of Willing & Francis, pay the nominal amounts.

Eventually, Barings saw a way to keep up the market for American debt in Britain despite the cumbersome transfer process insisted upon by the U.S. government. If proprietors would take their interest payments in the United States, they would avoid the British income tax, and Barings offered to take care of the foreign exchange transaction for a nominal commission. If the proprietors insisted on having payment in British pounds, however, the U.S. Treasury still had to provide funds to Barings, increasingly by bills of exchange drawn against cotton importers in Liverpool.[23]

Second, while Barings forwarded on the U.S. interest payments to their associates in Amsterdam, this was done initially by drawing bills on Amsterdam in Dutch guilders payable to the Dutch proprietors. The imposition of Napoleon's Continental Blockade, which became increasingly effective from 1807 on, however, required a change in tactics. Using the private means of communication between Barings in London and Hope & Co. in Amsterdam (letters carried by agents on fishing boats directly to the Netherlands, or circuitously to the German or French coast and then overland to Amsterdam) Barings held the American payments until Willink & Staphorst drew bills on Barings. For the interest payments on the Louisiana certificates held in Amsterdam, the proprietors could go directly to the offices of Willink & Staphorst apparently as the new system for transferring the American funds from London to Amsterdam was maintained until the fall of Napoleon in 1813.

Originally, the two houses in that city arranged as they had done traditionally to issue scrip in their own names based on the certificates they held. Their elaborate plan was described in detail for the benefit of Sir Francis and Henry Hope, as shown in Appendix E and was presented to Addington and Hawkesbury by Sir Francis to show the seriousness of the Dutch intent to finance at least $5 million of the Louisiana bonds. The elaborate printing and sub-division of the Dutch certificates, however, meant that while Baring Bros. in London would handle the original interest payments from the United States destined for the Dutch investors, it would be up to the two operations in Amsterdam to disburse the semi-annual interest payments to the certificate holders in the

[23] Perhaps drawn by Vincent Nolte in New Orleans?

Netherlands. It appears, moreover, that some of the certificate holders in Amsterdam would claim their interest payments in London. Some, apparently, even arranged to receive their interest payments in Philadelphia under the terms of a transferred stock certificate (See the example in Appendix A).

In the years immediately after the formal end of that war in February 1815 and then the end of the European war with Napoleon following June 1815, every country involved in the largest scale of military conflict to that time had to readjust its finances in order to cope with the uncertain challenges of peace-time recovery. The lessons learned by Alexander Baring and Pierre Cesar Labouchere in dealing with the financial obligations of the various belligerents over the years 1789–1815 were put to good use in the years immediately following. Their efforts would lay the basis for their individual fortunes, but they also signaled the future of international finance.

References

Adams, Donald R. Jr. 1972. "The Bank of Stephen Girard, 1812–1831." *The Journal of Economic History* 32 (4): 841–868.

McCraw, Thomas K. 2012. *The Founders and Finance: How Hamilton, Gallatin, and Other Immigrants Forged a New Economy*. Cambridge, MA: Belknap Press of Harvard University Press.

Taylor, Alan, 2010. *The Civil War of 1812: American citizens, British subjects, Irish rebels, & Indian allies*. New York: Alfred A. Knopf.

Taylor, Alan. 2012. *The Civil War of 1812: American Citizens, British Subjects, Irish Rebels, & Indian Allies*. New York: Alfred A. Knopf.

Walters, Philip G., and Raymond, Jr., 1944. "The American Career of David Parish." *The Journal of Economic History* 4 (2): 149–166.

CHAPTER 11

Lessons Learned, Applied, and Ignored

The second foreign sovereign debt after the American government securities to be listed officially on the London Stock Exchange's official price list, Edward Wetenhall's *Course of the Exchange*, was the 5% *rente* issued by the new French government. It appeared in the issue of August 20, 1816, five years after the Exchange had been listing the various American public stocks, albeit at irregular intervals. The French listing came well after the second restoration of Louis XVIII as the legitimate constitutional monarch of France following his return to Paris after Napoleon's defeat at Waterloo in June 1815.

The London market's evaluation of the French security was clearly less favorable than its opinion of the new American 7% bond. The price of the *rente* hovered between 55 and 60 percent of par, implying a yield of 9% while the American bond held at par. Even more telling was the persistent gap between the yield of the British 3% Consol and other issues. Issues of the 3% Consol had expanded enormously over the course of the successive wars with America and France (Fig. 11.1). Clearly, the French regime still had more to learn about the fundamentals of international finance if they were to compete again with the British, but that was also true of the American regime, now under the resurgent Republican party led by the Virginia Dynasty of Jefferson, Madison, and Monroe.

L. Neal, *The Forgotten Financiers of the Louisiana Purchase*, Palgrave Studies in the History of Finance,
https://doi.org/10.1007/978-3-031-56277-8_11

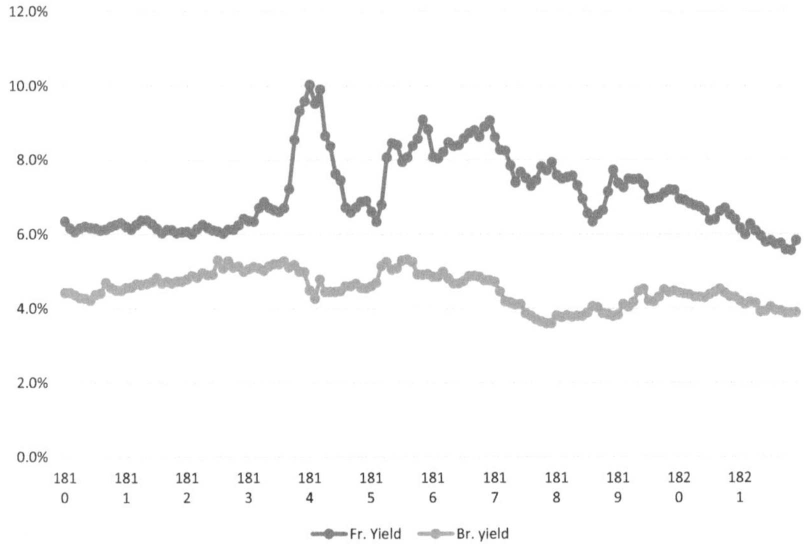

Fig. 11.1 Yields of French 5% and British 3% bonds, 1810–1821 (*Source* Wetenhall, *The Course of the Exchange*, 3% Consol, & Courtois (1877), average of French *rente* high/low prices monthly, Paris bourse)

The first lesson learned by the Americans was to restore the keystone of Hamilton's financial system, the Second Bank of the United States. Gallatin had objected to letting the First Bank of the United States fall to the wayside when its initial charter of 20 years had lapsed in 1811. Madison, who along with Jefferson had only reluctantly acquiesced to Hamilton's assumption of state debts back in 1790, continued to doubt the usefulness of Hamilton's Bank of the United States and allowed the Bank's operations to lapse when Congress failed to renew its 20-year charter in 1811. Consequently, he had no recourse to the Bank's lending power when he urged Congress to declare war against Britain in June 1812. It took the combined resources (and respective client bases) of Stephen Girard, David Parish, and John Jacob Astor to provide the financial underwriting for the War of 1812 that Alexander Baring and Pierre Cesar Labouchere had provided ten years earlier for the Louisiana Purchase. Worried whether their clients could continue to pay their subscriptions, Girard and Parish jointly presented detailed plans for a new Bank of the United States to A. J. Dallas, the Philadelphia lawyer who had replaced Gallatin as Secretary of the Treasury in 1814. Madison, after vetoing a greatly modified version of the Dallas-Girard-Parish proposal, finally approved the Second Bank of the United States on April 10, 1816. That lesson had been learned, if painfully, but not permanently, as Jackson would veto the renewal of the Second Bank's charter in 1836!

The first years of the Second Bank of the United States, however, did not persuade its opponents that it had been a mistake to end the first Bank of the United States. The determination of the re-chartered bank to force state-chartered banks to redeem their notes in specie only tended to exacerbate the existing shortage of coins. Stephen Girard, who remained on the Bank's Board of Directors despite his growing dismay at the quality of management, wrote to Alexander Baring in March 1817, hoping that he "will have induced some of your capitalists to invest in the United States Bank."[1] In fact, at the next meeting of the directors, a contract with Baring Bros. & Company was approved to obtain approximately $3,100,000 of specie, pledging as collateral more than $3,000,000 of the funded stock of the United States.[2] Later problems would arise in 1819, but rather than having been caused by the final redemption of the Louisiana bonds, they were due to the efforts of the Bank of England to build back its specie reserves so it could restore full convertibility of its bank notes as mandated by Act of Parliament in 1819. Further, Britain's eventual return to its prewar gold standard in 1821 caused additional problems and not just in the United States.[3]

The contract with Baring Bros. & Co. with the Second Bank of the United States took place at the same time that Alexander and Pierre Cesar were underwriting a series of huge loans to the French government.[4] After refusing to consider a loan at all when first approached in 1816, the two men, now formally the heads of their respective firms in London and

[1] Brown (1942), p. 144, fn. 84.

[2] Ibid., p. 145.

[3] The literature is extensive, as noted in Neal (1998), and continues with recent work in two Ph. D. dissertations: John Gent at the London School of Economics (2016) and Pamfili Antipa at the Paris School of Economics (2018).

[4] White (2001), analyzes the full sequence of loans and their consequences for the French economy.

Amsterdam, agreed to underwrite the first loan of 100 million *francs* on February 9, 1817. Eugene White summarizes the results;

> The bankers made out handsomely, selling the whole issue eventually for 108.3 m francs for a total profit of 12.7 million francs. . . . Barings and Hope quickly obtained new contracts for further debt issues to continue reparations payments. On 11 March 1817, an agreement was signed to issue another 100 m francs, followed by 115.2 m on 22 July 1817. The opposition by French bankers was tamed by including selected French houses in the new syndicates. Payment of reparations now appeared to be easy.
>
> (White, pp. 346–347)

Certainly, the finances of the French constitutional monarchy after Waterloo were in distress under the pressure of occupation by the Allied armies, so some kind of loan was required that would buy off the allied occupation forces, much as Portugal had needed to do in 1802, then to keep French forces from occupying the country. Then, it had been the endangered monarchy of Maria I that required foreign assistance. This time it was the tenuous monarchy of Louis XVIII that needed a loan orchestrated by Baring & Hope. It seemed natural to French officials and especially to Gabriel-Julien Ouvrard that Labouchere and Baring should be able to work their financial magic once again. The literature on the reconstruction loan to France that Baring and Hope jointly underwrote in 1817 is extensive, starting with Ouvrard's self-serving memoirs where he takes credit for manipulating the French officials and Alexander and Pierre Cesar into negotiations.

The research by Oosterlinck et al. (2014) makes a strong case that it was the first loan by Baring & Hope that began a convergence of the yield on French *rentes* to the benchmark yield of the British Three Per Cent Consul, as shown in Fig. 11.1.

They emphasize the correspondence between Wellington and Alexander Baring, the two primary decision-makers who, the authors argue, were critical for the success of the loan. They leave open, however, why Alexander was able at this time to have so much influence with Wellington. The role played by Baring Bros. in facilitating the American supplies to the Peninsular Army during Wellington's campaigns in 1810–1812, described above, surely was a factor. The authors also ignore the influence of Labouchere, who was a key participant in the negotiations that led to the issuance of the French bonds. While nearly half the first loan was sold in Paris, some to foreign opportunists such as David Parish and Vincent Nolte, an eighth was placed in Amsterdam through Hope & Co., and just under one-third with Baring Bros. clients in London.[5]

The materials in the Baring Archive, mentioned in passing by Kaplan (2006), and used sparingly by Greenfield (2016), highlight the central role played by Alexander in negotiating the initial loans and bringing a successful completion to the last one at the end of 1818. One enthusiastic letter to Alexander, written by the chief of police in Paris under Louis XVIII, Élie Decazes, who was effectively the head of government at the time, implores him to return to Paris, as "one hour of your conversation is worth more than a month of correspondence, and you could smooth out all the difficulties with ease!"[6] More letters were saved by Alexander, each praising his efforts in France and thanking him lavishly for his efforts at raising and marketing the series of loans.[7]

Decazes' letter in July 1818 was followed by an agreement between Hope & Baring and the Duc de Richelieu in October 1818, which amended the terms of the loan to enable France to delay issuing new *rentes* so the market price could stabilize. Vincent Nolte states, without elaboration, that Alexander's intervention in the Paris stock market was

[5] White, p. 346. "Table 3. First Reparation Loan 100 m francs." He notes that the distribution of the later loans is unknown, but the records of Hope & Company provided the placement of the first loan.

[6] BA, MS 204229/3, Letter of 6 July 1818 from Comte de Cazeres, "une heure de conversation ferait plus qu'un mois de correspondence et cette conversation pourrait suffire pour aplainer toute les difficultés et lever bien des obstacles."

[7] The papers were purchased by ING Barings in 1996. The papers form part of the papers of Sir Francis Baring's son Alexander, 1st Lord Ashburton. Alexander kept a number of his business papers at home, and they passed at his death in 1848 to his elder son William Bingham, 2nd Lord Ashburton. He died in 1864 when his widow, Louisa Lady Ashburton, inherited much of his estate at The Grange; and she took with her, along with much else, all the family papers including the business papers of 1st Lord Ashburton. Lady Louisa's only child, Mary, married in 1884 the 5th Marquess of Northampton and so, at some time, the Ashburton Papers went to Castle Ashby and remained there until 1996 as part of the Northampton Papers. In 1996 the current Lord Northampton placed the papers in auction. ING Barings purchased 'Box 7' which contained the French Reparation Loan [204228–204229] papers and a piece relating to a Russian Loan of 1820.

solely responsible for raising the price of French sovereign debt.[8] Nevertheless, Alexander's replies to some of the letters highlight his reliance upon Labouchere in Amsterdam, as well as in Paris and Aix-la-Chapelle, to deal directly with the various Parisian and German banking firms. He remarked that Labouchere would have a more difficult task than he was having in London.

Most interesting for revealing the importance of Alexander's role in London is a lengthy copy of an open letter he composed while in Paris in July 1818 to Nicholas Vansittart, then Chancellor of the Exchequer, with a copy to "His Grace," the Duke of Wellington.[9] Wellington, of course, had to convince the military leaders of the Allies—Austria, Prussia, Russia—to accept the French bonds as payments for maintaining both their troops in France and for their specific reparations. Vansittart, on his part, had serious financial difficulties in England, thanks to Parliament's repeal of the income tax, 18 March 1816. It was the income tax that provided the revenue throughout the war to keep up interest payments on the burgeoning British national debt. Further difficulties for continuing to service the huge increase in British national debt were looming as Parliament also determined, against the wishes of the Bank of England directors (including Alexander), to resume convertibility of Bank of England notes in gold at the pre-suspension rate. The Bank of England was tightening credit sharply to build back its bullion reserves. Alexander's letter, consequently, treads a fine line between the two powerful political figures as he explains how his revised contract with the French government can serve the interests of both men, Vansittart in London and Wellington in Paris.

While Alexander is responding to a communication from Vansittart, but is sharing his reply with Wellington so the Duke can add his views on the subject, Alexander frames the policy issue carefully:

> I am not quite sure that I understand the object you have in view, whether it is to realize the French stock belonging to the claimants or merely to avail yourself, for general purposes of the amount of the stock and of the English share of contributions to be settled at the Congress.

[8] Nolte, p. 275. "In No. 24" of the "Deutschen Freihafen," for 1848. See my article on "Lord Ashburton and the Baring house in London."

[9] BA, MS Item 204229.10, Paris, 2 August 1818, "Letter by AB to Nicholas Vansittart."

Alexander goes on to argue that the claimants, the individual Allied governments, take precedence over whatever other considerations were in Vansittart's mind. These could have been to cover the continued subsidies to the Allied troops occupying parts of France, or to cover the loss of revenue from the income tax, or to deal with the Bank's restrictions in view of the upcoming resumption of note convertibility. As the exact timing of realization of the claims of the Allied powers was yet to be determined at the upcoming conference in Aix-la-Chapelle (1 October 1818), it was feasible at the time to delay issuing new French bonds. That delay would stabilize the price of the existing French bonds and allow the Allies to cash the existing bonds at favorable terms for supplying their needs. Alexander's own interest was to delay the further issue of *rentes*, and force the Allies to take payment from their previous shares of the *rentes* in the meantime.

For Vansittart's immediate needs, Alexander could provide him bills of exchange at 2, 3, or 4 months, "or in any other shape to suit your purpose. These bills through the Bank would be as good as money, and I would recommend this transaction passing through Mr. Rothschild." Further, Alexander added,

> I should be afraid of engaging to convert the francs into pounds sterling at the present exchange, considering the large sum there will be to remit from hence & especially if the Bank is to be pressed to pay in specie; but on this part of the business a reasonable arrangement may be proposed which I will discuss with Mr. Rothschild. Should you wish to treat for the two operations together, the Banks & the contributions I have no objection, but as the sum will be large some time must be taken for the remittances; but I should think that six months would be sufficient and as before stated we would give you bills available at the Bank or else as when to answer your wants as they occurred.[10]

It is noteworthy that Alexander had been in England earlier to assure his re-election to Parliament before returning to Paris and then Amsterdam and, finally, to Aix-la-Chapelle for the Allied Congress. That political agreement in October 1818 arranged to remove the Allied troops from all of France while making secret arrangements among the Quadruple Alliance to enforce France to respect its new boundaries.

[10] Ibid.

Back at the home offices of Baring Bros. in London and Hope & Co. in Amsterdam, the bankers were processing payments from the United States as it began redeeming the outstanding Louisiana bonds. Part of the reason for the successful placement of the new French *rentes*, it is clear, was they served to replace the existing American bonds that had enjoyed a sustained market price during their 15-year existence. So continued the process of rolling over American sovereign debt, a process that continues to the present.[11]

The ingenuity and determination of Labouchere to establish and motivate the network of agents needed to carry out the Mexican silver scheme surely laid the basis for the ultimate success, not just of the bonds issued to finance the Louisiana Purchase, but of the American war bonds issued in the war of 1812. The central role played by Alexander and Pierre Cesar in coordinating these financial transactions across the Atlantic was duly recognized by Gabriel-Julien Ouvrard in France, Stephen Girard in Philadelphia, and by Gallatin, especially as he entered his final public role as American Ambassador to France (July 16, 1816–May 16, 1823), but also by the leading political figures of the time. Why then, has their role been so overlooked in the historiography of those tumultuous times?

The reason, perhaps, that the defining interventions of Alexander and Pierre Cesar have been ignored in the subsequent historiographies of American and French finance is that the essential elements of maintaining sovereign debt finance that they implemented successfully over the course of the finance of the Louisiana Purchase, essentially December 20, 1803 to October 1821, were fleeting, and ultimately ignored or misunderstood for the rest of the nineteenth century. This was especially the case in the United States, subject as the country has been to recurrent financial crises, which have punctuated its relentless economic growth over the following centuries. But another, perhaps more compelling, reason for the missing historiography is the departure of the main players from the scene after the completion of the Louisiana Purchase.

[11] The "present" being March-October 2023, when the Republican control of the House of Representatives threatened to default on the existing national debt of the United States for the first time in history.

References

Brown, Kenneth L. 1942. "Stephen Girard, Promoter of the Second Bank of the United States." *The Journal of Economic History* 2 (2): 125–148.

Courtois, Alphonse. 1877. *Tableaux des Cours des Principales Valeurs Négociées et Cotés aux Bourse des Effets Publics de Paris, Lyon, et Marseille du 17 Janvier 1797 (28 Nivose an V) à Nos Jours Relevés sur les Documents Officiels et Authentiques,* 3rd edn. Paris: Garnier Frères; Guillaumin & Cie.

Greenfield, Jerome. 2016. "Financing a New Order: The Payment of Reparations by Restoration France, 1817–1818. *French History* 30 (3): 376–400.

Kaplan, Herbert, 2006. *Nathan Meyer Rothschild and the creation of a dynasty: the critical years 1806–1816*. Stanford : Stanford University Press.

Neal, Larry. 1998. "The Bank of England's First Return to Gold and the Stock Market Crash of 1825." *Federal Reserve Bank of St. Louis Review* 7 (2): 53–76.

Oosterlinck, Kim, Loredana Ureche-Rangau, & Jacques-Marie Vaslin. 2014. "Baring, Wellington and the Resurrection of French Public Finances Following Waterloo." *The Journal of Economic History* 74 (4): 1072–1102.

White, Eugene N. 2001. "Making the French Pay: The Cost and Consequences of the Napoleonic Reparations." *European Review of Economic History* 5 (3): 337–365.

CHAPTER 12

Curtain Call: All the Players Should Take a Bow

François Barbé-Marbois, the "man who sold Louisiana," died in 1837, before the revolutions of 1848 ended the French monarchy, whether absolute or constitutional. His defining history of the Louisiana Purchase, initially published in French in 1829, then in English in 1830, ignored the key role played by both Alexander, who initiated the financial arrangements, and Pierre Cesar, who ensured the early payments to France. The main purpose of his history, however, was to extol the virtues of the Constitution of the United States, a worthy model for France as well and one that he had tried to implement repeatedly. His life as a devoted public servant, pledging sycophancy to whomever might be the titular ruler of France at the time, continued to be obscured in the bureaucratic routines of monitoring and auditing the public accounts of France under the constitutional monarchs, Louis XVIII, Charles X, and Louis-Philippe. Barbé-Marbois did try to reassure his American friends in the preface to his *History of Louisiana*, however, that the United States would survive the populism of Andrew Jackson who had just been elected President. He reassured his American readers that the strength of its laws, so well established under the Constitution, would carry them through. One wonders what postscript he might have added if he had written after Jackson closed the Second Bank of the United States.

L. Neal, *The Forgotten Financiers of the Louisiana Purchase*, Palgrave Studies in the History of Finance,
https://doi.org/10.1007/978-3-031-56277-8_12

Albert Gallatin, after leading the American delegation in Ghent to a successful treaty ending the War of 1812, certainly merited continuation in the administration of James Monroe as Secretary of State. Instead, he was shunted off abroad to serve, first as U.S. Ambassador to France (1816–1823) and then to the United Kingdom (1826–1827). Thereafter, he retired to private life, becoming the first president of the National Bank in the City of New York that was organized by John Jacob Astor in 1829. There he served until 1839, when he stepped down in favor of his son, James Gallatin, after assuring himself that he had provided for his family after decades of public service. Until his death in 1849, however, he became absorbed in the ethnography of Native Americans, favoring their assimilation into American culture as an alternative to forced relocation. He produced path-breaking studies of Native American linguistics and their geographical distribution throughout the new territories opened to more European immigrants as a result of the Louisiana Purchase. His other published works defended the Second Bank of the United States against President Jackson's veto and then attacked the war against Mexico by the Polk administration. Unlike his counterpart in France, he continued to feel free to express criticism of the policies in force in his adopted country when they did not measure up to the idealistic vision that had motivated his youthful migration to America.

Robert R. Livingston, after retiring from public life, returned to the life of a proper country gentleman at his estate of Clermont on the banks of the Hudson River in upstate New York. There, he could relish the sight of the regular steam-driven river boats invented by his friend, Robert Fulton, plying the river on regular schedules. He also enjoyed the handsome dividends on his investment in Fulton's enterprise, which had the monopoly privilege of steam-driven shipping on the waterways of New York. He died, however, in 1813, so it was left to his younger brother, Edward Livingston, to bring suit against the Ohio River company whose steamboat had brought the cannons down to New Orleans that Andrew Jackson could place atop the cotton bales he stole from Vincent Nolte's ship in order to become the hero of the Battle of New Orleans. Edward Livingston, one assumes, was key in assuring that the mural celebrating the Louisiana Purchase in the state capitol in Baton Rouge put only Robert R. Livingston next to Napoleon and Jefferson, and left out James Monroe.

James Monroe, dying in 1831, did manage to send Barbé-Marbois copies of several documents to add as appendixes to his history of

Louisiana, all designed to bolster Monroe's claim to fame for signing the conventions that constituted the Louisiana Purchase for the United States. Only in his memoirs does Monroe mention an emissary of the Baring firm who had informed him of the possibility of a $10 million loan to facilitate the purchase of New Orleans upon his arrival in Paris.

Later memoirs indicate that person was none other than Daniel Parker, whose death, 1 April 1829 in Versailles, brought an end to his attempts to return to the United States. There is no mention of Gallatin visiting Daniel Parker, whether in Paris or Draveil, while Gallatin was the U.S. Ambassador to France, 1816–1823. But, given the regular contacts of American officials with Daniel Parker throughout this period, it seems likely they did meet. What role Gallatin might have played in advising John Holker, who was pursuing his claims against Parker with renewed vigor, remains a mystery, but he surely should have been consulted by both men. Parker's sale of Draveil in 1821 suggests, however, that his run of luck had finally ended, well before his death in 1829.

David Parish, who took up the Mexican silver scheme in place of Daniel Parker, also tried to play a role in the placement of the French occupation loan in 1818. One of Alexander's letters suggests that Parish tried to cooperate with James Rothschild during the initial negotiations in Paris. Remaining in Europe, Parish moved to Vienna where he attempted to promote a public bank in Vienna in competition with the Rothschilds. When his bank promotion failed, however, he took the honorable course for failed financial speculators by drowning himself in the river Danube (27 April 1826).

Vincent Nolte, despite repeated losses in his various ventures with Baring & Hope, ending as one of the more notable victims of the Panic of 1837 in New Orleans, never contemplated suicide, despite risking demise in more than one duel. Instead, he continued after each setback to try a new enterprise, the wide range of which provided ample material for his colorful memoirs. None of them, however, succeeded in restoring the fortune he had enjoyed as the leading cotton factor in New Orleans before Jackson and Biddle waged their bank war against each other. His insights into the respective strengths of Alexander and Pierre Cesar are credible, even if perhaps more positive due to the repeated financial backings they provided him for his adventures along the way.

Finally, Pierre Cesar took seriously his initial attempt to retire from the heady world of haute finance in order to settle his family back in England, and it was only due to the affection of his brother-in-law that he resumed as titular head partner of Hope & Co. in Amsterdam in 1815, even while remaining firmly based in England. The venerable firm of Hope & Co. of Amsterdam, retained its name, but having been purchased outright by Alexander Baring in September 1813, was only resuscitated by Alexander on 1 January 1815 when the allied powers meeting in Vienna had confirmed that Belgium would be unified with Holland (Buist, pp. 68–69). For the immediate future it would be managed by Pierre Cesar Labouchere, now permanently based in England, and Pierre's colleagues Hieronymus Sillem (from Hamburg), Adriaan van der Hoop, and Pierre Firmin Lestapis, who had been active as clerks with procuration powers for the firm during the tumultuous period following the absorption of Holland into Napoleon's empire. While no one with the name of Hope remained as a partner or manager, in the circular announcing the new management, each individual signed his name as "Hope & Co."[1]

Pierre Cesar, on returning to Amsterdam and Paris to manage the details of the French occupation loans in 1818, maintained his pre-eminence among the lords of finance in Europe, until withdrawing from active participation in the firm in 1822. He left the sum of *cf* 750,000 as a passive partner, sharing in profits but not losses made by the remaining active partners. His estate of Hylands Park, purchased in 1815, became the focus of his continued art collection and experiments in horticulture. Today, the mansion is a "Council-run stately home and grounds hosting music festivals and family activities."[2] Never holding public office, whether in the Netherlands or France or England, and never writing up his memoirs, historians are left with deciphering his nearly illegible handwriting in correspondence preserved in the archives of Hope & Co in Amsterdam and in the Baring Archive in London. Nevertheless, his name, and his portrait, should always be linked with that of Alexander Baring, both major players in the successful origins of modern sovereign debt.

Alexander Baring, after re-organizing his father's firm as Baring Bros. in 1807, clearly found it more rewarding to be closely involved in the political developments in England. While his name was essential for dealing with the political authorities in Britain, France, and the United States, step by step he removed himself from active participation in the

[1] Buist, p. 377, "Circular of 1811 announcing the granting of power of procuration to Van der Hoop, Coesvelt and Lestapis."

[2] See more information at: https://en.wikipedia.org/wiki/Hylands_House.

Baring Bros. firm. Following his brother-in-law's example, he purchased a major estate, The Grange, at Northington in Hampshire.[3] Forsaking further adventures in American real estate, he sold off his holdings in Maine in 1830, but thereafter used his accumulating wealth to purchase other estates scattered around England, perhaps to avoid further unfavorable press from his political opponents and jealous merchant bankers. His few publications were provoked by seeing his opinions ignored or overridden by the majority vote in Parliament or the Court of Directors of the Bank of England. His father, already before his death in 1810, had tried to minimize public awareness of the profits made in the finance of the Louisiana Purchase, and Alexander had to continue that low profile. The contrast with his cajoling of American Treasury Secretaries to pay up their arrears on the U.S. government's accounts with Baring Bros. in 1813 nevertheless demonstrates his commitment to maintaining the reliable credit of the new Federal Government of the United States. His name, and portrait, therefore also deserve recognition as a founder of modern sovereign debt finance, along with that of Pierre Cesar Labouchere.

[3] See more information at: https://www.english-heritage.org.uk/visit/places/northington-grange/history/.

Appendix A. The U.S. Certificates for the Louisiana Purchase

Panel A: As directed by Sir Francis Baring to Alexander Baring

List of certificates of stock of which the interest to be paid in Amsterdam,

Certifs	200	of 200 Dollars each	$40,000
	200	400	80,000
	200	600	120,000
	400	800	320,000
	500	1200	600,000
	500	2000	1,000,000
	200	3000	600,000
	200	4000	800,000
	240	6000	1,440,000
Certs.	2640		5,000,000

Also, List of certificates of stock of which the interest to be paid in London,

Certifs	50	of 100 Dollars each	$5000
	100	500	50,000
	50	800	40,000
	500	1000	500,000
	500	2000	1,000,000
	500	3000	1,500,000
	500	4000	2,000,000
	231	5000	1,155,000
Certs. 2431			6,250,000

L. Neal, *The Forgotten Financiers of the Louisiana Purchase*, Palgrave Studies in the History of Finance,
https://doi.org/10.1007/978-3-031-56277-8

The certificates for Holland in the name of Hope & Co.—those for London in the name of Sir Francis Baring & Co. *(Baring Archives, NP1.A4.16).*

Panel B: As recorded by the U. S. Treasury (Winston and Columb, p. 197)

In the name of	Lot	Cert.	Amt.
Hope and Co.; Raymond and Theo. De Smeth; William and John Willink of Amsterdam, assignees of Hope and Co.;	1A	800	$1,250,000
and F. Baring and Co., or their assigns	1B	730	$1,750,000
F. Baring and Co., of London, Merchants	1C	1081	$2,500,000
F. Baring and Co., Hope and Co., Amsterdam	1D	1110	$2,000,000
	1E	800	$2,000,000
	1F	550	$1,750,000

"Interest upon the allotments designated A, B, and D was payable at Amsterdam; that upon the allotments designated C, E and F was payable at London....Alexander Baring gave his receipt for one third of the stock [packets E and F] --$3,750,000 on January 16, 1804."

Panel C: 1803, Dec. 21, Alex. Baring requests to the United States to issue the stock in certain designated amounts and to certain named persons. (Winston and Columb, pp. 222–224.)

Packet A, In the names of Hope and Company, Raymond & Theodore De Smith, and William and John Willink of Amsterdam, Merchants, Assignees of Hope and Company and Francis Baring and Company, or their Assigns, the Interest whereof to be paid in Amsterdam, viz.

100 Certificates of200 dollars each, is	20,000
100 Certificates of400 dollars each, is	40,000
100 Certificates of600 dollars each, is	60,000
100 Certificates of800 dollars each, is	80,000
100 Certificates of 1200 dollars each, is	120,000

(continued)

(continued)

150 Certificates of 2000 dollars each, is	300,000
50 Certificates of 3000 dollars each, is	150,000
60 Certificates of 4000 dollars each, is	240,000
40 Certificates of 6000 dollars each, is	240,000
	1,250,000

Packet B, In the names of Francis Baring & Company of London, Merchants, the Interest whereof to be paid in London:

50 Certificates of 100 dollars each, is	5000
100 Certificates of 500 dollars each, is	50,000
50 Certificates of 800 dollars each, is	40,000
200 Certificates of 1000 dollars each, is	200,000
200 Certificates of 2000 dollars each, is	400,000
200 Certificates of 3000 dollars each, is	600,000
200 Certificates of 4000 dollars each, is	800,000
81 Certificates of 5000 dollars each, is	405,000
	2,500,000

Packet C, In the names of Hope and Company, Raymond and Theodorew De Smith and William and John Willink of Amsterdam, Merchants, Assignees of Hope and Company and Francis Baring and Company, or their Assigns, the Interest whereof to be paid in Amsterdam, viz.

150 Certificates of 800 dollars each, is	120,000
150 Certificates of 1200 dollars each, is	180,000
200 Certificates of 2000 dollars each, is	400,000
70 Certificates of 3000 dollars each, is	210,000
60 Certificates of 4000 dollars each, is	240,000
100 Certificates of 6000 dollars each, is	600,000
	1,750,000

Packet D, In the names of Francis Baring & Company of London, Merchants, and Hope & Company of Amsterdam, Merchants, the interest whereof is to be paid in London, viz.

200 Certificates of 1000 dollars each, is	200,000
200 Certificates of 2000 dollars each, is	400,000
200 Certificates of 3000 dollars each, is	600,000
200 Certificates of 4000 dollars each, is	800,000
	2,000,000

Packet E, In the names of Hope and Company of Amsterdam, Merchants, and Francis Baring and Company of London, Merchants, the Interest whereof to be paid in Amsterdam, viz.

100 Certificates of 200 dollars each, is	20,000
100 Certificates of 400 dollars each, is	40,000
100 Certificates of 600 dollars each, is	60,000
150 Certificates of 800 dollars each, is	120,000
250 Certificates of 1200 dollars each, is	300,000
150 Certificates of 2000 dollars each, is	300,000
50 Certificates of 3000 dollars each, is	240,000
80 Certificates of 4000 dollars each, is	320,000
100 Certificates of 6000 dollars each, is	600,000
	2,000,000

Packet F, In the names of Francis Baring & Company of London, Merchants, and Hope & Company of Amsterdam, Merchants, the interest whereof to be paid in London, viz.

100 Certificates of 1000 dollars each, is	100,000
100 Certificates of 2000 dollars each, is	200,000
100 Certificates of 3000 dollars each, is	300,000
100 Certificates of 4000 dollars each, is	400,000
150 Certificates of 5000 dollars each, is	750,000
	1,750,000
Grand total	**11,250,000**

Appendix B. Initial Transfers of Louisiana 6% Stock by Baring Bros. (from Library of Congress, Baring mss. MMC 2475)

Name	*Amount*	*Date*
Gordon Coesvelt	$75,000	August 25, 1804
James Francis Mesturas	$4500	
Thomas Cooper	$1500	
William Holland	$49,000	
Madam Walburga Luckman	$3500	
Thomas Gilbert	$1000	
Samuel More	$100,000	February 21, 1805
William Dunlop	$104,000	
George Boyle	$70,000	
Alexander Adair	$17,000	
Richard Stainforth	$19,800	
William Holland		$22,000
William Morgan		$5000
Thomas Palmer	$9000	June 8, 1805
Fenwick Bulmer	$2000	
William Holland	$15,000	
William Dunlop	$104,000	
George Boyle	$70,000	
Alexander Adair	$17,000	
Richard Stainforth	$19,800	

(continued)

L. Neal, *The Forgotten Financiers of the Louisiana Purchase*, Palgrave Studies in the History of Finance,
https://doi.org/10.1007/978-3-031-56277-8

(continued)

Name	*Amount*	*Date*
William Morgan	$5000	
William Holland	$13,000	
William Holland	$6500	Jan 30, 1806 (#s 137, 138, 59)
Thomas Palmer	$4800	
George William Erving,	$22,800	(Boston, MA)
John Stanley, Lisbon $10,000	21 July 1806	
Dame Walburga Luchner	$6000	
Thomas Palmer	$8400	24 January 1807
William Bingham Estate[1]	$300,000	4 August 1807
William Bingham, Junior	$10,000	
George Bowles	$42,000	
Thomas Palmer	$9400	
Henry Wadding	$6000	
Peter Cesar Labouchere	**$100,000**	**23 October 1807**
Edward Holland	$18,000	(from William Holland, 15 May 1810)
Anne Rushout	$4500	17 July 1810

[1] William Bingham ($300,000) distributed to 5 joint executors of his estate: Robert Gilmore, Charles Willing, Thomas Haynes Willing, Alexander Baring & Henry Baring.Total $1,275,000 in all.

Appendix C. Examples of Stock Certificates

(Original dimensions, 10.5 by 5.5 inches.)

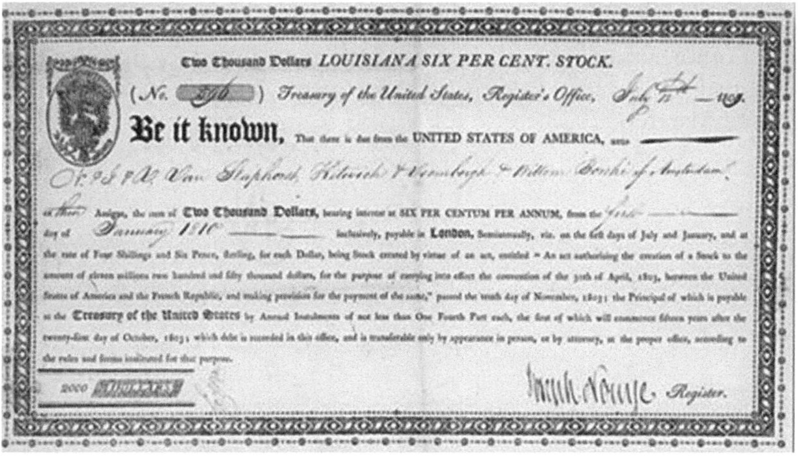

Two Thousand Dollars LOUISIANA SIX PER CENT. STOCK.

(No.) Treasury of the United States, Register's Office,

Be it known, That there is due from the UNITED STATES OF AMERICA, unto

Assigns, the sum of Two Thousand Dollars, bearing interest at SIX PER CENTUM PER ANNUM, from the

day of inclusively, payable in London, Semiannually, viz. on the first days of July and January, and at the rate of Four Shillings and Six Pence, sterling, for each Dollar, being Stock created by virtue of an act, entitled "An act authorising the creation of a Stock to the amount of eleven millions two hundred and fifty thousand dollars, for the purpose of carrying into effect the convention of the 30th of April, 1803, between the United States of America and the French Republic, and making provision for the payment of the same," passed the tenth day of November, 1803; the Principal of which is payable at the Treasury of the United States by Annual Instalments of not less than One Fourth Part each, the first of which will commence fifteen years after the twenty-first day of October, 1803; which debt is recorded in this office, and is transferable only by appearance in person, or by attorney, at the proper office, according to the rules and forms instituted for that purpose.

2000

Register.

Two Thousand Dollars *LOUISIANA SIX PER CENT. STOCK.*
(No. 596) *Treasury of the United States, Register's Office, July 12th—1809.*
National Archives and Records Administration.
Transcript:

L. Neal, *The Forgotten Financiers of the Louisiana Purchase*, Palgrave Studies in the History of Finance,
https://doi.org/10.1007/978-3-031-56277-8

Be it known, That there is due from the UNITED STATES OF AMERICA, unto, N. & J. & R. van Staphorst, Ketwich & Voombergh & William Borski of Amsterdam, or their Assigns, the sum of **Two Thousand Dollars,** bearing interest at SIX PER CENTUM PER ANNUM, from the first day of January 1810 inclusively, payable in **London,** Semi-annually, viz. on the first days of July and January, and at the rate of Four Shillings and Six Pence, sterling, for each Dollar, being Stock created by virtue of an act, entitled "An Act authoring the creation of a Stock to the amount of eleven millions two hundred and fifty thousand dollars, for the purpose of carrying into effect the convention of the 30th of April, 1803, between the United States of America and the French Republic, and making provision for the payment of the same," passed the tenth day of November 1803; the Principal of which is payable at the **Treasury of the United States** by Annual Instalments[sic] of not less than One Fourth Part each, the first of which will commence fifteen years after the twenty-first day of October 1803; which debt is recorded in this office, and is transferable only by appearance in person, or by attorney, at the proper office, according to the rules and forms instituted for that purpose.

Source: https://lewis-clark.org/media/loupur_stock-certif.jpg, accessed March 6, 2023.

Appendix D. Addington's Order for Barings to Stop Payments

Downing Street

Dec. the 16th—1803

Dear Sir,

Having reflected very seriously on the subject of our conversation on Wednesday last, I am decidedly of opinion, that, considering the peculiar circumstances of the present War with France, and the avow'd purpose of the enemy to employ all their resources with a view to their projected invasion of this Kingdom, His Majesty's government would not be justified in allowing any subjects of His Country to facilitate at this time such pecuniary arrangements as may subsist between other foreign powers, & the government of France. I have therefore to desire that you would decline being a party to any remittances to France on Account of the Debt due from the United States of America in Consequence of the cession of Louisiana; and if there should be any sums of money on the continent destined by you to the liquidation of this debt, & you should have the means of withdrawing them, or of diverting them into other channels, I fully rely on your doing so.

There is no objection to your stating to your correspondents, as your justification, if you shall deem any justification necessary, that you have

L. Neal, *The Forgotten Financiers of the Louisiana Purchase*, Palgrave Studies in the History of Finance,
https://doi.org/10.1007/978-3-031-56277-8

adopted this line of Conduct in consequence of the direct interposition of His Majesty's Government.

I have the honor to be, with great regards, Dear Sir,

Your faithful,
& obedient servt:
Henry Addington

Sir Francis Baring Bart.
(Baring Archives, NP1.A4.28)

Appendix E. The Dutch Plan for Selling and Managing the U.S. Bonds

NP1.A4.30 in Baring Archives

Article 1	This American stock has interest at 6 pct. per annum payable by the Government of the United States, in Amsterdam at the expense & risk of the said government without any deduction on account of the exchange or of any other nature whatsoever
Article 2	The Capital of the Stock according to the decree of the United States of America is repayable in three equal yearly instalments with the interest to the period of those instalments of which the first shall take place at the latest at the expiration of 15 years from the 1 January 1804 and the two other instalments at the expiration of the two following years, so that the whole capital will be paid off, & extinguished in the years 1821
Article 3	The abovementioned Capital American Stock thus become a Property in common, shall not exceed the amount of five million dollars, but the directors & depositaries hereafter mentioned reserve to themselves the faculty of confining it to a smaller sum, they also reserve to themselves the faculty of acting in the execution of this plan in the manner which they may find most consistent with the general interest of the concerned, according to existing circumstances
Article 4	This original American stock shall be

placed in the names of
Messrs. Hope & Co.
R. & F. deSmeth
Wm. & G. Willink

L. Neal, *The Forgotten Financiers of the Louisiana Purchase*, Palgrave Studies in the History of Finance,
https://doi.org/10.1007/978-3-031-56277-8

as representing the Participants& interested in this Community, and shall remain for this purpose in the possession & under the direction of these three houses until the final liquidation of the concern, and the capital of this stock shall be divided into convenient partial certificates registered in the names of the said gentlemen depositaries who shall keep them for the advantage & for the account & risk of the united concern, accompanied with the notarial documents usual in this kind of stock and in associations of this nature

Article 5 The shares in this Concern shall be of 400 Dollars of the abovementioned Capital American Stock, which at the evaluation of 50 stivers current money of Holland per Dollar represent one thousand gilders of that currency. *[LN: 20 stuivers = 1 guilder; 20,000 stivers = 1000 guilders]*

Article 6 Of the amount of the annual interest of the stock there shall be divided by the Directors & Depositaries to the concerned f55 per annum on each share making this an interest of 5 ½ pct. per annum according to the evaluation of the f1000 above stated

Article 7 The fund arising from the annual ½ pct. (NB above the 5 ½ pct. paid to the concerned) excedent received on the American stock shall be employed by the Directors & Depositaries in the purchase of shares in the capital of this concern & which shares shall be extinguished to the profit of the same, the same rule shall be observed with regard to the surplus of interest which will remain in consequence of these interim purchases & extinction of shares bought up

Article 8 When the partial reimbursement of the Capital American Stock shall take place the amount of this reimbursement shall be employed in the reimbursement of a proportional number of the shares in this Concern, to be decided by lot and the said reimbursement shall provisionally be of f1000 per share, according to the evaluation of said f1000 before stated, and the shares thus paid off shall be furnished with a mark indicating the reimbursement thereof and delivered to the bearer to serve as a title or claim to the proportion of the advantage which may result to the united concern after the reimbursement of all the shares in the same manner (except those which shall have been bought in for account of the common concern) & according to the above evaluation

Article 9 After the final reimbursement of the whole Capital stock belonging to the concern, an account shall be rendered to the interested in it or holders of shares unextinguished, of the result, after payment of the f1000 per share unextinguished as above stated, & the said result (or profit), shall be divided in equal portions among the holders of the unextinguished shares against the delivery of the said shares which will then become finally annulled

Article 10 From & after the 1 July 1804 every holder of one or more unreimbursed share may demand a sum of original American stock equivalent to that represented by said share or shares, or 400 Dollars Capital for each share, which Capital shall be delivered by the Depositaries & Directors to those who may require it, by means of a power of attorney in due form for the transfer of such stocks in the United States, and this against a cession of the said shares in which the portion in the result of the concern, shall revert to the association conformably to article 8

Article 11 The shares shall be delivered by the Depositaries & Directors signed by them respectively at their expense & without any charges whatever to the subscribers

Article 12 To every share shall be annexed seventeen coupons for the year repartition of f55 per share signed by such person or persons as shall thereto be qualified by the Depositaries & Directors, & in the case of reimbursement before the expiration of the last year, conformably with Art. 8, the Coupons not due shall be given up with the shares to which they belong to the said Depositaries & Directors in order to be cancelled & annulled

Article 13 The subscription to or participation in this association is from this time open to all who may incline to interest themselves in it, at the Counting houses of Messrs. Berck & Berck for & in behalf of Messrs. The Depositaries & Directors, provided that such subscription be in the proper name of the subscribers, & indicating the number of shares of 400 Dollars each, which he desires to subscribe for

Article 14 Every subscriber shall be bound to furnish at the date of his signature to the Depositaries & Directors 10 pct. Of the amount of his subscription being according to the evaluation Art. 5 upon each share, 40 Dollars or *f*500 current money of Holland

Article 15 Every subscriber will receive for their provisional payment a receipt (recepisse) acknowledging the said payment & the capital sum of such subscription, these receipts will in due time be exchanged for partial certificates allowing 5 ½ pct. interest upon the Capital Sum therein specified & subscribed and that notwithstanding the said Subscriber will only have paid provisionally 10 pct. which interest shall be reckoned from the date of the furnishment until the 1 Jan'y 1804, from which date the annual repartitions mentioned in Art. 6 will be reckoned

Article 16 Those of the Subscribers who may prefer to furnish the amount of their subscriptions in full, may be permitted so to do, & there shall be allowed them at the time of the Exchange of their receipts 5 ½ pct interest on the amount reckoning from the 1st day of the month preceding that in which the payment shall have been made, until the date from which the said annual repartitions commence

Article 17 The shares in this concern shall be delivered by the Depositaries & Directors the 1 Jan'y 1804, or as soon after as possible, @ the exact period of the delivery shall be announced in the Gazettes of Amsterdam, Harlem, Leyden, the Hague, & of Rotterdam

Article 18 The subscribers shall be bound to come & retire the Shares for which they have subscribed within the term of three months after the said announcement shall have been made, and on delivering up their receipts to pay to the Depositaries & Directors.The remainder of the Capital of their subscription estimated as above, & consequently *f*900—on every share of 400 dollars American stock with the interest due on *f*1000 from the 1 Jan'y 1804 to the day in which the payment is completed—and in case of neglect or delay on the part of the Subscribers to retire their shares & acquit themselves in proper time, they will forfeit all right & title to this association in favor & to the profit of the farther interested therein, & their receipts shall be considered as null & void

Article 19	If from this time to the 1 Jan'y 1804 the Depositaries & Directors should find themselves inclined to reduce, or to annul the present transaction, they do reserve to themselves that faculty, on giving notice thereof in the Gazettes abovementioned, and in this case they will repay to each subscriber the whole of the provisional furnishment made by him on account thereof, together with the interest thereon stipulated by the above Art. 15 & 16, & calculated to the day for which the reimbursement shall be indicated as payable by the said Subscription

Appendix F. Sir Francis Baring's "Estimate" of Profits

11,250,000 dollars at 4/6 is	£2,531,250.---
52,000,00 at 24.10 is	£2,122,250.---
difference at par	£409,000
deduct at 2%	£50,652
remains	£358,350
£358,350 at 24.10 is frs.	7,779,575
paid	52,000,000
frs.	59,779,575
The lowest value is	95%
The installments being for 2 years leaves a profit on the interest for 1 year at 6%^	6%
Real value	101%
Deduct for charges, suppose	3
or a defalcation of 2% as above	98

(Baring Archives, NP1.A4.44)

[The calculations first convert both dollar and franc obligations into pound sterling at fixed exchange rates, to show a net profit of £358,350, which is then calculated back in francs, to show a 13% overall gain, presumably to counter claims that the firms had extracted extravagant profits from their role in financing, a claim made repeatedly by Albert Gallatin, for example].

L. Neal, *The Forgotten Financiers of the Louisiana Purchase*, Palgrave Studies in the History of Finance,
https://doi.org/10.1007/978-3-031-56277-8

References

Adams, Donald R. Jr. 1972. "The Bank of Stephen Girard, 1812–1831." *The Journal of Economic History* 32 (4): 841–868.

Adams, Henry, ed. 1879. *The Writings of Albert Gallatin*, 3 vols. Philadelphia: J. B. Lippincott & Co.

Alberts, Robert C. 1969. *The Golden Voyage; The Life and Times of William Bingham, 1752–1804*. Boston: Houghton-Mifflin.

Allis, Frederick, Jr. ed. *William Bingham's Maine Lands 1790–1820*. Publications of the Colonial Society of Massachusetts, Vol. 36. Portland: The Anthoensen Press.

Antipa, Pamfili. 2018. "The Interactions Between Monetary and Fiscal Policies in Britain during the French Wars." Unpublished Ph.D. Dissertation, Paris School of Economics.

Austin, Peter E. 2007. *Baring Brothers and the Birth of Modern Finance*. London: Pickering & Chatto.

Barbé-Marbois, François. 1796. *Réflexions sur la colonie de Saint-Domingue: ou Examen approfondi des causes de sa ruine, et des measures adoptées pour la rétablit . . .* Paris: Chez Garnery.

Barbé-Marbois, François. 1829. *Histoire de la Louisiane et de la cession de cette colonie par la France aux États-Uniés de l'Amérique Septentrionale: précédé d'un discourse sur la constitution des aux États-Unis*. Paris: Firmin-Didot.

Barbé-Marbois, François. 1830. *The History of Louisiana, particularly the cession of that colony to the United States of America with an introductory essay on the Constitution and government of the United States* (tr. William Beach Lawrence). Philadelphia.

L. Neal, *The Forgotten Financiers of the Louisiana Purchase*, Palgrave Studies in the History of Finance,
https://doi.org/10.1007/978-3-031-56277-8

Barbé-Marbois, François. 1796. *Discours de Barbé-Marbois sur la resolution relative à la retenue sur la matières d'or & d'argent à convertir en espèces séance du 16 frimaire an 5*. Paris: Impriméric nationale.

Baring, Alexander. 1808. *An Inquiry into the Causes and Consequences of the Orders in Council; and an Examination of the Conduct of Great Britain towards the Neutral Commerce of America*. London: J. M. Richardson.

Bergeron, Louis. 1978. *Banquiers, négociants et manufacturiers parisiens du Directoire à l'Empire*. Paris: Mouton Éditeur.

Bianchi, Serge, E. Rapoport, and J.-L. Aubert. 1984. *Histoire d'un domaine, du château seigneurial de Draveil à la cité coopérative Paris-Jardins*, Association les amis d l'histoire du Château de Draveil et la cité coopérative Paris-Jardins.

Bizardel, Yvon. 1972. *Les américains à Paris pendant le revolution*. Paris: Calmann-Lévy.

———. 1975. *The First Expatriates: Americans in Paris During the French Revolution*, Translated by June P. Wilson and Cornelia Higginson. New York: Holt, Rinehart, and Winston.

Bordo, Michael and Eugene N. White, 1991. "A Tale of Two Currencies: British and French Finance during the Napoleonic Wars." *The Journal of Economic History* 51 (2): 303–316.

Borneman, Walter R. 2004. *1812: The War that Forged a Nation.* New York: HarperCollins.

Branda, Pierre. 2007. *Le Prix de la Gloire: Napoléon et l'Argent (Divers Histoire)*. Paris: Librairie Arthème Fayard.

Brecher, Frank W. 2006. *Negotiating the Louisiana Purchase: Robert Livingston's mission to France, 1801–1804*. Jefferson, N. C.: McFarland & Co.

Brown, Kenneth L. 1942. "Stephen Girard, Promoter of the Second Bank of the United States." *The Journal of Economic History* 2 (2): 125–148.

Brown, Margaret L. 1937. "William Bingham: Eighteenth Century Magnate." *The Pennsylvania Magazine of History and Biography* 61 (4): 387–434.

Brown, Stuart Gerry. 2017. *The Autobiography of James Monroe*. Syracuse, NY: Syracuse University Press.

Buel, Richard, Jr. 2011. *Joel Barlow: American Citizen in a Revolutionary World*. Baltimore: The Johns Hopkins Press.

Buist, Marten G. 1974. *At Spes Non Fracta: Hope & Co. 1779–1815*. Amsterdam: Bank Mees & Hope NV.

Cerami, Charles A. 2003. *Jefferson's Great Gamble: The Remarkable Story of Jefferson, Napoleon and the Men Behind the Louisiana Purchase*. Naperville, IL: Sourcebooks.

Chase, Eugene Parker. 1929. *Our Revolutionary Forefathers: The Letters of Francois, Marquis de Barbé-Marbois, during his Residence in the United States as Secretary of the French Legation, 1779–1785*. New York: Duffield & Co.

Chernow, Ron. 2005. *Alexander Hamilton*. New York: Penguin Books.

Childs, Francis Sergeant. 1940. *French Refugee Life in the United States, 1790–1800: An American Chapter of the French Revolution*. Baltimore, MD: The Johns Hopkins University Press.

Chinard, Gilbert. 1931. *The Correspondence of Jefferson and Du Pont de Nemours, with an Introduction on Jefferson and the Physiocrats*. Baltimore, MD: The Johns Hopkins Press.

Clark, John G. 1970. *New Orleans, 1718–1812: An Economic History*. Baton Rouge: Louisiana State University Press.

Cohen, Felix. 1948. "Original Indian Title." *Minnesota Law Review* 32: 35–36.

Compton, Charles. 1833. *A Treatise on Tontine: In Which the Evils of the Old System are Exhibited, and an Equitable Plan Suggested for Rendering the Valuable Principle of Tontine more Beneficially Applicable to Life Tontines*. London: Effingham Wilson, Royal Exchange.

Cope, S. R. 1983. *Walter Boyd: A Merchant Banker in the Age of Napoleon*. London School of Economics and Political Science: Alan Sutton.

Costa, Fernando Dores. 2008. "Army Size, Military Recruitment and Financing in Portugal during the Period of the Peninsular War—1808–1811." *e-Journal of Portuguese History* 6 (2): 1–27.

Courtois, Alphonse. 1877. *Tableaux des Cours des Principales Valeurs Négociées et Cotés aux Bourse des Effets Publics de Paris, Lyon, et Marseille du 17 Janvier 1797 (28 Nivose an V) à Nos Jours Relevés sur les Documents Officiels et Authentiques* (3rd edn). Paris: Garnier Frères; Guillaumin & Cie.

Cowen, David. 2000. "The First Bank of the United States and the Securities Market Crash of 1792." *The Journal of Economic History* 60 (4): 1041–1060.

Cutterham, Tom. 2018. "'A Very promising Appearance': Credit, Honor, and Deception in the Emerging Market for American Debt, 1784–92." *William and Mary Quarterly* 75 (4): 623–650.

Daniel, De J. Hippolyte. 1837. *Biographie des hommes remarquables de Seine-et-Oise*. Paris: J. Angé.

De Albuquerque, Tomás Pinto. 2016. "Qual o papel das redes na contrução da carreira de um grande homem de nogócios e sua relevância para o funcionamento do Imperio?" Unpublished Master's Thesis in Modern History, Universidade Nova de Lisboa.

DeConde, Alexander, 1976. *This Affair of Louisiana*. New York: Charles Scribner's Sons.

De Knight, William F. 1900. *Currency of the Country and of the Loans of the United States, from the Earliest Period to June 30, 1900*. Washington, DC: Government Printing Office.

Deviosse, Jean. 1989. *L'homme qui vendit la Louisiane, récit*. Paris: Olivier Orban.

Duffy, Michael. 1987. *Soldiers, Sugar, and Seapower: The British Expeditions to the West Indies and the War against Revolutionary France*. Oxford: Clarendon Press.

Dungan, Nicholas. 2010. *Gallatin: America's Swiss Founding Father*. New York: New York University Press.

Edling, Max M. 2014. *Hercules in the Cradle: War, Money and the American State, 1783–1867*. Chicago: University of Chicago Press.

Egan, Clifford. 1983. *Neither Peace nor War: Franco-American Relations 1803–1812*. Baton Rouge, LA: Louisiana State University Press.

Ferguson, E. James. 1961. *The Power of the Purse: A History of American Public Finance, 1776–1790*. Chapel Hill, NC: University of North Carolina Press.

———. ed. 1971. *Selected Writings of Albert Gallatin*. Indianapolis, IN: Bobbs-Merrill.

Fichter, James R. 2010. *So Great a Proffit: How the East Indies Trade Transformed American Capitalism*. Cambridge, MA: Harvard University Press.

Fiechter, Jean-Jacques. 1983. *Un diplomate américain sous la Terreur: les années européennes de Gouverneur Morris, 1789–1798*. Paris: Fayard.

Flandreau, Marc and Juan H. Flores. 2009. "Bonds and Brands: Foundations of Sovereign Debt Markets, 1820–1830." *Journal of Economic History* 69 (3): 646–684.

Fugier, Andre, 1930. Napoleon et l'Espagne, 1799–1808, 2 vols., Paris: Librairie Felix Alcan.

Furstenberg, François. 2015. *When the United States Spoke French: Five Refugees Who Shaped a Nation*. New York: Penguin Press.

Gallatin, Albert. 1796. *A Sketch of the Finances of the United States*. New York: William A. Davis.

Gallatin, Alert. 1879. *The Writings of Albert Gallatin*, edited by Henry Adams. Vol. 1. New York: J. B. Lippincott.

Gemeente Archief Amsterdam, 654 *Inventaris van het archief van de Firma Daniel Crommelin en Soonen, sedert 1859 Tutein Nolthenius en De Haan, Inventaris nummer* 201 "Brieven aan Daniel Parker te Londen, 1790. Koncepten, opgesteld door H. Fijnje."

Gent, John A. 2016. "Abundance and Scarcity: Classical Theories of Money, Bank Balance Sheets and Business Models, and the British Restriction of 1797–1818." Unpublished Ph.D. Dissertation, The London School of Economics and Political Science.

Gilpin, W. Freeman. 1922. "The American Grain Trade to the Spanish Peninsula, 1810–1814." *The American Historical Review* 28 (1): 24–44.

Glijeses, Piero. 2016. "Napoleon, Jefferson, and the Louisiana Purchase. *The International History Review* 39 (2): 237–255.

Greenfield, Jerome. 2016. "Financing a New Order: The Payment of Reparations by Restoration France, 1817–1818. *French History* 30 (3): 376–400.

Griffith, Rob. 2017. "The Commerce of Treachery: The Selling of Suriname, 1799." Guest Post on https://adventuresinhistoryland.com/2017/11/10/the-commerce-of-treachery-the-selling-of-suriname-1799-by-rob-griffith/, accessed December 21, 2020.

Hamilton, Alexander. 1790. *First Report on the Public Credit.* Accessed March 15, 2020: https://founders.archives.gov/documents/Hamilton/01-06-02-0076-0002-0001

Hassler, Gene. 1988. *An Illustrated History of U. S. Loans, 1775–1898.* Port Clinton, OH: BNR Press.

Hickey, Donald R. 2012. *The War of 1812: A Forgotten Conflict. Bicentennial Edition.* Urbana, Chicago, and Springfield, IL: University of Illinois Press.

Hidy, Ralph W. 1949. *The House of Baring in American Trade and Finance: English Merchant Bankers at Work, 1763–1861.* Cambridge, MA: Harvard University Press.

Hill, Peter P. 2012. *Joel Barlow, American Diplomat and Nation Builder.* Washington, DC: Potomac Books.

Hill, Peter P. 2005. *Napoleon's Troublesome Americans: Franco-American Relations, 1804–1815.* Washington, DC: Potomac Books.

Hitsman, J. Mackay. 1968. *The Incredible War of 1812.* Toronto: University of Toronto Press.

Hotson, Anthony. 2017. *Respectable Banking: The Search for Stability in London's Money and Credit Markets since 1695.* Cambridge: Cambridge University Press.

Ingram, T. L. n.d. "Sir Francis Baring and the Loans for Portugal, 1797–1803. Unpublished Paper, Baring Archive.

Jacoud, Gilles. 1996. *Le billet de banque en France (1796–1803), de la diversité au monopole.* Paris: Éditions L'Harmattan.

Jefferson, Thomas. 1930. *Correspondence between Thomas Jefferson and Pierre Samuel du Pont de Nemours, 1798–1817*, edited by Dumas Malone, Translations by Linwood Lehman. Boston & New York: Houghton Mifflin Company.

Jennings, Robert M., Donald F. Swanson, and Andrew P. Trout. 1988. "Alexander Hamilton's Tontine Proposal." *The William and Mary Quarterly*, 45 (1): 107–115.

Jimenez Codinach, Guadalupe. 1991. *La Gran Bertana y La Independencia de México, 1808–1821.* México: Fondo de Cultura Economica.

Jones, Robert F. 1992. "*The king of the Alley*," *William Duer, Politician, Entrepreneur, and Speculator.* Philadelphia: American Philosophical Society.

Jonker, Joost, and Keetie Sluyterman. 2000. *At home on the world markets: Dutch international trading companies from the 16th century to the present.* The Hague: Sdu Uitgevers.

Journal de Palais. 1819. “Presentant la Jurisprudence de la Cour de Cassation, et des Cours d’Appel De Paris et des autres departements.” T. 54 & 2, art. 72, 321–359.

Jusselin, Maurice. 1957. “Le Trafic Américain sur les biens nationaux.” *Mémoires de la Société Archeologique d’Eure-et-Loir* XX: 147–155.

Kaplan, Herbert, 2006. *Nathan Meyer Rothschild and the creation of a dynasty: the critical years 1806–1816.* Stanford : Stanford University Press.

Kearney, John Watts. 1968. *Sketch of American Finances, 1789–1835.* New York: Greenwood Press.

Kennedy, Roger G. 2003. *Mr. Jefferson’s Lost Cause: Land, Farmers, Slavery, and the Louisiana Purchase.* New York: Oxford University Press.

Knodell, Jane Ellen. 2017. *The Second Bank of the United States: “Central” Banker in an Era of Nation-Building, 1816–1836.* London and New York: Routledge.

Kukla, Jon, 2003. *A Wilderness So Immense: The Louisiana Purchase and the Destiny of America.* New York: Anchor Books.

Labouchere, Joan. 2023. E-mail Communication with Genealogy of Pierre Cesar Labouchere.

Labouchere, M. G. 1913. “Un financier diplomate au siècle dernier: Pierre-César Labouchère (1772–1839).” *Revue d’Histoire Diplomatique* 27 (3): 425–455.

———. 1914. “Un financier diplomate au siècle dernier: Pierre-César Labouchère (1772–1839).” *Revue d’Histoire Diplomatique* 28 (1): 74–97.

———. 1916. “L’Annexion de la Louisiane aux États-Unis et les Maisons Hope et Baring.” *Revue d’Histoire Diplomatique* 29 (1): 423–455.

Lee, Robert. 2017. “Accounting for Conquest: The Price of the Louisiana Purchase of Indian Country.” *The Journal of American History* 103 (4): 921–942.

Lewis, James E. 2003. *The Louisiana Purchase: Jefferson’s Noble Bargain?* Charlottesville, VA: Thomas Jefferson Foundation.

Liss, Peggy K. (1983). *Atlantic Empires: The Network of Trade and Revolution, 113–1826.* Baltimore: The Johns Hopkins University Press.

Lyon, E. Wilson (1942, 2nd printing 1974). *The Man Who Sold Louisiana.* Norman, OK: University of Oklahoma Press.

MacDonald, James, 2003. *A Free Nation Deep in Debt: The Financial Roots of Democracy.* New York: Farrar, Straus and Giroux.

Marichal, Carlos. 2007. *Bankruptcy of Empire: Mexican Silver and the Wars between Spain, Britain and France, 1760–1810.* Cambridge: Cambridge University Press.

Mathiez, Albert. 1930. *Girondins et Montagnards.* Paris: Firmin-Didot et Cie.

May, Gregory. 2018. *Jefferson’s Treasure; How Albert Gallatin Saved the New Nation from Debt.* Washington, DC: Regnery History.

McCraw, Thomas K. 2012. *The Founders and Finance: How Hamilton, Gallatin, and Other Immigrants Forged a New Economy*. Cambridge, MA: Belknap Press of Harvard University Press.

McCullough, David. 2019. *The Pioneers: The Heroic Story of the Settlers Who Brought the American Ideal West*. New York: Simon & Schuster.

McGrath, Tim. 2020. *James Monroe: A Life*. New York: Dutton.

Meagher, Thomas M. 2017. *Financing Armed Conflict, vol. 1, Resourcing US Military Interventions from the Revolution to the Civil War*. New York: Palgrave Macmillan.

Milevsky, Moshe A. 2015. *King William's Tontine: Why the Retirement Annuity of the Future Should Resemble the Past*. Cambridge: Cambridge University Press.

Miller, Robert J. 2008. *Native America, Discovered and Conquered: Thomas Jefferson, Lewis and Clark, and Manifest Destiny*. Lincoln and London: University of Nebraska Press.

Morales, Lisa. 2009. *The Financial History of the War of 1812*. Unpublished Ph.D. Dissertation, Department of History, University of North Texas.

Moreira, Cristina and Jari Eloranta. 2011. "Importance of 'Weak' States during Conflicts: Portuguese Trade with the United States during the Revolutionary and Napoleonic Wars." *Journal of Iberian and Latin American Economic History* 29 (3): 393–423.

Myers, Margaret G. 1970. *A Financial History of the United States*. New York: Columbia University Press.

Neal, Larry, 1990. *The Rise of Financial Capitalism: International Capital Markets in the Age of Reason*. New York: Cambridge University Press.

———. 1998. "The Bank of England's First Return to Gold and the Stock Market Crash of 1825." *Federal Reserve Bank of St. Louis Review* 7 (2): 53–76.

———. 2015. *From Babylon to Bernanke: A Concise History of International Finance*. Cambridge: Cambridge University Press.

Nolte, Vincent. 1854. *Fifty Years in Both Hemispheres, or, Reminiscences of the Life of a Former Merchant*. New York: Redfield.

O'Brien, Patrick Karl and Nuno Palma. 2023. "Not an Ordinary Bank but a Great Engine of State: The Bank of England and the British Economy. *Economic History Review*.

Oosterlinck, Kim, Loredana Ureche-Rangau, & Jacques-Marie Vaslin. 2014. "Baring, Wellington and the Resurrection of French Public Finances Following Waterloo." *The Journal of Economic History* 74 (4): 1072–1102.

Orbell, John. 1985. *A History of Baring Brothers to 1939*. London: Baring Brothers & Co., Limited.

———. 2008. "Baring, Alexander, first Baron Ashburton (1773–1848)." *Oxford Dictionary of National Biography*.

Parker, Daniel. *Daniel Parker Letter Book, 1781–1816 (inclusive)*. Mss: 761 1781–1783 P238, Baker Library Special Collections, Harvard Business School.

Perkins, Edwin J. 2004. *American Public Finance and Financial Services, 1700–1815*. Columbus, OH: Ohio State University Press.

Pinaud, Pierre-Francois. 1990, "Guerre et Finances de 1792 a 1815: Le service de la Tresorerie aux Armees." *Revue Historique* 283 (1): 53–69.

Poniatowski, Michel. 1976. *Talleyrand aux États-Unis, 1794–1796*. Paris: Librairie Académique Perrin.

Quinn, Stephen and William Roberds, 2024. *How a Ledger Became a Central Bank: A Monetary History of the Bank of Amsterdam*. Cambridge: Cambridge University Press.

Rice, Howard C. 1937. "James Swan: Agent of the French Republic, 1794–1796." *The New England Quarterly* 10 (3): 464–486.

Riley, James C. 1978. "Foreign Credit and Fiscal Stability: Dutch Investment in the United States, 1781–1794." *The Journal of American History* 65 (3): 654–678.

———. 1980. *International Government Finance and the Amsterdam Capital Market, 1740–1815*. Cambridge University Press.

Roberts, Andrew. 2014. *Napoleon: A Life*. New York: Viking.

Rydjord, John. 1938. "Napoleon and Mexican Silver." *The Southwestern Social Science Quarterly* 19 (2): 171–182.

Saricks, Ambrose. 1965. *Pierre Samuel Du Pont de Nemours*. Lawrence, KS: The University of Kansas Press.

Saulnier, Eugene. 1916. "l'Hôtel du Ministère des Colonies: Hôtel de Montmorin." *Revue de l'Histoire des Colonies Françaises* 77–94.

Schama, Simon, 1992. *Patriots and Liberators: Revolution in the Netherlands, 1780–1813*. New York: Vintage Books.

Schachtman, Tom. 2019. *The Founding Fortunes: How the Wealthy Paid for and Profited from America's Revolution*. New York: St. Martin's Press.

Silva, Andrée Mansuy-Diniz. 2006. *Portrait d'un homme d'État: D. Rodrigo de Souza Coutinho, Comte de Linhares, 1755–1812. (V. II. L'homme 'État, 1796–1812)*. Lisbon: Fundação Calouste Gulbenkian.

Silveira, Luis Espanha da. 1987. "Aspectos da Evolução das Finanças Publicas Portuguesas (1800–1827)." *Análise Social* 23 (3): 505–529.

Smith, Philip Chadwick Foster. 1984. *The Empress of China*. Philadelphia: Philadelphia Maritime Museum.

Sparrow, Elizabeth. 1999. *Secret Service: British Agents in France 1792–1815*. Woodbridge, Suffolk: The Boydell Press.

Stabile, Donald R. 1998. *The Origins of American Public Finance: Debates over Money, Debt, and Taxes in the Constitutional Era, 1776–1836*. Westport: Greenwood Press.

Stephen, James. 1805. *War in Disguise: Or, the Frauds of the Neutral Flags.* London: J. Hatchard.

Stevens, John Austin. 1883. *Albert Gallatin.* Boston: Houghton, Mifflin and Company.

Stourm, René. 1902. *Les Finances du Consulat.* Paris: Guillaumin et Cie.

Sylla, Richard. 2007. "Reversing Financial Reversals: Government and the Financial System since 1789." In *Government and the American Economy: A New History*, edited by Price Fishback et al. Chicago: University of Chicago Press.

———. 2008. "The Political Economy of Early U. S. Financial Development." In *Political Institutions and Financial Development*, edited by S. Haber, D. C. North, and B. R. Weingast. Stanford: Stanford University Press.

———. 2009. "Comparing the US and UK Financial Systems, 1790–1830." In *The Origin and Development of Financial Markets and Institutions*, edited by Jeremy Atack and Larry Neal. Cambridge: Cambridge University Press.

———. 2011. "Financial Foundations: Public Credit, the National Bank, and Securities Markets. In *Founding Choices: American Economic Policy in the 1790s*, edited by Douglas A. Irwin and Richard Sylla. Chicago: University of Chicago Press.

———. 2016. *Alexander Hamilton: The Illustrated Biography.* New York: Sterling.

Sylla, Richard, Robert E. Wright, and David J. Cowen, 2009. "Alexander Hamilton, Central Banker: Crisis Management during the U. S. Financial Panic of 1792." *The Business History Review* 83 (1): 61–86.

Taylor, Alan. 2006. *The Divided Ground: Indians, Settlers, and the Northern Borderland of the American Revolution.* New York: Alfred A. Knopf.

Taylor, Alan, 2010. *The Civil War of 1812: American citizens, British subjects, Irish rebels, & Indian allies.* New York: Alfred A. Knopf.

———. 2012. *The Civil War of 1812: American Citizens, British Subjects, Irish Rebels, & Indian Allies.* New York: Alfred A. Knopf.

———. 2016. *American Revolutions: A Continental History, 1750–1804.* New York & London: W. W. Norton & Co.

Taylor, George Rogers, 1950. Ed. *Hamilton and the National Debt: Problems in American Civilization.* Boston: Heath and Company.

Tearle, David. 2017. *Merchants of War: Barings Bank and William Bingham, Revolutionary Bankers from the War of Independence to the Louisiana Purchase.* Modbury, Devon, UK: The Incorporated History Press.

Thorold, Algar. 1913. *The Life of Henry Labouchere.* New York, London: G. P. Putnam's Sons.

Unger, Harlow Giles. 2005. *The French War Against America: How a Trusted Ally Betrayed Washington and the Founding Fathers.* New York: John Wiley & Sons.

United States, Department of the Treasury, *Annual Reports, 1801–1823.* Accessed at https://fraser.stlouisfed.org/

Valmori, Niccolò. 2023. *Banking and Politics in the Age of Democratic Revolution.* Oxford University Studies in the Enlightenment. Liverpool: Liverpool University Press.

Van Meter, Suzanne R. 1977. "A Noble Bargain: The Louisiana Purchase." Unpublished Ph.D. Dissertation, Indiana University, Department of History.

Ver Steeg, Clarence L. 1953. "Financing and Outfitting the First United States Ship to China." *Pacific Historical Review* XXII (1): 1–12.

Ver Steeg, Clarence. 1954. *Robert Morris: Revolutionary Financier: With an Analysis of His Earlier Career.* Philadelphia: University of Pennsylvania Press.

Veru, Peter. 2021a. "Pieter Stadnitski Sharpens the Axe: A Revolutionary Research Report on American Sovereign Finance, 1797." *Research in Economic History.*

Veru, Peter. 2021b. "The French bonds: The Little-known Bidding War for France's Holding in American Debt, 1786–1790. *Financial History Review* 28 (2): 259–280.

Walters, Philip G., and Raymond, Jr., 1944. "The American Career of David Parish." *The Journal of Economic History* 4 (2): 149–166.

Walters, Raymond, Jr. 1957. *Albert Gallatin: Jeffersonian Financier and Diplomat.* New York: The Macmillan Company.

Warren, Elizabeth. 1976. *The Role of American Diplomacy in the Louisiana Purchase.* M.A. Thesis in History, Portland State University.

White, Eugene N. 2001. "Making the French Pay: The Cost and Consequences of the Napoleonic Reparations." *European Review of Economic History* 5 (3): 337–365.

Williams, Greg H., 2009. *The French Assault on American Shipping, 1793–1813: a history and comprehensive record of merchant marine losses.* Jefferson : McFarland & Co.

Wilkins, Mira. 1989. *The History of Foreign Investment in the United States to 1914.* Cambridge, MA: Harvard University Press.

Winter, Pieter J. van. 1977. *American Finance and Dutch Investment, 1790–1815: With an Epilogue to 1840.* English Adaptation of the Rev. Version of the Dutch Original ed. Prepared for Publication with the Author's Assistance by James C. Riley, 2 vols., New York: Arno Press.

Wright, Robert E. 2002a. *Hamilton Unbound: Finance and the Creation of the American Republic.* Westport, CT: Greenwood Press.

———. 2002b. *The Wealth of Nations Rediscovered: Integration and Expansion in American Financial Markets, 1780–1850.* Cambridge: Cambridge University Press.

———. 2008. *One Nation Under Debt: Hamilton, Jefferson, and the History of What We Owe.* New York: McGraw-Hill.

Wright, Robert E., and David J. Cowen, 2006. *Financial Founding Fathers: The Men who Made America Rich*. Chicago: University of Chicago Press.

Ziegler, Philip, 1988. *The Sixth Great Power: A history of one of the greatest of all banking families, the House of Barings, 1762–1929*. New York: Alfred A. Knopf.

Index

A

Adams, John, 19, 37, 57, 83, 92, 120, 121
Adams, John Quincy, 83, 84
Addington, Henry, Prime Minister, 1801–04, xvi, xix, 20, 79, 107, 109, 139, 141–145, 153, 158, 179, 201, 227, 228
Aix-la-Chapelle, 208, 209
Astor, John Jacob, 185, 193, 194, 196, 204, 214
Azilum, 95, 105

B

Babut, 72
Baguenault, 72, 73, 154
Bank of England, vii, 36, 107, 108, 170, 176, 205, 208, 211, 217
Bank of Pennsylvania, 91, 137
Bank of the United States, 4, 14, 35, 38, 49, 56–58, 60, 63, 65, 71, 79, 80, 91–93, 97, 98, 118, 137, 139, 140, 178, 179, 194, 204, 205, 211, 213, 214
Banque de France, 5, 54, 73, 88, 161, 168, 170
Barbé-Marbois, François, ix, xv, xvii, xix, xx, 4, 5, 9, 10, 13, 14, 18, 23, 25, 28, 60, 63, 64, 80, 83–88, 96, 104, 138, 139, 143, 144, 155, 158–163, 166–171, 213, 214
Baring & Co., John & Francis, 3, 125
Baring, Alexander, viii–x, xv–xix, 2, 4, 6, 10, 12–14, 17–23, 25, 27–29, 31, 34–36, 39–41, 44, 50, 53, 55–58, 60–70, 72–76, 78–81, 83, 90, 93–101, 103, 105, 111, 112, 115, 116, 120, 126, 132, 135–137, 139–141, 143, 145, 147, 149–158, 164–166, 172, 173, 175–178, 181–185, 189, 190, 197–200, 202, 204–210, 213, 215–217, 219, 220, 223, 224

L. Neal, *The Forgotten Financiers of the Louisiana Purchase*, Palgrave Studies in the History of Finance,
https://doi.org/10.1007/978-3-031-56277-8

Baring Archive, vii–ix, 4, 10, 13, 17–21, 23, 26, 27, 36, 38, 40, 41, 43, 45–48, 53, 55–57, 59, 61, 62, 66–70, 72, 76–79, 94, 97, 103, 106, 108, 109, 111, 112, 116, 125, 126, 141, 143, 147, 148, 151–154, 156–158, 164, 166, 179, 207, 216
Baring, Sir Francis, viii, xv, xvii, xx, 7, 10–14, 20, 23, 26, 28, 34, 36, 38–41, 44, 46, 48, 50, 53, 56–58, 60–62, 67, 68, 72, 74, 79–81, 93, 96, 99, 111–113, 115–117, 137, 141, 144, 147, 149–151, 157, 164, 165, 175, 176, 183, 185, 199, 200, 207, 219, 220, 228, 233
Barlow, Joel, 119, 122, 123, 127, 128, 130, 189
Bills of exchange, 23, 28, 61, 73, 76, 77, 81, 105, 111, 117, 141, 144, 149, 191, 201, 209
Bingham, William, xv, xviii, 4, 12, 14, 38, 41, 56, 61, 90, 94, 95, 97, 98, 105, 111, 119, 137, 141, 152, 207, 224
Bird, Savage, and Bird, 78
Boehm, Edmund, 41, 42
Bonaparte, King Louis, 182
Bonaparte, Louis Napolèon, 182
British pound, 36, 66

C
Caisse d'Amortissement, 35, 168
Caisse de Service, 168, 170
Cazenove, Théophile, 94
Chevalier de la Luzerne, 83, 85
Citizen Genêt, 18
Coesvelt, William Gordon, 103
Consols, 3 Per Cent, vii, 65, 203, 204
Constable, William, 47
Continental Blockade, 13, 33, 136, 174–176, 178, 183, 186, 194, 201
Coup of 18 Fructidor, 87
Cour des Comptes, 88, 168, 169
Cour des Comptes, xx

D
Dallas, A.J., 132, 199, 205
De Smeth, 14, 72, 74, 76, 79, 81, 141, 144, 145, 149, 150, 152, 154–156, 182, 220
Desprez, Médard, 161
Doctrine of Discovery, 6, 7
Duer, William, 44, 105, 117, 118, 122, 123, 130
Du Pont de Nemours, Pierre-Samuel, xvi, 63, 78, 98, 104, 112, 117
Dutch East India Company, 36
Dutch guilder, 66, 97

E
Embargo Act, xx, 49, 190
Empress of China, 117, 130
Exchange Bank of Amsterdam, 36

F
Fox Blockade, 177
French franc, 28, 66, 80
French *rentes*, 55–57, 59, 62, 75, 79, 80, 206, 210
Friendship Hill, 90, 91

G
Gallatin, Albert, ix, 2, 4, 13, 14, 22, 29, 36, 37, 40, 55, 58, 88, 89, 97, 98, 119, 135, 137, 147, 149, 168, 197, 200, 214, 233
Gênet, Citizen, 105

Gilmor, Robert, 135, 141
Girard, Stephen, 185, 193, 194, 196, 202, 204, 205, 210, 211

H
Haiti, xvii, xviii, 34, 62, 77, 85, 86, 190, 193
Haitian revolution, 34
Hamburg, 12, 33, 102–105, 125–127, 133, 164, 166, 183, 186, 216
Hamilton, Alexander, xv, 2, 6, 12, 22, 25, 35, 36, 39, 41, 44, 57, 62, 66, 97, 120
Hinchman, Thomas, 41, 42, 46, 47
Holker, John, 44, 117, 118, 120, 130, 132, 133, 215
Hope & Co., vii, xv, xix, xx, 3–5, 11, 12, 14, 20, 23, 27, 28, 59–61, 68, 78, 100, 101, 103, 104, 110, 125, 126, 135, 139, 141, 144, 145, 149, 150, 152, 154, 156, 158, 163, 166, 171, 172, 174, 181–183, 186, 187, 197, 201, 207, 210, 216, 220, 229
Hope, Henry, viii, xvii, xx, 11–14, 20, 34, 50, 53, 58, 60, 61, 67–70, 74, 76, 77, 79, 80, 90, 93, 99–102, 107, 109–112, 116, 126, 136, 137, 142, 149, 151, 152, 154, 155, 157, 158, 173, 175, 181, 183, 185, 201
Hope, John Williams, 151, 152, 155, 157, 163, 164, 181, 183, 187
Hottinguer, 72
Huskisson, William, 104

I
Insinger, 72

J
Jackson, Andrew, xx, 8, 190–193, 213, 214
Jefferson, Thomas, viii, xvi, 8, 14, 22, 37, 63, 77, 85, 120–122, 195

K
King, Rufus, xvi, 79
Knox, Henry, 94, 119

L
Labouchere, Pierre Cesar, viii–x, xv, xvii, 4, 10, 12–14, 17, 19–23, 29, 34, 35, 50, 53, 58–65, 68, 70, 72, 73, 75, 76, 78–81, 83, 97, 99–103, 106, 108, 109, 115, 126, 144, 149, 152, 155, 157, 158, 160, 165, 166, 172, 173, 175, 181–185, 202, 204–206, 210, 213, 215–217
LaFayette, Marquis de, 89
Lancaster Turnpike, 91
Laussat, Pierre-Clément, xvii, xviii, 7, 77
Leclerc, General Charles, 77
Lestapis, Armand Pierre, 166
Lewis and Clark expedition, viii, 7
Lincoln, Levi, 93, 97
Liquidated debts, xv, 39–41, 71
Livingston, Edward, 192, 193, 214
Livingston, Robert R., xvi–xix, 5–10, 14, 23, 25–28, 62–65, 67, 70, 81, 88, 98, 112, 115–117, 132, 138, 143–145, 155, 164, 192, 214
Louisiana Purchase, vii–x, xv, xvii, xviii, 1, 3, 6, 7, 11, 13, 17, 19, 21, 22, 24–29, 33–35, 38, 48, 49, 53, 62, 64, 72, 78, 80, 81, 88, 93, 96, 98, 101, 102, 108, 111, 112, 115–117, 127, 130,

133, 136, 140, 141, 143, 159, 163, 172–174, 181, 182, 185, 189, 192, 200, 204, 210, 213–215, 217, 219
Louisiana Territory, 1, 3, 4, 6–8, 23–25, 34, 49, 56, 63, 65, 76, 77, 81, 93, 149, 163
Ludlam, William, 45

M
Madison, James, xvii, xviii, 7, 14, 22, 38, 64, 65, 89, 91, 92, 97, 137, 139, 174, 176, 186, 190, 195–197, 203–205
Matthiesen & Sillem, 102
Mexican pesos, 66
Mollien, Nicolas-François, 167
Monroe, James, xvii, xviii, 4, 5, 7, 9, 10, 14, 18, 20, 23, 25, 26, 49, 62, 64, 78, 86, 87, 115, 184, 195, 214
Montmorin, Comte de, 121, 128
Moore, Elizabeth, 85
Morris, Gouverneur, 4, 18, 46, 47, 86, 105, 119, 121, 123, 133, 171, 190
Morris, Robert, 46, 47, 91, 95, 105, 117–119, 121, 130, 133

N
Napoleon Bonaparte, viii, xv–xx, 3, 4, 6–10, 13, 14, 20, 21, 24, 27, 33–36, 48, 49, 54, 55, 64, 65, 73, 77, 78, 80, 87, 88, 93, 104, 106, 107, 113, 136, 138, 141–143, 151, 155, 158–172, 174–178, 181–187, 194, 201–203, 214, 216
Native Americans, 1, 6, 26, 214
Necker, Jacques, 46, 92, 121, 123
Négociants Réunis, 88, 160–162, 167
New Orleans, xvi–xviii, xx, 2, 4–8, 18, 20, 24, 34, 49, 53, 56, 57, 59, 63–65, 76–80, 93, 98, 100, 102, 112, 116, 117, 135, 140, 141, 143, 158, 166, 170, 186, 189–193, 201, 214, 215
Noailles, Vicomte de, 95, 105
Nolte, Vincent, xix, 100–102, 112, 166, 170, 183, 185, 186, 189, 190, 192, 201, 207, 214, 215

O
Ohio Company, 123
Orders in Council, 13, 175–178, 182–184, 186, 194
Orthez, 100
Ouvrard, Gabriel Julien, xix, 160–164, 166, 170–172, 185, 186, 206, 210

P
Paper pound, 36, 107, 176
Parish, David, xix, 164, 166, 170, 171, 173, 182, 185, 186, 189, 193, 195, 196, 204, 207, 215
Parker, Daniel, xv, xviii, 4, 5, 12–14, 18, 38, 41, 44, 46–48, 62, 63, 70, 96, 106, 112, 115–117, 119–125, 127–130, 161, 164, 185, 189, 215
Perregaux, 73
Pitt, William, xix, 104, 107, 165, 168, 184
Portuguese bonds, 54, 74–76, 108, 109, 153
Portuguese loan, 55, 69, 72, 107, 111, 112, 117, 155, 182
Preemption, 1, 7

Q
Quasi-War, xvi, 2, 4, 19, 25, 56, 62, 96, 113

R
Rente, 31, 203, 204
Rogers, Samuel, 41, 45–47
Rosanna, 62, 96, 106, 117, 125–129, 133
Russian bonds, 163, 186

S
Saint-Domingue, 34, 85
Sargent, Nathaniel, 62, 125, 127, 133
Savage, Bird & Bird, 69
Savary, Jean, 90
Scioto Company, 118, 122, 123, 128
Seguin, Armand, 161
Shaw, Samuel, 118, 130
Smith, William Stephens, 120, 121
Sovereign debt, vii, x, 13, 21, 22, 31, 34, 37, 38, 44, 48, 69, 146, 151, 175, 179–181, 186, 198, 200, 203, 208, 210, 216, 217
St. Domingue, xv, xvi, 34, 55–57, 61, 63, 77, 78, 80, 86, 96, 102, 105, 160
  Haiti, 56
Surinam, 12, 96, 102–104, 106, 125–127
Swan, James, 122, 124

T
Talleyrand, Charles-Maurice de, xvii, xviii, 6, 9, 14, 19, 62, 64, 67, 70, 94, 95, 98, 104, 105, 110–113, 116, 117, 164, 166
Talon, Amer, 86
Talon, Antoine Omer, 95, 96, 103, 104
Three Per Cent Consol, 31, 139
Tontine, xv, 39–41, 43–48, 62
Toussaint l'Ouverture, xvi, 34, 77
Treaty of Amiens, 9, 31, 33, 48, 55, 72, 111
Treaty of Mortefontaine, xvi, 3, 8, 9, 56, 113
Treaty of San Ildefonso, xvi, 8, 9, 25, 49
Treaty of Subsidies, 160
Truce of Amiens, ix, xvi, 31, 34, 109, 117

U
U. S. dollar, 66, 80, 97

V
Vanlerberghe, Ignace-Joseph, 160
Vansittart, Nicholas, 208
Van Staphorsts, 146
Vergennes, Comte de, 86

W
Wall, Charles, 72, 176
War of 1812, x, xx, 11, 36, 49, 132, 137, 151, 174–176, 179, 180, 185, 189, 190, 193, 195–200, 204, 214
Waterloo, x, 3, 203, 206, 211
Wellesley, Lord Richard, 182
Wellington, Duke of, 21, 165, 172, 178, 180–182, 187, 206, 208, 211
West Florida, 56, 57, 59, 63, 65, 78
Wetenhall's *Course of the Exchange*, 11, 179, 203
Willink, 14, 41, 72, 76, 79, 81, 141, 144–146, 149, 150, 152, 155, 182, 201, 220, 221, 229
Willink Bros/Willink brothers, 14, 41, 76, 152, 182

The manufacturer's authorised representative in the EU is Springer Nature Customer Service Centre GmbH, Europaplatz 3, 69115 Heidelberg, Germany. If you have any concerns regarding our products, please contact ProductSafety@springernature.com

Printed and bound by CPI Group (UK) Ltd, Croydon, CR0 4YY
01/10/2026
02225894-0005